NOTES

ON

THE LATE REVISION

OF

THE NEW TESTAMENT VERSION.

BY THE
REV. DANIEL R. GOODWIN.

WIPF & STOCK · Eugene, Oregon

Wipf and Stock Publishers
199 W 8th Ave, Suite 3
Eugene, OR 97401

Notes on the Late Revision of the New Testament Version
By Goodwin, Daniel R.
ISBN 13: 978-1-5326-0898-8
Publication date 10/19/2016
Previously published by Thomas Whittaker, 1883

ADVERTISEMENT

A portion of these Notes, with the Introduction, have appeared in the "American Church Review," for which they were originally prepared; and this must be at once the explanation and the excuse for the assumption of certain modes of expression belonging to the style of the reviewer.

NOTES ON THE LATE REVISION OF THE NEW TESTAMENT VERSION.

INTRODUCTION.

THESE notes have a subordinate and restricted purpose. They are not intended as a thorough review, or as the complete basis of a final judgment. They look only at a part of one side of the case.

1. They are not intended at all to point out the merits of the Revision, but only some of its faults. It is freely and fully admitted that the Revisers have made important corrections and many improvements. Indeed it were passing strange if so many biblical critics, selected from the ripest scholarship of Great Britain and America, after devoting so many years to their task, had failed to make such emendations. No scholar of even the most moderate pretension could have failed to make many such in far less time. Though this would seem, therefore, no great ground of boasting, we cheerfully accord the Revisers all the credit they can claim on this score. But the counterbalancing faults, if such there be, must be considered before making up a final judgment. We propose to furnish from this quarter some of the material for such a judgment.

2. We set aside all reference to changes in the Greek text, and the consequent changes in the version. In this department lie the most interesting and important questions of criticism. In most of these alterations, and in some of the most important, we are free to say that, in our humble judgment, the Revisers are right. But we pass this question by entirely.

3. In our strictures upon the other changes introduced into the version by the Revisers we may sometimes call in question the accuracy or the propriety of their translation in itself considered; but more frequently we shall call in question the necessity or importance of the changes, under the rule by which they professed to be guided—viz., "to introduce as few alterations as possible into the text of the Authorized Version consistently with faithfulness." Some have seemed to think it a sufficient justification of any change, that it is, in any degree, an improvement; and to assume that, in such a case, faithfulness required it. But the rule just cited is, and was evidently intended to be, a special restriction; it is a restriction, moreover, which was doubtless in consonance with the purpose of Convocation, and which commends itself to the general approval of the Christian community. The Revisers professed to act under it. But could they have understood, can any intelligent man understand, that rule to mean simply that they were to introduce no alterations which, in their judgment, would not be, in some degree, improvements? To suppose such to be the meaning of the rule were to stultify the Committee who made it and who were to act under it: for it would imply that the Committee thought it necessary solemnly to guard themselves against making alterations which they should judge to be no improvements at all; and a Committee for whom such a solemn resolution should have been necessary were certainly a Committee beneath the task assigned to them, not to say beneath contempt. In considering, therefore, any alteration in the version we shall regard it as pertinent to ask, not only, Is this a correct translation? or, Is it, in some critical sense or degree, an improvement upon the Authorized Version? but, *Is it required by faithfulness?* And we shall regard this last question as having a different meaning and bearing from the others.

4. We shall avoid setting our own mere opinion or judgment against that of so many learned men, the ripest scholars of the age; and rarely shall we thus set our own reasonings merely; but, in most of our animadversions, we

shall undertake to show that the Revisers are inconsistent with themselves ; and thus we shall appeal to them as their own judges. When any of these inconsistencies are palpably shown, it may be replied that they are mere oversights. They may be mere oversights ; but, even so, none would be more earnest or glad to have them corrected than the learned Revisers themselves. And, after all, the question is not how far the Revisers may be excused for faults and inconsistencies, if they have committed any, but whether, with such faults and inconsistencies, their work is such as it ought to be for the purpose for which it was intended—to become a final substitute for the Authorized Version.

5. Whenever, and in so far as, any alterations involve in any degree theological, or dialectic, or doctrinal considerations, if we differ from the Revisers, we shall not regard it as temerariously pitting our solitary and insignificant authority against that of the ripest scholars and greatest theologians of the age, but we shall take to our side the forty-seven translators of the Authorized Version. Those men, if they had not had the opportunity of studying the modern grammars and lexicons of the Greek, if they had not seen the recently discovered manuscripts and the latest improved text, were yet, in sound theological learning and in dialectic training, the undoubted peers of the best linguists and critics " of to-day."

6. We shall proceed upon the assumption that a good translation from Greek into English must not only express the exact sense of the Greek, but must also express it in English, in good English, pure, idiomatic English ; not only in English words, but in English style and construction. If it cannot be expressed in good English, it cannot be translated, but must, so far, be left to scholars and commentators to paraphrase and explain. The nearest approximation to the exact sense of the Greek which can be made in good idiomatic English, without offending the English taste or ear, is the best English translation that can be made. To invent a sort of Greek-English *patois*, to resort to a tyro's construing, with a view of giving the English reader a kind of *fac-simile* of the Greek, is not to

translate into English at all. Languages differ in the collocation of words as well as in the words themselves; and often the proper order is to be determined by an appeal to the ear or to usage, not to logic, and still less from the English to the Greek. So, too, for the repetition or variation of words. A repetition, which may be a positive beauty in one language, may, in a given connection, be simply barbarous or positively offensive in another. So, oftentimes, with the use of more general or more specific terms. In English a traveller goes to *see* the world, we do not say he goes to *behold* it; though the ancient Greek might use the more specific word θεωρέω, to behold or view. In English a man *sees* a wolf coming, we do not say he *beholds* him; and we should say, "what you see me have," not "what you behold me having." Also, in English there are certain established phrases or forms of expression which have so long been used as the correspondents to certain Greek phrases, that to change them in order to secure a so-called literal or exact translation would be sheer pedantry—a new coining of an artificial English; as, *e.g.*, if "the kingdom of heaven" were Grecized into "the kingdom of the heavens," or "the children of Israel" into "the sons of Israel."

7. It is not necessary to faithfulness of translation that a given word in one language should always—while retaining the same intrinsic meaning—be rendered by the same word in another language. The rendering may be varied in view, not only of the intrinsic meaning, but of the general air and associations of the different passages, or of the habits of expression in the different languages, or of their comparative copiousness of diction. Suppose, *e.g.*, that Shakespeare were to be translated into Persian verse—it would not give a fair idea of him to Persian readers, if, where the Persian poetic diction should have a hundred terms for one English epithet, the same Persian term should be used throughout for this same English word; even though this English word had the same intrinsic meaning in all the cases. The translators of 1611 recognized this principle, and they purposely and professedly

varied their renderings accordingly. In some cases they may have pushed the application of the principle farther than was necessary or even proper. In strictly parallel passages there would seem to have been no good reason for such variations. And yet even in these extreme cases, if, in every passage, the sense of the Greek was accurately conveyed in the English, and if our ears and our biblical literature had become habituated and conformed to the variation, there would seem to have been no sufficient reason for making a change in what was already received. Certainly faithfulness to God's Word did not require the change, for confessedly the true meaning of that Word was already, in each case, accurately rendered. But, it is said, if the same sense is found expressed in English in two forms, the reader will naturally infer that the form of expression in the original also is different, and if it is not, he will be deceived ; we answer, the common English reader ought to be, and is, satisfied if he has the true sense of the original accurately expressed in good English. Not to one in ten thousand of such readers does it ever occur to make such an inference at all. And as for critical students, they have no right to make any such inference in regard to the Authorized Version ; because the translators have given express notice that they did not hold themselves bound by any such rule of iron uniformity or literal correspondence. Translations are not made for the special accommodation of comparative critics.

On the other hand, however, when the Revisers have adopted and expressly announced this principle of uniform correspondence, they are bound to adhere to it, otherwise they may deceive all their readers. Consistency would require them to conform to it in connection with identical constructions as well as of identical words. Yet they freely render : "when he had taken it, he went," and "he, when he had taken it, went ;" or "he took it and went," "having taken it, he went," "taking it, he went"—all with complete indiscriminateness. Indeed they expressly tell us that they propose to introduce the participial construction into the English—they do not say always, but *more frequently;* thus acknowledging that they retain and use variety. But, passing by this, whenever they have varied the rendering of a given word while used in the same sense, they are chargeable with a serious fault, because, with their professions, they lead their readers to erroneous inferences. Besides, even if they were consistent in all these cases, we contend that it would be a consistency not required by "faithfulness," and, therefore, lying beyond their province. Under this head they have brought in a vast amount of "*consequential*" *damages* which, we contend, the readers of the New Testament are not bound to pay.

8. As to the use of the article. In this respect it was very generally supposed that the Authorized Version stood in special need of large emendations, in the light of the scholarship " of to-day." Indeed there was a multitude of grammarians and critics, who, to determine whether to put " the" or " a" before any English noun in the singular number, thought it necessary to inquire only whether there was or was not an article before its Greek correspondent; and, for the plural number, they required the article to be inserted or omitted in the English, just as it was in the Greek: and they were clamorous to have the New Testament version corrected accordingly. These have got small comfort from the Revisers, but more, we fear, than they deserved. Our Revisers were far above any such sweeping, schoolmaster ideas. They had a scholarship far too broad and generous for such narrow and Procrustean notions. They knew that the rules for the insertion or omission of the article in Greek were in many cases different from the usage of the English; that those rules were subject to many exceptions in good Greek usage, and that there were many cases where the article was inserted or omitted without any general reason which we can discover. Moreover, the use of the English article is far from being reducible to fixed and universal rules, but varies from time to time and from man to man. Locke wrote an " Essay concerning human understanding." We now say it was concerning " the human understanding." And the use of the article with "*reason*" has varied and even vibrated in

the course of two hundred years. Accordingly, the insertion or omission of the article in a translation will depend largely upon the good taste and good judgment of the translator, in view of the genius of the two languages and the drift and scope of the discourse, rather than of any formal rules. If in these respects we have great reason to defer to the Revisers, have we not equal reason to defer to the translators of 1611 ? We think the Revisers have, in this particular, yielded to the vulgar clamor more than was called for, and have made changes not required by faithfulness. But, after all, in innumerable instances they have inserted the article in English where it is omitted in Greek, and often omitted it in English where it is inserted in Greek. Where there is no Greek article before a singular noun they have sometimes inserted "a" and sometimes not; and they have even inserted "a" for the Greek article itself. Where, in all this, they have diverged from the Authorized Version, they are, in many cases, undoubtedly right; but, in many other and most important cases—*quære?* Their authority is greatly shattered if it can be shown that they are inconsistent with themselves. Take for instance the insertion or omission of the article before the word "heaven." We can only say, in all humility, that it surpasses our ingenuity to find or guess by what rule or rules they were guided. They have omitted the article alike when the Greek inserts and when it omits it; and in many instances, as far as we can see, have inserted or omitted it arbitrarily. Yet in multitudes of these cases they have altered the Authorized Version. Can any one show how or why, taken as a whole, the Authorized Version is not, in this case of the article with the word "heaven," as faithful to the Greek and as good English as is the Revision, with all its studied improvements? The contortions by which the Revisers elsewhere seek to express the presumed distinction indicated by the absence of the Greek article are something ludicrous.

9. Another great hue and cry has been persistently raised against the Authorized Version for its numberless blunders in the rendering of the Greek aorist tenses.

From the multitude and noise of these critics, all radiant and blatant with the new light and fresh inspiration from the modern apocalypse of the mysteries of Greek grammar, one might suppose that the learned translators of 1611 were simple ignoramuses in regard to the structure of the Greek language. It seems to have been assumed by many—and modern English scholars have given too much countenance to the idea—that the Greek aorist was of course to be rendered by the English simple preterite throughout, or that every departure from this rule must justify itself by irrefragable proofs as an extraordinary exception or even as a solecism ; or else be condemned as a false translation. But, on mature examination, the facts are found to be : (*a*) That this rule holds, with any degree of strictness, only in sustained narrative discourse ; (*b*) In numberless instances the English employs its compound preterite or perfect where the Greek uses the aorist ; and that not in the Bible only, or from the influence of the Latin Vulgate upon our former translators, but in our current discourse, from the influence, it may be, of the Latin language upon the structure of the English. Each language has its idioms ; and other European tongues have gone farther in this direction than we—the Italian, the French and the German familiarly using their compound preterites where we in English should use the simple preterite ; (*c*) In poetical and prophetic composition, in the epistolary and conversational style, in personal addresses and exhortations, in impassioned utterances, in teaching, in brief or fragmentary statements of fact—in short, in a very large part of Holy Scripture—the Greek uses the aorist where the English would naturally use the perfect ; and that so freely, that in such cases no *a priori* probability can be claimed for the preterite over the perfect, as the proper English translation of the Greek aorist.

The Revisers, far wiser critics than the average of the later school—though we think they have been too much influenced by the clamors of these absolutists—have, in by far the greater number of instances, we should judge, followed the former translators in rendering the aorist by the

English perfect. In some of their divergences in this particular they are probably right ; but, in many if not in most of these cases, we must take the liberty of siding with the translators of 1611 rather than with the Revisers. They themselves have rendered the aorist by the English perfect too often to claim that the mere fact of the Greek form being aorist proves that the English must be preterite. Whether the English should be perfect or preterite must very often be determined by the general character and drift of the discourse, by the immediate context and the nature of the case, by general analogy and, perhaps, by doctrinal considerations, as well as, especially, by the natural English idiom. And for sound sense and good judgment in these particulars, it is no want of due respect to the learned Revisers to say that we think we have as good reason to defer to the authority of the translators of 1611 as to theirs. Some cases are beyond all question of any party, as when the demoniac child falls as one dead, insomuch that many said, $\mathring{a}\pi\acute{e}\vartheta\alpha\nu\varepsilon\nu$. This is the Greek aorist ; but the English must be " he is dead ;" it cannot be " he died."

10. As to the number of the changes made by the Revisers. We see it set down at 35,000, and, though we have made no enumeration ourselves, we should judge that estimate to be not far from the truth. Now the number of changes recognized by them in the Greek text, including those in the margin with the rest, is about 5500; by far the greater part of which are of the least possible importance ; and, of the others, a large number are still of very doubtful authority, the best textualists changing their minds from edition to edition. But, as we have before said, we now dispute none of these new readings. If to these we add, say 10,000 changes more, as having been required by what could reasonably be called faithfulness to the original, we think a very generous allowance will have been made ; for we cannot include in this class the cases where the Revisers have been inconsistent with themselves, or have substituted mere Grecisms of expression or of construction for idiomatic English. There will then remain nearly 20,000 changes either wanton,

or trifling, or consequential, or Grecisms, or inconsistencies —or, perchance, proposed improvements of the English style; as in their elaborate reconstructions of "also," "therefore," etc. As to this last class of changes, we leave the English reader to judge whether in general, for good English style, the Revision is superior to the Authorized Version.

These notes may seem very extended, and some of them very minute; but we protest against the inference that they are exhaustive. They are, after all, but specimens, and even random specimens at that. They are the result of one cursory examination of the Revision, currently jotted down, and afterward expanded with cross-references, and shaped so as to make them, at least in some degree, readable. A subsequent review of any chapter has always brought up a new crop of queries and objections; they are still as thick as August blackberries. Should such a review as this have been undertaken by another person, there can be no doubt that a very large part—not unlikely the largest part—of the passages and points animadverted upon would have been different from those here criticised, and many of them probably much more striking and important than any included in these notes.

In concluding these introductory statements, we must allude to one trifling point which we have not seen referred to—probably because it is so trifling—but which may have some significance. We refer to the spelling "judgement," adhered to by the Revisers throughout. Is this a specimen of the changes which they judge to be required by faithfulness? Did they borrow it from the translators of 1611? If so, why did they not give us "wisedome" also—for such is the spelling of King James's translators. How far this newly introduced archaism of spelling "judgement" for *judgment* may have become prevalent in England we do not know; but "judgment" is the spelling of Johnson's Dictionary, of all the Oxford Bibles, we believe, for centuries, and of the best editions of English standard authors from about the year 1700. Why then this change? Do the Revisers propose to appear in the *rôle* of spelling-reformers?

Before the Revision was undertaken, it had always been put forward as one important and leading reason for making it, that the English language had greatly changed in nearly 300 years, and that the translation needed to be accommodated to modern use. But the Revisers have made it a principle to remove no archaisms, provided they were intelligible. In avoiding many changes of this kind, we think they were right. But, in fact, instead of diminishing the archaisms, they have increased and intensified them; not only retaining "which" for "who," " or" for "ere," "be" for "are ;" and " wot," " wist," " alway," etc. ; but sometimes putting " alway" for " always," " the which," for " which," etc. ; and multiplying the use of " howbeit," " straightway," etc.

In what follows we expect to commit many oversights; but it is due to ourselves to remind our readers that we have not had the aid of twenty others to revise and correct our solitary work.

ST. MATTHEW.

I.

18. "Had been betrothed," for "was espoused ;" but verse 20, "thought," and ii. 1, "was born." These are all alike for aorist participles in the genitive absolute, depending on aorist verbs.

21. " It is he that shall save," for " He shall save"= αὐτὸς σώσει. But (1) the Revisers have elsewhere translated αὐτός by "he" most frequently, as in Matt. xiv. 2; xxi. 27; Mark iv. 27; Col. i. 17, 18, etc., etc. ; frequently by " he himself," as in Luke x. 1; John vi. 6, etc. ; and sometimes by "himself" alone, as in Matt. viii. 17: but nowhere else, out of more than a hundred places, have they ever translated it by this phrase, "it is he that." Wherefore, then, this special translation here? (2) If, and so far as, this phrase differs in sense from "he" or "he himself" or " himself," it differs, we apprehend, from the true sense of the original, in which there is implied, we think, something peculiar, inherent, spontaneous, absolute, and not merely

demonstrative or antithetical. (3) This rendering is, at best, not a translation but a paraphrase, and this is its decisive condemnation. "It is he that shall save" is not a translation of αὐτὸς σώσει; but of αὐτός [or ἐκεῖνος or οὗτος] ἐστιν ὁ σώσων: see Luke xxiv. 21; John ix. 37; xiii. 26; xiv. 21; Acts x. 42; compare Matt. xi. 19; Luke xxii. 23, 28, etc.

23. "The virgin" for "a virgin" = ἡ παρθένος. So they have put "the sower" for "a sower" (Matt. xiii. 3, etc.). This is well enough, but is the change necessary? After all, the sense remains substantially the same; for who can doubt that, however personally definite ἡ παρθένος may have been in the mind of the prophet, in the mind of the evangelist the application had become generalized? So that "the virgin" means "she (or the person or the woman) who is a virgin;" just as "the sower" means "he (in fact any man) who is a sower." So the Revisers have rendered ἡ γυνή "a woman," John xvi. 21; τῷ ψεύδει "a lie," Rom. i. 25; τοῦ ἀνθρώπου "a man," Rom. vii. 1; 1 Cor. ii. 11; τῇ πόρνῃ "a harlot," 1 Cor. vi. 16; and τὰ δαιμόνια "devils" in instances unnumbered.

They have also substituted here "which is, being interpreted," for "which, being interpreted, is!" How important! how necessary to faithfulness! for is not that the order of the Greek? Why did they not add "with us God" for "God with us"?

II.

2. "Saw" for "have seen" = εἴδομεν, and then "are come" = ἤλθομεν.

4. "Gathering" for "when he had gathered"= συναγαγών. So, at verse 11, "opening" for "when they had opened" = ἀνοίξαντες. Is this necessary? But see xiv. 23, "After he had sent" for "when he had sent"= ἀπολύσας; Mark xiv. 23, "when he had given thanks" = εὐχαριστήσας. (Compare Matt. xxvi. 27, "gave thanks, and" = εὐχαριστήσας—the A. V. is not bound to be uniform even in parallel passages, but the Revisers are.) See also Acts xxi. 2, 3, 4, where we have "having found" twice

for "finding" = εὑρών, and "when we had come," etc., for an aorist participle; and all these, like συναγαγών and ἀνοίξαντες, belonging to the subjects of aorist verbs. So also, at verse 9, "they having heard" for "when they had heard."

13. "Until I tell thee" for "until I bring thee word."

18. "A voice was heard in Ramah" for "In Ramah was there a voice heard." Are these changes necessary to faithfulness?

23. "That he should be called" for "he shall be called" = ὅτι κληθήσεται. The original familiarly mixes both constructions; but why, in English, should one be necessarily substituted here for the other? See Matt. xvi. 7; Mark i. 15, 37, etc., where, as in almost innumerable similar cases, they render in the *oratio recta* without the ὅτι. Was it any of their business to modify the rendering here in view of the difficulty of finding the prophecy referred to?

III.

3. "The voice of one crying," as A. V., though there is no article in the Greek. But see "An unknown God," Acts xvii. 23. "Make ready" for "prepare" = ἑτοιμάσατε, though "make" is repeated immediately after. They have often rendered this verb by "prepare," as in Luke xxiii. 56; xxiv. 1; John xiv. 2, 3; 1 Cor. ii. 9; 2 Tim. ii. 21; Philem. 22; Heb. xi. 16; Rev. viii. 6; ix. 7; xii. 6; etc. Perchance the learned Revisers saw some nice distinction to which they felt bound to be faithful, and their translation might be well enough in itself; but was a *change* necessary?

7. "Warned" for "hath warned" = ὑπέδειξεν. Was this necessary to faithfulness?

17. "Am well pleased" = εὐδόκησα, and so also at xii. 18. Very well; but what becomes of faithfulness to the aorist?

IV.

3. "And the tempter came and said to him" for "And when the tempter came to him he said." Here the new

text changes the place of "to him;" but it is still implied with προσελθών—see viii. 2, new text; viii. 25 and xxviii. 18. But is the change of construction required by faithfulness? Either mode of construction for the Greek participial clause is allowed in English; and according to its avowed principles, the A. V. uses now one and now the other. The Revisers had just used the construction with "when" in a perfectly parallel case of the Greek. What then prompted the change here? It could not be faithfulness to the Greek. Was it to improve the English by varying the form of expression and preventing the disagreeable recurrence of similar sounds? But this is scarcely consistent with their own principles in their multitudinous consequential changes. Surely the simple English reader would infer that the Greek construction was different in the two cases here, where they make the English construction different—would infer it quite as likely, and with quite as much damage to his exact knowledge of the Word of God, as he would infer that there were different words in Greek for "immediately" and "straightway," if, in otherwise parallel passages in St. Matthew and St. Mark, one of the English words were used in one case and the other in another. And as to their regard for the English ear, look at their harsh and slavish repetitions of "enter," Matt. xxiii. 13; of "mad," Acts xxvi. 24, 25; and of "subject," 1 Cor. xv. 27, 28. But to see the finishing touch put to the changes required by faithfulness, turn to Matt. xxv. 3. There they substitute "the foolish, when they took their lamps, took no oil with them" for "the foolish took their lamps, and took no oil with them." There the Greek participial construction is precisely the same as here at Matt. iv. 3, but the change they make is precisely the reverse. Is this faithfuness? or is it wantonness? or what is it? It is far from being a solitary instance of such inconsistencies.

4. "It is written" (not "it has been written") = γέγραπται. That we have, in English, this form of the perfect passive is noted here for further use; but see v. 10. Note also, "by" = ἐπί: "out of" = διά.

7. "Again, it is written" for "it is written again." But see verse 4, where they did not say, with the Greek, "Not by bread alone shall man live."

15. "The land of Zebulun and the land," etc. No article in the Greek.

17. Why not follow the Greek faithfully and say "the kingdom of the heavens"?

23. "Disease" (νόσον) and "sickness" (μαλακίαν) for "sickness and disease." Very nice and well. But then in verse 24 they should have said "all who were ill," etc., instead of "all who were sick," for the Greek expression has, in form, no relation to μαλακίαν, though the simple English reader might think so. "The sick" are sick with "diseases," see here and at Luke iv. 40. Here and at Matt. x. 1, θεραπεύειν (νόσους) is "to heal;" at Luke ix. 1 it is rendered "to cure." What will the simple reader think?

V.

3. "In spirit" = τῷ πνεύματι. But see John xi. 33, "in the spirit."

8. "In heart" = τῇ καρδίᾳ: not "in the heart." Yet at verse 1 they carefully put "the mountain" for "a mountain," and at viii. 12, etc., "the weeping" for "weeping."

9. "Sons" for "the children;" but, for article, see iv. 3, 6.

12 and 45. "In heaven" = ἐν τοῖς οὐρανοῖς: see vi. 20, where "in heaven" = ἐν οὐρανῷ.

18. "Heaven and earth" = ὁ οὐρ. and ἡ γῆ. But see Acts iv. 24.

21, 27, 33, 38, 43. "Ye have heard" = ἠκούσατε—not "ye heard."

32. "Is put away;" why not "has been put away"? See verse 10.

34. "The throne of God" for "God's throne." Why? Does "God's word" mean anything else than "the word of God"? Would swearing by "God's throne" be swearing by "a throne of God"?—Articular nicety.

35. "The footstool of his feet" for "his footstool." What dialect of English is this? Grant that the Greek

has this redundant form, must we use it, English or no English?

37. "Of the evil *one*" = ἐκ τοῦ πονηροῦ.

39. Why not "the evil *one*" for τῷ πονηρῷ also? Do the Revisers mean "the evil *one*" and "him that is evil" to have the same or a different import?

45. "That ye may be" (not "may become") = γένησθε.

VI.

2. "When therefore" for "Therefore, when" = ὅταν οὖν. And so, often. But does faithfulness require this change? Is a translator bound to follow the order of the Greek words? Besides, which is the most logical English? Does the illation refer to the clause with "when," or to the clause on which that depends? But see vii. 20. It is true that in this last phrase ἄραγε is for "therefore" and stands first in Greek; but is any English reader to infer that "therefore" has a different sense here in English because it has a different position? The truth is, in English "therefore" may stand first or second in a clause, and the question here is about the necessity of a *change*.

2, 5, and 16. "Have received" for "have" = ἀπέχουσιν. What then would ἀπεσχήκασι mean? In Philemon 15 the Revisers put "have" for "receive" = ἀπεχῇς!

4 and 6. "In secret" = ἐν τῷ κρυπτῷ: not "in the secret *place*."

5. "To stand and pray" for "to pray standing" = ἑστῶτες προσεύχεσθαι. Yet they claim to have improved the translation by a freer use of the participial construction in English.

6. "Having shut" for "when thou hast shut." But see iv. 2, vii. 6, etc., etc.

7. "Gentiles" for "heathen" = ἐθνικοί (ethnics). But ordinarily "Gentiles" is for ἔθνη.

Ἐν is rendered "for" (their much speaking).

9–11. In the Lord's Prayer the Revisers have refrained from making many changes which consistency with the changes elsewhere made would require. But if such changes were demanded by faithfulness at all, they were most strenuously demanded precisely in the most familiar and oft-repeated passages. Here, however, the order is freely varied from the Greek to accommodate English idiom and even English rhythm. If they had followed their own precedents, the Prayer would have read something like this: "Our Father which (or, even thou that) art in the heavens; Hallowed be thy name. Come thy kingdom. Come to pass (or accomplished be) [see i. 22 and v. 18] thy will, as in heaven, so on earth. Our bread which is (or, even that which is) daily, give us to-day." As to "the evil *one*" for "evil," we think the preponderating evidence from New Testament usage and from early testimony is in favor of their translation. Still, as there is much room for doubt, and as "evil" includes all that is contained in the other expression, perhaps they would have done better if they had interchanged their text and marginal reading; or had put "the evil" into the text here and at John xvii. 15, as the A. V. had done in the latter passage.

14. Their painful faithfulness in the construction of "also" should have led them to say here: "you also shall your heavenly Father forgive." See also verse 21.

26. "Are not ye" for "are ye not." How important!

27, 28. Note the difference between the Greek and the English in the order of *emphasis*. Here they leave the Greek and follow the English.

30. "If . . . doth so clothe" for "if . . . so clothe." This was to avoid "clotheth." But they might have accomplished this purpose by simply retaining the subjunctive form in the English; as they have done at vi. 23 (ad fin.) Luke xi. 36; 1 Pet. iv. 17; Phil. iv. 8; Rom. xii. 18; Matt. viii. 31; xiv. 28; xxvi. 39; 1 Cor. xiv. 5; Rom. viii. 9, 17, etc.

33. "His kingdom and his righteousness." The first "his" is not in the Revisers' text.

34. "Will be" for "shall be." But is it not an assurance, of the nature of a promise, rather than of a mere prediction?

VII.

3. "Beholdest" = $\beta\lambda\acute{\epsilon}\pi\epsilon\iota\varsigma$. But see xix. 26.
6. "Under" = $\acute{\epsilon}\nu$ = among.

9. "Shall ask him for a loaf" for "ask bread "= αἰτήσει ἄρτον. There is no "him" in the Greek; it is not needed in English; and it makes confusion with the next "him." See 10th verse.

12. "All things therefore" for "therefore all things." As at vi. 2; but see verse 20.

13. "Many be they that enter in thereby" for "many there be which go in thereat." What's the difference? They often render ἔρχομαι by "go." See Matt. xxiii. 13, note.

15. "False prophets, which" = τῶν ψευδοπροφητῶν, οἵτινες. But what has become of the article? Is it not as essential to the prophets as it is to the mountain, or to the weeping and gnashing? If they had rendered οἵτινες by "for they," as at Phil. iv. 3, they might have retained the article with "false prophets" without any ambiguity.

16. "By their fruits ye shall know them." The Revisers have changed the order of the A. V. here to conform to the order in the Greek, and in verse 20 of A. V.; but at xii. 33 they have forgotten themselves, and returned to the order of the A. V. at this verse 16.

20. "Therefore" for "wherefore" = ἄραγε. What is the difference?

27. "Smote" for "beat" = προσέκοψαν (?).

28. "When Jesus ended" for . . . "had ended." But see Mark vii. 17; Luke xxii. 14; John xiii. 31; xxi. 15; Acts xi. 2; Rev. v. 8, etc.

29. "Taught" = ἦν διδάσκων. But see xix. 22, "was one that had" = ἦν ἔχων.

VIII.

1, 5. Aorist participles in dative rendered by "when" and the pluperfect.

6. "In the house" for "at home" = ἐν τῇ οἰκίᾳ. Why not, then, put "is laid," or "hath been laid," for "lieth" = βέβληται?

12. "Cast forth" for "cast out" (ἐκβάλλω). But see verse 16 and xxii. 13. And then "the weeping and gnashing of teeth" (τῶν ὀδόντων).

14. "Lying" for "laid and" = βεβλημένην καί: and yet "footstool of his feet"!

16. Why not say, "And all that were sick he healed," after the Greek order? See their translation at xx. 26.

19. "A" for "a certain" = εἷς; also at ix. 18. "There came" for "came" (?).

25. "Save, Lord" for "Lord, save us" = Κύριε, σῶσον. What now about faithfulness to the Greek? "We perish," not "we are perishing;" why not? See 2 Cor. ii. 15.

26. "There was a great calm," not "there followed" = ἐγένετο. But see Rev. xi. 15, 19, etc.

31. "Herd of swine" (τῶν χοίρων). See τὸ ὄρος. Cf. vii. 6.

IX.

6. "On earth" = ἐπὶ τῆς γῆς. See x. 34.

8. "Which had given" = τὸν δόντα—not "even him which," nor "which gave."

12. "But when he heard it he said"—not "but he, when he heard it, said" = ὁ δὲ ἀκούσας εἶπεν. But see xii. 2; xxi. 38, etc., etc.

13. "I desire mercy" for "I will have mercy" = Ἔλεον θέλω. So at xxvii. 43, etc.; but which is the simpler English? As for ambiguity in the A. V., the phrase is never used in the other sense without "on" or "upon" following.

31. "But they went forth and spread" for "But they, when they were departed, spread" = οἱ δὲ ἐξελθόντες διεφήμισαν. But see Acts iv. 24, etc.; also above at verse 12.

36. "Not having a (shepherd)" for "having no" = μὴ ἔχοντα ποιμένα. But see x. 9; xiii. 5, 6; Rev. iii. 2.

X.

2. "The first" = πρῶτος. No Greek article.

8. "Received" for "have received." Is this spoken of as a past historical event, or as a present fact?

16. "Serpents" = οἱ ὄφεις: "doves" = αἱ περιστεραί. But see xxi. 12 and Mark iv. 7, "the thorns;" "the weeping and gnashing;" "the sower," etc., etc.

17, 18. The order is here changed to conform to the Greek, while at verse 5 a change is made in just the contrary sense. Are these changes 'required by faithfulness? They make no change in the meaning, and it is difficult to see how they mend the English.

21. "The father" = $\pi\alpha\tau\acute{\eta}\rho$, English idiom; but "his" should also be "the;" and will not the distinction made in the translation, between "brother" and "the father," lead the English reader to suppose a distinction in the Greek?

23. "Gone through" for "gone over" = $\tau\epsilon\lambda\acute{\epsilon}\sigma\eta\tau\epsilon$. (?) "The next" should be "the other" = $\tau\grave{\eta}\nu\ \acute{\epsilon}\tau\acute{\epsilon}\rho\alpha\nu$—if we *must* have the article.

24. "A disciple" for "the disciple." But see next verse, and see verses 21 and 35, and 2 Tim. ii. 24.

25. "Be" = $\gamma\acute{\epsilon}\nu\eta\tau\alpha\iota$—not "become."

28. "Be not afraid of" for "fear not." This is to render the $\acute{\alpha}\pi\acute{o}$ following; but what difference does it make in the sense?

32, 33. "Him will I also confess" (and so A. V.). In the Greek the "him" comes last. But see Rev. viii. 2, where the A. V. is altered to conform to the Greek.

35. "A man," "the daughter" (bis); no Greek article in either case. "A man's foes" certainly means, to unsophisticated ears, "the foes of a man," and yet the Greek is $\acute{\epsilon}\chi\vartheta\rho o\grave{\iota}$ $\tau o\tilde{v}\ \acute{\alpha}\nu\vartheta\rho\acute{\omega}\pi o v$, "foes of the man." See xii. 43.

XI.

2. "Now when John heard (for 'had heard') in prison the works of the Christ (for 'of Christ'), he sent" = $\acute{o}\ \delta\grave{\epsilon}$ $\prime I\omega\acute{\alpha}\nu\nu\eta\varsigma\ \acute{\alpha}\kappa o\acute{v}\sigma\alpha\varsigma,\ \kappa.\tau.\lambda.$ The Revisers do not make here their pet emendation: "Now John, when he heard . . . sent;" as see xii. 2, 43; Mark vi. 16, etc., etc. It may as well be "had heard" as "heard," see iv. 2; with "hear," "see," etc., either form may be used. The $\tau o\tilde{v}\ X\rho\iota\sigma\tau o\tilde{v}$ here is taken not from John's point of view, but from the evangelist's when he wrote, and may as properly be rendered "Christ" as "the Christ;" and even if taken from John's point of view, "the Christ" would beg the question about which John asked.

3. "He that cometh" for "he that should come" = ὁ ἐρχόμενος = "he that is to come," or "that shall come" They have rendered it "is to come" at Rev. i. 4, 8, and iv. 8, etc.; and in like manner they have rendered τὰ ἐρχόμενα.

4, 7. "Go your way" for "go;" "went their way" for "departed" (πορεύω). But see xxviii. 19.

5. "The blind," etc. Article inserted six times with A. V.—not "blind men," etc.; and so, often; and so, right. This is our idiom. See xxi. 14.

6. "Shall find no occasion of stumbling in" = σκανδαλισθῇ ἐν. Elsewhere they are more brief, and render: "be stumbled," "stumble," "be offended." See xiii. 21, 57, etc.

7. "To behold," for "to see" = θεάσασθαι. But see vi. 1; xxiii. 5; Mark xvi. 14; John vi. 5; Acts xxi. 27; Rom. xv. 24, etc. The ἰδεῖν which follows in the next verse shows that this has the same meaning; see xiii. 17.

12. "Men of violence," for "the violent" = βιασταί. Why did not they say at verse 5 "blind men" for "the blind," to show their reverence for the Greek article, or rather, for its absence? See also verse 25.

14. "Which is to come" for "which was for to come" = ὁ μέλλων ἔρχεσθαι. But see John xii. 4; Acts xxvi. 22; Rom. v. 14; Heb. ii. 5; vi. 5; ix. 11; x. 1. In Hebrews it is translated "to come"—not "which is to come;" and it probably means "which was to come," i.e., "which was predicted and expected."

16. "In the market places" for "in the markets" = ἐν ἀγοραῖς. No article.

19. "Is justified"—aorist in Greek.

25. "Of heaven and earth." Both with article in Greek. Cf. Acts iv. 24.

25, 26. Aorist rendered preterite for perfect. (?)

27. Aorist rendered perfect. See John xvii. 2. "Willeth"—not "desireth" = βούληται. See Mark xv. 15; Acts xxii. 30; xxiii. 28; xxv. 22; xxvii. 43, etc. Compare John xviii. 39.

XII.

2. "But the Pharisees, when they" for "but when the Pharisees, they." But see verse 24, where the Revisers reverse their construction, with the same Pharisees and the same Greek construction! See also xi. 2; ix. 12.

12. "How much is a man of more value" for "how much is a man better." If they must change, suppose they had said, "Of how much more value"?

"To do good" for "to do well" = καλῶς ποιεῖν, not even καλὸν ποιεῖν. Which is the more faithful? See 2 Thess. iii. 13; Acts x. 33; 1 Cor. vii. 37, 38; 2 Cor. xi. 4, etc.

20. "Judgement" = τὴν κρίσιν: so A. V.

21. "The Gentiles" = ἔθνη: so also A. V.

24. "The prince" = ἄρχοντι. Why not "prince" or "a prince"? See Mark iii. 17, etc.

27, 28. Article omitted twice—τὰ δαιμόνια.

33. "The tree is known by its fruit;" but see the correction of A. V. at Matt. vii. 16.

40. Note how the order of time and place in the Greek is inverted in the English.

"The belly of the whale" for "the whale's belly"! When we compare this and v. 34 with 2 Tim. ii. 24, I am almost tempted to infer that the learned Revisers supposed "the whale's belly" might mean "a belly of the whale." But how many bellies had the whale?

42. "The queen of the south." No articles in Greek. But see 2 Tim. ii. 24 again.

43. "The unclean spirit, when he" for "when the unclean spirit ... he." But this is departing from the structure of the Greek; and the ambiguity which they would remove is as much in the Greek as in the English of the A. V. This change of construction therefore is as much required in our Lord's own words (if he used the Greek) as in the English. And what has become of their painful faithfulness to the exact text? See xxi. 38, etc., etc., etc. Here they assume and translate a text for which there is not the slightest authority. Besides, they might have reached their

purpose by substituting, from the margin, "it" for "he," referring to the demon.

46. "His" for the article only, twice.

XIII.

2. "Beach" for "shore." How necessary.
3. "The sower" for "a sower" = ὁ σπείρων. But why change? Does ὁ σπείρων here mean any definite particular sower? Does it not mean indifferently "the sower" or "a sower," *i.e.*, "he that" or "one that sows"? See John v. 45; and viii. 50, "one that seeketh" = ὁ ζητῶν: and Mark iv. 26, "casts seed," τὸν σπόρον:—the generic article.
17. Preterites for perfects (?).
"To see" = ἰδεῖν: "see" = βλέπετε. Cf. xi. 7, 8.
18. "Hear then ye" for "hear ye therefore" (?).
24. "Is likened" = ὡμοιώθη.
27. "Didst thou not" for "didst not thou" (?).
28. "Hath done" (aorist); why not "did"?
(No marginal note.) "Wilt thou"—not "desirest thou." But see Matt. xxvi. 15.
30. "Time" = καιρῷ.
34. "Without" = χωρίς.
"In parables unto the multitudes" for "unto the multitude in parables." "Parables" here is the emphatic word, and the A. V. is the natural English.
36. "Left" for "sent away" = ἀφείς (?).
39. Why not "the angels" as well as "the end"? Both are predicates, and both without the article.
44. "In" = ἀπό—"of," "from," or "for;"—why "in"?
46. "Sold" = πέπρακε—perfect co-ordinated with aorists, and all here rendered preterite. But see i. 22, γέγονεν.
48. Order changed; see xxi. 12, etc., for the Greek order.
50. "Furnace of fire," τοῦ πυρός. Also, as at verse 42, "the weeping" (ὁ), and "of teeth" (τῶν).
57. "Were offended" = ἐσκανδαλίζοντο. But see xi. 6.
58. "Unbelief" = ἀπιστίαν—not "disbelief." But see Mark xvi. 16.

XIV.

1. "Report concerning Jesus" for "fame of Jesus" = ἀκουὴν Ἰησοῦ (?). "Is risen" = ἠγέρθη—not "is raised" or "was raised." But see Mark xiv. 28; John ii. 22; Matt. xxvi. 32; Rom. viii. 34, etc. "These powers" = αἱ δυνάμεις (?).

9. "Was grieved" for "was sorry" = ἐλυπήθη. But see xvii. 23; xviii. 31; xix. 22; xxvi, 22, 37; Mark x. 22 ("sorrowful" for "grieved"!); xiv. 19; John xvi. 20; 2 Cor. ii. 2, 4, etc.

14. "Had compassion on" for "was moved with compassion towards" = ἐσπλαγχνίσθη. So xv. 32. But see xviii. 27; xx. 34. In this last case they put "moved with compassion" *for* "had compassion"!

16. "They have no need to go away" for "they need not depart" = οὐ χρείαν ἔχουσιν ἀπελθεῖν. Had they need or did they need to make this change? As for "depart" it is true the Greek word is rendered just before "go;" and the same is true of their "go away." The Revisers not unfrequently render ἀπελθεῖν "depart," as at Acts xvi. 40.

17. Note that here οὐκ .... εἰ μή means "but" = "only;" while at xv. 24 it means "not .... but:"— English idiom.

22. "To enter into" for "to get into" (a boat) = ἐμβῆναι (not εἰσελθεῖν). (?)

23. "After he had sent" for "when," etc. = ἀπολύσας. Why not "sending," as at ii. 11?

24. "Distressed" for "tossed" = βασανιζόμενον — of the boat, by the waves. (?)

25. "Upon" for "on;" and so at 28, 29. Why? How vastly important, and intensely necessary!

29. "Went down and walked" for "when he was come down he walked." But see "when he saw" in the next verse, also for an aorist participle. Should the reader be led to suppose the Greek construction different in the two cases? Do the Revisers study variety of expression? But see "straightway," etc. By the way they have, in the

next verse, inadvertently left "immediately" (instead of "straightway," their archaic pet) for εὐθέως, as also at xxiv. 29. So difficult is it to hold split hairs steadily in view, or, perhaps, they have split the hair a second time.

33. "The Son of God;" compare xxiii. 31.

XV.

5. "That wherewith thou mightest have been profited by me is given *to God*" for "It is a gift, by whatsoever thou mightest be profited by me" = Δῶρον, ὃ ἐὰν ἐξ ἐμοῦ ὠφεληθῇς. "To God" is not translation, but paraphrase or exposition. Compare this with their painstaking faithfulness in adhering to the Greek order and emphasis in other cases. The A. V. is here by far the more faithful to the original, and gives the same sense as their version, and that as clearly as the Greek gives it; and, moreover, has retained the right grammatical tense for ὠφεληθῇς. See, by analogy, Luke xvi. 30, 31.

9. "The precepts" for "the commandments" = ἐντάλματα. While they were making their correction they might as well have made it accurate and said, "precepts" or "injunctions."

12. "Were offended"—not "stumbled," and that though their rendering here might stumble the reader—quite as naturally as in any of the passages where they have introduced the other translation.

14. "If the blind guide the blind"—"guide" for "lead"? And nothing to distinguish the singular number. There is no article in the Greek, but it is literally "if blind lead blind" or "if a blind man lead a blind man." For do we not naturally speak of a blind man's being "led," rather than "guided"?

"A pit" for "the ditch" (no article); but is not the A. V. the true sense in current English? Just before the Revisers say, "is cast into the draught," although "draught" has no article in the Greek.

32. "Would" for "will." Is this necessary, and is it exactly the sense? He refers to what he *wills*, not to what he *would*. He is resolved upon what he will and will not do.

33. "In a desert place" for "in the wilderness" = ἐν ἐρημίᾳ. But the article is familiarly supplied in such cases after ἐν; and see 2 Cor. xi. 26.

XVI.

1. "From heaven" = ἐκ τοῦ οὐρανοῦ—not "out of the heaven," as elsewhere.
2, 3. "The heaven" for "the sky" = ὁ οὐρανός.
5. "Forgot" for "had forgotten." But it must be "had forgotten" with any construction; the forgetting must be antecedent to their coming to the other side, and so the Greek implies. If we must change the A. V., would it not be better to say, "And being come to the other side, the disciples had forgotten," etc.; *i.e.*, they then found it out?
7. "Perceiving" = γνούς.
8, 11. "Perceive" for "understand" = νοεῖτε (?).
19. "On earth," "in heaven"—article in Greek.
29. "In no wise" for "not" = οὐ μή. But see xxiii. 39; xxiv. 35, etc., etc.
24, 25. "Would" for "will" = θέλει = wills to. The simple future after "if" would be "shall," never "will." There could therefore be no ambiguity. But see xxiii. 4.
27. "To every man" = ἑκάστῳ. Elsewhere they often change "every" to "each," making questionable English.

XVII.

5. "My beloved Son" = υἱός μου ὁ ἀγαπητός—not "a son of mine, even the (or my) beloved." But see xxv. 40; Luke ix. 35; Mark v. 15; 1 Cor. xv. 38; Rev. iii. 2; Gal. ii. 20.
8. "Lifting up" for "when they had lifted up" = ἐπάραντες. See xiv. 23; Acts xxi 2, 4; cf. Acts i. 9.

"No one" for "no man;" and so, often. But in the next verse they say "no man." Does οὐδείς mean "no one" and μηδείς "no man"? Or did they fear an inference as to Christ's humanity?

13, 25. How necessary to faithfulness are these changes in the order of the words!

26. "Therefore the sons are free" for "then are the chil-

dren free" = ἄραγε ἐλεύθεροί εἰσιν οἱ υἱοί. "Sons" may be more accurate than children; but why "therefore" for "then"? As to arrangement, the A. V. is clearly nearer the order and emphasis of the original.

27. "Lest" = ἵνα μή—not "that not." But see John xii. 35; Col. ii. 4; iii. 21; Phil. ii. 27, etc.

"Cause to stumble," and so xviii. 6. But see xv. 12. "Stumble" is ambiguous as well as "offend."

XVIII.

3. "Turn" for "be converted" = στραφῆτε. (?) "Little children" = τὰ παιδία. Article?

7, 8, 9. "Occasions," etc. = τῶν σκανδάλων: "the occasions," etc. = τὰ σκάνδαλα: "life" = τὴν ζωήν. "The eternal fire"—(not "the fire which is," or "even that which is") = τὸ πῦρ τὸ αἰώνιον: "the hell of fire" (not "the hell of the fire")—τοῦ πυρός.

12. "Which goeth astray," for "which is gone astray;" present participle = "which is straying," or "is gone astray."

16. "Two witnesses or three," for "two or three witnesses." Is not this a piece of hypercriticism? The A. V. gives the usual English phrase. See Heb. x. 28 and 2 Cor. xiii. 1; and "the kingdom of heaven." See also Deut. xvii. 6 and xix. 15.

18, 19. "On earth" (thrice),—τῆς: "in heaven" (twice), —τῷ: "in heaven" = ἐν οὐρανοῖς. See also xvi. 19; but compare xxiii. 9.

20. "In my name," Gr. εἰς.—Note and cf. xxviii. 19.

32. "Called" for "after that he had called." But see xiv. 23. Either way is well enough; but why change, and that, first one way and then another?

XIX.

1. "Beyond Jordan," τοῦ; and so at John i. 28; iii. 26; but, Matt. iii. 13, they say "to the Jordan," and Mark i. 9, "in the Jordan." The established English usage has Jordan without the article (in the Palestinian point of view), even in the nominative case; see Joshua iii. 15, "Jordan

overfloweth." If this is an archaism it is no more unintelligible or ambiguous now than is "which" for "who," or "or" for "ere," or "howbeit," or "straightway."

5. "His father and mother" for "father and mother." The A. V. is literal and plain. In the Greek there is no article.

11. "All men . . . not" = οὐ πάντες, = "not all men." Cf. 1 Cor. vi. 12, and x. 23.

20. "Have observed" for "have kept" = ἐφυλαξάμην. (?)

22. "Was one that had" for "had" = ἦν ἔχων. But see vii. 29; Mark i. 22, etc.

23. "It is hard for a rich man to enter" for "a rich man shall hardly enter." Here the A. V. is exactly literal with tense, adverb and all.

24. What is the difference, to a simple reader, between "a needle's eye" and "the eye of a needle"? Do the Revisers suppose that "a needle's eye" means "an eye of a needle," *i.e.*, "one of the eyes of a needle"? And do they intend to insinuate this meaning? A needle is ordinarily cycloptic, or, at the least, monoptic. But ah! the Greek article! Or must St. Matthew be conformed to St. Luke?

25. "Astonished exceedingly" for "exceedingly amazed;" —consequential.

26. "Looking upon them said" for "beheld them and said" = ἐμβλέψας εἶπεν. But see vii. 3 and xxvi. 27.

27. "Lo" for "behold" = ἰδού. But see i. 20, 23; ii. 1, 9; x. 16; xx. 18, 30, etc., etc. What hair is split here? "Then" for "therefore" = ἄρα. But see at xvii. 26 "therefore" for "then" = ἄραγε. What hair is split again here?

30. The Revisers show here that the sense can be conveyed in English without inserting the article; and their manipulation is skilful. But what is gained, by their change, in faithfulness to the Word of God? See x. 2.

XX.

1. "*That is*" should be "*that was.*" So the American Revisers.

7. "Hath hired" = ἐμισθώσατο. 10. "Would receive" = λήμψονται.

17. "As Jesus was going up" for "Jesus going up" = ὁ Ἰησοῦς ἀναβαίνων. Which is the more faithful? and what of participial constructions?

19. "Shall be raised up" for "shall rise again." In the Revisers' text ἐγερθήσεται is put for ἀναστήσεται. But see xiv. 2; xxvii. 63, 64; xxviii. 6; Mark xvi. 6; etc.

21. "What wouldst thou?" for "what wilt thou?" *i.e.*, "what wilt thou have?" = τί θέλεις; (?)

23. "*It is for*" for "*it shall be given to.*" The latter insertion keeps up the connection, and is as true as the other. "Hath been prepared" for "is prepared." But see γέγραπται.

25. "Their great ones" for "they that are great" = οἱ μεγάλοι. At Mark x. 42, "their great ones" = οἱ μεγάλοι αὐτῶν (so also A. V.). But is not a pronoun as important as an article? What has become of their zeal for infinitesimal exactitude in conforming to every particle of the text, in bringing out the slightest differences in different passages, and particularly in their new text? See "a needle's eye," "the belly of the whale," "two witnesses or three;" see also xix. 30; and their contortions to keep the article out, and yet to get it in, at Gal. ii. 20, etc., etc. If the A. V. had given the same rendering here as in St. Mark, although there was no αὐτῶν in the text, or if, the αὐτῶν being in the text, they had translated as they did, the Revisers would have shown no more than a reasonable breadth of the critical mind in leaving the translation unchanged. But the change they have made only combines pettiness with inconsistency. We beg pardon for speaking plainly. If we are asked why make so much ado about a trifling oversight? we answer that, if an oversight, it is an oversight in making a petty correction; and what we most object to all along is precisely the pettiness of the greater part of the corrections the Revisers have indulged in.

26. "Not so shall it be among you" for "it shall not be so among you" = οὐχ οὕτως ἔσται ἐν ὑμῖν. But Cf. ix. 13; viii. 16, 25; xii. 33; xv. 5; xxi. 12, 33; xxiii. 1, 2, 3,

etc. And why not say "not all" (οὐ πάντες) at xix. 11, and be logically as well as literally correct?

27. "Would" for "will." The simple future would be "shall." There is no ambiguity therefore in the A. V.

XXI.

5. "Riding" =ἐπιβεβηκώς. Did they see the perfect, or did they render by consequence? "The foal of an ass" = υἱὸν ὑποζυγίου. Why not "a foal of an ass," or at least, "an ass's foal"?

8. "Cut and spread." These are imperfects; why not, "went on cutting and spreading"?

10. "The prophet, Jesus, from Nazareth" for "Jesus, the prophet of Nazareth." Ὁ ἀπὸ N. = "who is," or, in the most approved style, "even he that is." How happened they to forget this?

12. Why did not the Revisers say, "And the tables of the money changers he overturned," and thus imitate the change of order in the Greek, as at xiii. 48; a change which may contain some latent emphasis or, perchance, some mystery?

16. "Did you never read" for "have ye never read." But see xii. 3, 5; xix. 4; xxii. 31; etc.—where οὐκ instead of οὐδέποτε : but what of it? Does the latter require the tense to be altered here? See also v. 21, 27, etc., etc.

23, 24. Why didn't they say: "In what authority?"—instead of "by" = ἐν, as elsewhere?

28, 41. "The vineyard" for "my vineyard;" because the μοῦ has fallen out of their text. But they find the article enough for the possessive pronoun in numberless instances; see verse 31, John xix. 30, etc., etc., and compare xx. 25.

33. Why not, "another parable hear ye"? See xx. 26; xxiv. 32, etc.

38. "But the husbandmen, when they saw, said" for "but when, etc., they said." But see ix. 12; xi. 2.

"Let us take." But their text is changed to σχῶμεν = "let us have" or "hold"—not seize or take = κατάσχωμεν.

41. " Miserable" for "wicked" = κακούς. (?)

42. "The head of the corner." No articles. Cf. xxiii. 15.
44. "Scatter as dust" for "grind to powder" = λικμή-σει. (?) Observe it is done by a falling stone.

XXII.

2. "Is likened" = ώμοιώθη. 3. Why not "bid the bidden" or "call the called"? See Acts xxvi. 24, 25.
4. "Made ready" for "prepared." See "ready" immediately afterwards.
6. "Entreated shamefully" for ". . . spitefully = ὕβρισαν. No *shame* in the word, but wanton *violence* and *outrage*. Cf. Mark xii. 4; Luke xx. 11, where "shamefully" is right.
11. "To behold (for see) the guests" = θεάσασθαι. But see vi. 1; xxiii. 5; Mark xvi. 14; Acts viii. 18, etc. So this strange English is not enforced by the Greek.
13. "Hand and foot" = πόδας καὶ χεῖρας, "feet and hands;" but see "the footstool of his feet," and the "two witnesses and three," etc.
21. Why not say "the things that are Cæsar's to Cæsar, and the things that are God's to God" and thus continue "faithful" to the Greek? See Mark v. 15.
34. "But the Pharisees, when they heard . . . gathered," for "but when the Pharisees heard, they were," etc. See xii. 2, 24.
36. "The great" = μεγάλη : 38, "the great" = ἡ μεγάλη. Both are predicates.
39. "A second" for "the second" (also in margin). But see Mark xii. 31, "the second," alike in both cases, no article.
40. "The whole law" for "all the law" = ὅλος ὁ νόμος. But why not, then, say, at verse 37, "thy whole heart," "thy whole soul," etc.; and see Matt. iv. 23, 24; ix. 26, 31, etc.; also Acts ii. 2, "all the house;" x. 22, "all the nation;" xi. 28, "all the world" (with A. V.); and compare Matt. xxiv. 14, "the whole world" (with A. V.). Why, then, must faithfulness make a change here?
42. Τοῦ Δαβίδ. The τοῦ here belongs to Δαβίδ in the

genitive. So, probably, the τοῦ before the list of names in St. Luke's genealogy of Christ, Luke iii. 23-36; and, if so, "the son" there, (both words), should be printed in italics (as being inserted), after the A. V.

43. "In the Spirit" = ἐν πνεύματι. So, then, it seems the absence of the article rather than its presence shows πνεῦμα to be the Holy Spirit. Compare Matt. v. 3.

XXIII.

4. "They will not move them" = οὐ θέλουσι. Here there might be ambiguity; but see xvi. 24; xxvi. 15.

9. "On the earth;" but see xvi. 19; xviii. 18, etc. The change proposed in this verse by the American Revisers is well enough in itself, but unnecessary. See John viii. 53.

13. If this repetition of "enter in" is required by faithfulness, then they should have "bid" "the bidden" to the marriage. Besides, they were bound to complete their improvement here by rendering, "for ye enter not in yourselves, neither suffer ye them that are entering in to enter (in)." They themselves render εἰσελθεῖν, "come under," Matt. viii. 8 and Luke vii. 6; "come into," Matt. xvii. 25; and "go in" or "went in," John x. 9,—here it is "enter in" and "go in" in immediate succession—; Acts i. 21; x. 27; xi. 3; xvii. 2; Mark xv. 43; Luke xi. 37; xv. 28; xxiv. 29; Matt. xxv. 10. And Liddell and Scott define it "to go or come in." Yet in some twenty or thirty cases they have changed "go in" to "enter in," with no more necessity than here, or in the passages just referred to.

15. "A son" for "the child." 31. "Sons" for "the children." Predicates or in apposition. See xiv. 33; xxiv. 8.

22. "The heaven" for "heaven;" and then, verse 23, the article omitted three times and three times. See verse 24, where "strain out" is right; but "the" is no more required with "gnat" and "camel" than with "mint, anise, and cummin," in verse 23.

39. Οὐ μή = simply "not;" and so Mark xiii. 3; Matt. xxiv. 35; xxvi. 29, etc., etc. But see Matt. xvi. 28.

XXIV.

9. "All the nations" for "all nations"—and so, often. But what is the faithful difference in the sense?

13. "To the end" = εἰς τέλος.

15. "When therefore ye see" for " when ye therefore shall see" = ὅταν οὖν ἴδητε. But see, for " shall," Mark xiii. 7; Luke xvii. 10, etc.; and for " therefore," Matt. xxv. 28.

22. "Except those days had been shortened no flesh would have been saved;" but they " shall be shortened." This, in English, is incongruous. Is it required by the Greek? Is not the rule that enjoins it contradicted by this fact of the language? See xxvi. 24. In St. Mark the construction of the parallel passage is consistent, being framed throughout from the prophetic or predestinate point of view.

27, 37. Is the change of order necessary to faithfulness, or was it to improve the English expression?

29. "Stars shall fall from heaven," ἐκ τοῦ οὐρ. "Powers of the heavens," τῶν οὐρ.: 30. "Sign in heaven," ἐν τῷ οὐρ.: " Clouds of heaven," τοῦ οὐρανοῦ : 31. " End of heaven," οὐρανῶν : 36. "Angels of heaven," τῶν οὐρανῶν : 35. "Heaven and earth," ὁ οὐρ. and ἡ γῆ. See Acts iv. 24.

32. " Now from the fig-tree learn her parable." Greek order, but see xx. 26; xxi. 33. No pronoun for " her," but see xxi. 28, 41.

42. This = ἐκεῖνο : and so A. V.

XXV.

18. " Digged in the earth" = ὤρυξε γῆν.

20, 22. "Lo" for " behold" = ἴδε. But see 65 ; Mark ii. 24; xi. 21, etc., etc. " He that received" for " he that had received" = ὁ λαβών. Cf. John xiii. 26 ; Heb. xi. 17.

21, 23. "Hast been" = ἧς. Why not " wast"? But who can exactly measure the depths of faithfulness?

24. " He that had received" = ὁ εἰληφώς. But it is manifestly co-ordinated with ὁ λαβών.

25, 27. "Thine own" for " that is thine" = τὸ σόν, not τὸ ἴδιον.

26. "Wicked" = πονηρέ, not "evil," and so Luke xix.
22. But see Matt. xii. 45; xvi. 4; Luke xi. 26; Col. i. 21;
2 Thess. iii. 2, etc., etc.

28. "Take ye away, therefore, from" for "take therefore from" = ἄρατε οὖν ἀπό. The "ye" is not expressed in the Greek; and see xxiv. 15.

37. "Athirst" for "thirsty" = διψῶντα. This painstaking emendation seems to have been made because (with A. V.) the Revisers have "athirst" at verse 44. But why stop at this? If διψῶντα must be "athirst," how should ἐδίψησα remain "I was thirsty"? Their shortest way would have been, if they *must* correct so flagrant a piece of unfaithfulness in the A. V., to put "thirsty" for "athirst" at verse 44, and then all would have been harmonious.

40. "One of these my brethren, *even* of these least" for "one of the least of these my brethren" = ἑνὶ τούτων τῶν ἀδελφῶν μου τῶν ἐλαχίστων. But the second "these" is not in the Greek. See the "daily bread" of the Lord's Prayer, for the construction.

XXVI.

2. "Cometh" for "is" = γίνεται: 5. "arise" for "be" = γένηται: 54, "be" = γενέσθαι.

7. "Exceeding precious" for "very precious" = βαρυτίμου:—exceeding faithful!

9. "The poor" = πτωχοῖς (no art.). Why not say, at verse 11, "For the poor ye have always with you, but me ye have not always;" thus taking advantage of the Greek initial and of the English final emphasis? But compare John xii. 8. If they must change there, why not also here?

12. "Did" = ἐποίησε: 13. "Hath done" = ἐποίησε. Note a painstaking reconstruction, and all to secure the presumed logical place for "also."

15. "Are ye willing to" for "will ye" = θέλετε; but see xxiii. 4; Acts xxv. 9.

15. "Weighed" = ἔστησαν:—a possible but at least a doubtful sense here.

17. "Of unleavened bread" for "of the feast of unleavened bread" = τῶν ἀζύμων. Faithfulness to the sense?

To the syllables? But what has become of the article? "Make ready" for "prepare." (?)

18. "Time" = καιρός.

19. "Appointed" for "had appointed" = συνέταξεν. But "had appointed" expresses in the English the strict relation of the time. See xxviii. 16; Luke xxiv. 24.

21. "Betray" = παραδώσει : but, at 16, "deliver" = παραδῷ is substituted for "betray," as "deliver" had been used just before. Why not make the change there as well as here? *Must* the A. V. be altered? Besides, the Revisers are not afraid of verbal repetitions. Rather they are bound to make them after the Greek. See 1 Cor. xv. 28, etc.

24. "Good were it for that man if he had not been born" for "it had been good," etc. But see xxiv. 22. Surely if ἦν conditioned by εἰ with an aorist indicative can mean "were" (= "would be,") ἐσώθη *with* ἄν, and conditioned in like manner, can mean "would be saved" instead of "would have been saved." It would really seem as if the A. V. must be corrected, render as it may. If it renders "had been," then "were" or "would be;" if it renders "would be," then "would have been" or "had been." But see John xv. 22, 24, where they follow the A. V.

25. "Is it I, Rabbi?" for "Master, is it I?" But see "Save, Lord," viii. 25. "Hast said" = εἶπας.

26, 27. "He" inserted before "gave" in 26 but not in 27. "A cup" for "the cup." Their text omits the article. But is any article needed in the Greek phrase? See verses 74 and 75.

28. "Is shed," not "is being shed." Cf. Acts ii. 47 and 2 Cor. ii. 15, etc. "Unto remission of sins" for "For the remission of sins" = εἰς ἄφεσιν ἁμ. But at Luke i. 77, they render ἐν ἀφέσει "in the remission;" and see verse 45, "unto the hands" = εἰς χεῖρας.

37. "Sore troubled" for "very heavy" = ἀδημονεῖν. (?)

43. "Heavy" = βεβαρημένοι = "weighed down."

44 and 42. "A second time," "a third" for "the" etc. O faithfulness! How many second and third times were there? But see Mark xiv. 72 and Acts x. 15.

45. "Unto" for "into" = εἰς. (?) And how important!

50. "Laid hands," τὰς χεῖρας: but at 45 "unto the hands," χεῖρας: and at verse 51 "his hand," τὴν χεῖρα. Why not say here "their hands" and be exact and consistent—and correct the A. V. at the same time?

52. "With" = ἐν: and "the" is inserted twice with "sword."

56. "Is come to pass." Misleading?

64 and 39. "Nevertheless" = πλήν. This particle seems to have been a special exercise to the faithful and consequential ingenuity of the Revisers. It is used in the N. T. about thirty times, and they have corrected the A. V. fifteen times. In Matt. xi. 22, 24; Luke x. 14; xi. 41; xii. 31; xix. 27, and Rev. ii. 25, they put "howbeit" for "but;" in Luke x. 11, 20, and Phil. iv. 14, they put "howbeit" for "notwithstanding;" in Luke xiii. 33, xviii. 8, and 1 Cor. xi. 11, they put "howbeit" for "nevertheless;" in Phil. i. 18; iii. 16, they put "only" for "nevertheless;" in Luke xxii. 42; Eph. v. 33, as here in Matt. xxvi. 39, 64, they have suffered "nevertheless" to remain. In Matt. xi. 22, 24, where they put "howbeit" for "but," the phrase in the Greek is the very same as here, where the "nevertheless" is retained, viz., πλὴν λέγω ὑμῖν. Now, as far as the sense is concerned, it could make no real difference whether "but" or "howbeit," or "notwithstanding," or "nevertheless" were used—"nevertheless" is one of the most clumsy—; and if they had used the simple "but" (or "yet," or "and yet") in all cases it might have been well. But they seem to have had a special fancy for the antiquated "howbeit," which the A. V. has never used as the translation of πλήν: and—for consistency's sake and consequential faithfulness —have retained all the others in different places, except "notwithstanding." Where they put "only" for "nevertheless," "but" would have done as well, or "nevertheless" might have been left, as here.

65. "Hath spoken," "have heard," for aorists.

74, 75. "The cock crew." No article in the Greek. Why did they not say: "a cock crew;" as, "he took a cup," at verse 27?

XXVII.

7. "Strangers" = τοῖς ξένοις. (article?) "With them" = ἐξ αὐτῶν.

8. "The field of blood;" ἀγρός. See Acts xvii. 23 and Mark iii. 17.

14. "He gave him no answer, not even to a word" for "he answered him to never a word" = οὐκ ἀπεκρίθη αὐτῷ πρὸς οὐδὲ ἓν ῥῆμα. (?)

"15. "At the feast" (marg. "a") = κατὰ ἑορτήν. Why not say, "at feast time"—if we must split hairs about articles, or may insert anything whatever except only an article? See Gal. ii. 20.

17. "When therefore" for "therefore when." But which is most *logical* in English? Do they think to express any difference in the sense?

18. "Had delivered" = παρέδωκαν :19, "have suffered" = ἔπαθον.

24. "See ye to it" = ὄψεσθε = "ye shall see to it." (?)

26. "Jesus he scourged and delivered" for "when he had scourged Jesus, he delivered him" = τὸν δὲ Ἰησ. φραγελλώσας παρέδωκεν. Which has the right air and tone? See verses 50 and 54.

27. 29. "Kneeled down" for "bowed the knee" = γονυπετήσαντες. "To kneel" is "to bow the knee," or "to fall upon the knees." Whence comes the added "down"? It is a curious illustration of punctilious faithfulness and consistency in correcting the A. V. that at Matt. xvii. 14 they put "kneeling" for "kneeling down;" at Mark i. 40 they retain "kneeled down;" and at Mark x. 17 they have simply "kneeled;" and all for the same Greek word, γονυπετέω.

33. "The place of a skull" for "a place," etc. Right, but remarkable. No article in Greek. Suppose the A. V. had said "the place," what would they have done? It is true they have left "the field" at verse 8; but see Mark iii. 17.

43. "Desireth" for "will have" = θέλει. (?)

45. "There was" = ἐγένετο. Why not "there came, arose, or followed"? See verse 24; Rev. xi. 15, etc.

46. "Loud" = μεγάλη. But see Rev. v. 2, 12; viii. 13; xiv. 7, 9, 15; where "loud" is faithfully changed to "great." "Hast forsaken," aorist.

49. "Cometh" for "will come." The sense is undoubtedly future though the tense is present.

52. "Were raised" for "arose" = ἠγέρθη. But see verses 63 and 64, etc., etc.

54. Compare the construction with verses 50 and 26. "The things that were done" = τὰ γενόμενα—not "the things that came to pass." But see xxviii. 11.

Marg. "A son of God." There seems no occasion for this marginal reading. It is not called for by the rule of the Greek article; see verse 43, etc., etc. And as to the centurion being a heathen, it is not certain that he was not like the centurion of Matt. viii. 5–10 and Acts x.; and it is probable that he knew about the claims of Jesus from the Jewish point of view, for most likely he was with Pilate, and had heard the charge made by the Jews before Pilate: "We have a law and by our law he ought to die, because he made himself the Son of God;" at which words Pilate, who before had been startled by the message from his wife, was the more afraid. But, finally, if the centurion must be supposed to speak from the purely heathen point of view, his exclamation should be translated, not "a son of God," but "the son of a god." The Revisers might suggest, "a son of a god," or "a god's son;" but these expressions are forced and artificial, and foreign to the English idiom, or, at least, very unnatural and unusual.

63. "We remember," aorist. "I rise again" for "I will rise again;" but the sense is undoubtedly future.

XXVIII.

1. "To see" = θεωρῆσαι—not "behold." 4. "Quake" for "shake." (?)

6, 7. "Is risen" = ἠγέρθη —not "was raised."

9. "Took hold of his feet" for "held him by the feet" = ἐκράτησεν αὐτοῦ τοὺς πόδας. Note the proper force of the verb. Was this change required?

14. "Rid you of care" for "secure you."

18. "Came to them and spake unto them" for "came and spake unto them" = προσελθὼν ἐλάλησεν αὐτοῖς. But see iv. 3, where they correct the A. V. by putting "came" for "came to him" as a translation of the same Greek word in the same construction.

"Authority" for "power" = ἐξουσία; but at Mark ii. 10 they render "power."

"Hath been given" for "is given" = ἐδόθη. (?)

19. "Make disciples of all the nations" for "teach all nations." "All the nations" cannot differ much in sense from "all nations;" only in form it brings out more sensibly the incongruity with "making disciples."

"Baptizing into the name," εἰς τὸ ὄνομα. But at x. 41. they render εἰς ὄνομα "in the name;" and see 1 Cor. x. 2.

20. "Commanded" for "have commanded;" but see verse 16, "had appointed"—both for aorists. If an aorist becomes pluperfect after another aorist, why should it not become perfect after a present tense? Besides, "commanded" would seem to refer to some particular, though indefinite, time. Can we suppose our Lord to have had in mind any such reference? We must read from his point of view, and not from our present position. Cf. Luke xxiv. 44; but the limitation of time there expressed is not expressed here, and what right have we to presume it to be implied? See Acts i. 2.

ST. MARK.

I.

4. Why is "the" retained before "baptism" and omitted before "remission"? Which required the change, faithfulness to the English or to the Greek? Cf. Luke i. 77 and Acts ii. 38. And as to the "unto" for "for," the A.V. put "unto" in the margin; but "for" is the settled English use, as see the Nicene Creed; and compare "the kingdom of heaven."

6. "Had" inserted for "with." The A.V. is literal and correct. For the construction of participles with the verb "to be," compare xiii. 25, and compare the latter with Matt. xxiv. 29.

8. "Baptized" for "have baptized;"—but compare verse 11, and 1 Cor. ix. 15; Col. iv. 8; Philem. 19, 21, etc., etc.

11. "Out of the heavens" for "from heaven" = ἐκ τῶν οὐρανῶν: but compare the Lord's Prayer, and the "kingdom of heaven," τῶν οὐρ.: also John iii. 31; 1 Thess. i. 10; Rev. x. 4, xiv. 13, etc.; where we have "in heaven" = ἐν τοῖς οὐρ. (as commonly elsewhere); and "from heaven" = ἐκ τῶν οὐρ., "cometh from heaven;" and "a voice from heaven," ἐκ τοῦ οὐρ.—not "out of heaven."

35. The *participial* construction of the A. V. wantonly changed.

37. "Are seeking" for "seek." But why not the same change at iii. 32, if faithfulness required it here?

II.

10. "Power" = ἐξουσίαν: changed to "authority" at iii. 15, and so, generally. But cf. Luke v. 24; xii. 5; John x. 18; xix. 10, 11; Acts v. 4; viii. 19; Rom. xiii. 1, 2, 3; and particularly Luke xxii. 53; Acts xxvi. 18; 1 Cor. vii. 37.

12. "Amazed" = ἐξίστασθαι:—but another verb is translated "amazed" at i. 27; and this verb is translated "is beside himself" at iii. 21.

17. "A" for "the;" and what's the difference? "The righteous" has no article in the Greek.

26. "Gave also to them," should be, if they *will* split hairs, "gave to them also"—their rule being, apparently, to put "also" after the word which in Greek follows the καί. 28. "Even" for "also." (?) At iii. 19, ὃς καί is rendered "who also."

III.

1, 3. "His" is put twice for the article only, unnecessarily. Indeed "a hand" was as near the sense as "his hand;" it was one of the man's hands.

9. "Lest" = ἵνα μή:—but see Col. iii. 21.

10. Here the A. V. follows the Greek order; and does it not give the sense, and is it not good English? Compare the painful transpositions of the Revisers at v. 15, in order

to conform to the Greek construction. And as to "that they might touch" for "to touch" = ἵνα ἄψωνται, compare their own translation at iv. 21, where "to be put" = ἵνα τεθῇ!

15. "Devils" = τὰ δαιμόνια. But see verse 22, and "the mountain" at verse 13; and vi. 7.

17. "Them he surnamed" for "he surnamed them." The A. V. follows the order of the Greek. Cf. Rev. viii. 2. "Sons" for "the sons;"—indifferent, but see Matt. xxvii. 34.

25. "Will not be able" for "cannot"= δυνήσεται :— so also at viii. 4. But "cannot" in English is either present or future; and "will not be able" looks as if not only a different tense but a different verb were used in the Greek. See Luke xvi. 2; where "can" is for the future.

26. "Hath risen up" for "rise up" = ἀνέστη. If ἀνέστη must be "hath risen up," then surely ἐμερίσθη (although displacing μεμέρισται) should be "hath been divided." But better say, "is risen up" (or "riseth up"), and "is divided." Both forms represent the perfect in English.

IV.

12. βλέπω = "see," and ἰδών = "perceive."

16. "Are sown," not "are being sown" = σπειρόμενοι. Cf. Acts ii. 47; 2 Cor. ii. 15. And compare "the sower" = ὁ σπείρων, verse 14, with "seed" = τὸν σπόρον, verse 26; and with ὁ κατηγορῶν, ὁ ζητῶν, and τὸν κρίνοντα, at John v. 45; viii. 50; xii. 48. With these last compare "There shall be the weeping and gnashing," and especially Mark i. 7, "there cometh he that is mightier than I."

19. "Entering in," not "going in" = εἰσπορευόμεναι, not εἰσερχόμεναι: see vii. 15-20. 21. "Is brought" = ἔρχεται.

28. Three articles inserted. What prevented their saying, "first a blade, then an ear, then full corn in the ear"?

34. Change of order needless; see the displacement of "he saith unto them," in verse 35.

37. "Insomuch that" for "so that" = ὥστε. But why?

Here is another of the Greek particles which seems to have sorely exercised the hypercritical faithfulness of the Revisers. They have changed its rendering from "therefore" to "wherefore" at 1 Cor. iii. 21; iv. 5; v. 8; xv. 58; 2 Cor. v. 17, and Phil. iv. 1. But they have admitted that it may be translated "therefore" by retaining that rendering at Rom. xiii. 2; and will they tell us the faithful difference in any of these cases between "therefore" and "wherefore"? They have changed "wherefore" to "so that," at Matt. xix. 6; Rom. vii. 12; Gal. iii. 24; iv. 7; and to "so then" at Phil. ii. 12; and "so then" to "so that" at Mark x. 8. They have changed "insomuch that" to "so that" at Mark ii. 2, but "so that" to "insomuch that" at xv. 5 and at Acts xix. 12, retaining "so that" at verses 10 and 16. But Luther, the Vulgate, and the whole English Hexapla render ὥστε in this verse 12 just as they do in verses 10 and 16; and, with one or two exceptions, they all disagree with all the changes here made by the Revisers. Now no new lights of Greek grammar or lexicography can be appealed to in defence of these changes; for the same Greek word is used throughout and in the same connection, *i.e.*, with the indicative mode. All the renderings of the A. V. are retained by the Revisers, only they are differently distributed, and the most cumbrous and obsolescent—"insomuch that"—is here introduced, and so multiplied. The right distribution must be determined by the nature of each case, by the context, and the propriety of English expression under the circumstances; and of these particulars any intelligent English reader may be as good a judge as the ripest Greek scholar. To such readers we cheerfully leave the judgment. But if any authority must be appealed to on these points, we humbly venture to set not only that of the translators of 1611, but that of the Vulgate, of Luther, and of the whole English Hexapla, against that of the Revisers. It is not a question of Greek scholarship, but of good common-sense. This may serve as a sample of the petty, if not wanton, changes, whose constant recurrence and vast multitude constitute our chief ground of complaint against the Late Revision. The worst of it is, they undermine our confidence in the judiciousness of really important alterations.

V.

4. "Had strength" for "could" = ἴσχυε. So at ix. 18 and Luke xx. 26, " were not able" for " could ;" and at Luke xvi. 3, "have not strength" for " can." The English reader can judge whether these changes are required for the sense ; for, that the Greek word does not require them will be seen by referring to Matt. viii. 28 ; xxvi. 40 ; Mark xiv. 37 ; and Acts xxv. 7, where they render this verb by "could ;" and Phil. iv. 13, where they render it by " can."

15. "Behold" for "see" = θεωροῦσι : and so at verse 38 and at iii. 11, and often elsewhere. But see Matt. xxviii. 1 ; John ix. 8 ; etc. "*Even* him that had" = τὸν ἐσχηκότα. For this laborious construction, compare the " daily bread" of the Lord's Prayer and Matt. xvii. 5. But τὸν ἐσχηκότα is rendered "him that had"—not "had had"—in the same tense with τὸν δαιμονιζόμενον="him that was possessed;" unless the latter is conceived—as indeed it may, if not must, be—in the pluperfect tense ; in which case the present participle is rendered as pluperfect, while the perfect participle, in precisely the same construction, is rendered as a simple preterite ! Had the man the legion still ? Now τὸν ἔχοντα, in this connection, as being governed by a preterite verb, would mean "him that had ;" shall we put the same for τὸν ἐσχηκότα ? In Rom. vi. 7, an aorist participle is rendered as a perfect, " he that hath died ;" and here a perfect is rendered as a simple preterite, and that when thrown into a time antecedent to the preterite verb that governs it ! This passage must evidently have been thoroughly studied, as it is so carefully reconstructed. And observe τὸν δαιμονιζόμενον is not rendered "him that was being possessed ;" as see Acts ii. 47, etc. For tenses cf. Acts iv. 13.

19. Aorist and perfect coördinated ; and both should be rendered perfect.

39, 40, 41. Here we have three aorist participles, and each followed by the present indicative,—one rendered by " when he was entered in," another by " having put them all out," and the third by "taking." Why this change of tense?

And as for the variety of construction, see "mad," "madness," "mad;" "subject," "subjected," "subject;" Acts xxvi. 24, 25; 1 Cor. xv. 27, 28.

VI.

7. An imperfect and an aorist are coördinated, and both translated by the preterite. Is this the reason for twice inserting "he"? Amazing faithfulness! See verse 13.

9. "To go" inserted for "be;" but the A. V. is the simpler. There is no "go" in the context.

13. Here all three imperfects are rendered preterites; and "they" is not repeated.

14. "Had become" for "was" = $\dot{\epsilon}\gamma\dot{\epsilon}\nu\epsilon\tau o$. "Is risen" = $\dot{a}\nu\dot{\epsilon}\sigma\tau\eta$. "These" = $a\dot{\iota}$.

16. "But Herod, when he heard thereof, said," for "But when Herod heard thereof he said" = $\dot{a}\kappa o\dot{\nu}\sigma a\varsigma$ $\delta\dot{\epsilon}$ $\dot{o}$ $\accentset{\cdot}{H}\rho\omega\delta\eta\varsigma$ $\dot{\epsilon}\lambda\epsilon\gamma\epsilon\nu$. How important! But see xv. 39; Matt. ix. 8, 12, etc. "He is risen" = $\dot{\eta}\gamma\dot{\epsilon}\rho\vartheta\eta$:—not "is raised" nor "was raised;" but see xiv. 28; and Matt. xxvi. 32; etc., etc.

17. Pluperfects for aorists right through; but, 18, "said" for "had said." Is not the A. V. right? Common-sense, and not the Greek grammar, must decide.

19. "Set herself against" for "had a quarrel against" = $\dot{\epsilon}\nu\epsilon\tilde{\iota}\chi\epsilon\nu$? "Grudge" might, perhaps, have been better than "quarrel." "Desired" for "would have" = $\ddot{\eta}\vartheta\epsilon\lambda\epsilon\nu$. But see verses 26 and 48, and Matt. xiv. 5.

23. "The half." No article in the Greek. This is a good illustration of idiom.

34. For change of construction, see v. 39. "Hath compassion" for "was moved with compassion;" see Matt. xiv. 14, note.

56. "He entered" = $\epsilon i\sigma\pi o\rho\epsilon\dot{\nu}\epsilon\tau o$: imperfect; but see vii. 15, "going into" for "entering into." "The country,"—no article in the Greek nor in the A. V.

VII.

7. "The precepts." No article in the Greek, and none needed in the English.

11. "Mightest have been" for "mightest be" = ὠφειλή-
θης: also "given" for "gift"? See also Matt. xv. 5, and note.
15-20. "Going into" for "entering into;" but see vi. 56; iv. 19; etc. "Goeth out," but in 15 and 20 "proceedeth out,"—all from ἐκπορεύομαι. But see "mad, madness, mad," Acts xxvi. 24, 25. And see Matt. xxiii. 13.

VIII.

1. Change of construction entirely unnecessary; in English, as in Greek, "great" is here of course in the singular number, and "having" in the plural, from the nature of the case.
4. "Shall be able" for "can;" see iii. 24, 25, also Luke xvi. 2. "In a desert place" for "in the wilderness;" see 2 Cor. xi. 26.
24. "I see men" = τοὺς ἀνθρώπους.
31. "By" for "of" = ὑπό: but see xiii. 13.
33. "Turning about" for "when he had turned about" = ἐπιστραφείς. But at verses 6 and 7 it is "having given thanks" for "gave thanks and" = εὐχαριστήσας: and "having blessed" for "blessed and" = εὐλογήσας: while at xiv. 22, 23 it is "when he had blessed" for "blessed and" = εὐλογήσας, and "when he had given thanks" = εὐχαριστήσας. See xiv. 22, note.
34, 35. "Would" for "will" = θέλει, θέλῃ. Compare vi. 19, 26, 48.
38. For the change of construction, compare iii. 17.

IX.

1. "There be some here of them that stand by" for "There be some of those standing here." This elaborate change is made because the position of ὧδε in the text had been changed from τῶν ὧδε to ὧδε τῶν. But does not the insertion of "by" make a bald tautology? And for the place of ὧδε note the construction of viii. 4. But ah! revising faithfulness! Mint, anise, and cummin!
13. "Have done" = ἐποίησαν, coördinated with a perfect; but it might have been rendered by the preterite, as if

contradistinguished from the accompanying perfect, as well as any of the aorists in John xvii.; and before at v. 19.

17. "I have brought" = ἤνεγκα.

18. "Were not able" for "could not;"—what's the faithful difference? But, it may be said, the Greek is ἴσχυσαν and not ἠδύναντο: then see Luke viii. 43, etc. And see verse 28, showing that the meaning of the two verbs is the same.

22. "Hath cast" = ἔβαλε.

29. "Is dead" = ἀπέθανε. For the change of construction, compare Matt. xxvi. 26. Could faithfulness require the change in one place and not in the other? and if so, in which was the greater faithfulness required?

39. "By" = ἐν, twice. Why did they not say "in"?

33. "When he was in the house" for "being in the house" = ἐν τῇ οἰκίᾳ γενόμενος. How is the A. V. to escape castigation? If it has the Latin construction, the participial is substituted, see verse 26 and viii. 33;—and if it has the participial construction, the Latin circumlocution must take its place. For rendering the aorist participle here as present, see again viii. 33, etc., etc.

34. Note that διελέχθησαν after γάρ is rendered by a pluperfect; and μείζων is rendered "the greatest."

41. "In no wise" for "not" = οὐ μή. But see xiv. 31.

42 "Were" for "is" = ἐστίν, in the simple direct indicative. Then, "were hanged" is for an indicative present with "if," and "were cast," in the same construction, for an indicative perfect. This may all be very well; but see the construction "it is better" in the following verses, with the aorist infinitives all rendered present. And then what has become of faithfulness to the original? See verse 1; xi. 24, etc.

X.

13. Is there no "ancient authority" for "those who brought them" = τοῖς προσφέρουσιν? The words are retained by Tischendorf in his eighth edition. S. and V. omit them.

15. "In no wise" for "not" = οὐ μή: unnecessary.—see Matt. xxiii. 39; Mark xiii. 2; xiv. 31, etc.

18. "*Even*" for "*that is.*" Faithfulness to the original! "Save" for "but" = εἰ μή: but cf. 1 Cor. viii. 4; and see Luke iv. 26, 27; Rev. ii. 17; Matt. v. 13; xii. 24; xv. 24, etc., where they as faithfully put "but" for " save."

25. " A needle's eye," again, for "the eye of a needle." See Matt. xix. 24, note.

26. " Then who" for " who then." The difference?

27. Another change of construction which utterly ruins the rhythm. As to the Greek order, see their own construction at iii. 17, and Matt. xxii. 21.

51. " What wilt thou?" But at verse 36 it is " what would ye?" The Revisers, after all, are no more consistent than the A. V.

XI.

10. Should they not have said "the coming kingdom" = ἡ ἐρχομένη βασιλεία, and saved the repetition of " the kingdom"? There is no article with the Greek noun.

17. "A house" for " the house;" but it is a predicate, and see Matt. xxvii. 33, etc. Was it to be one of the houses of prayer for " all the nations" or " the house" of prayer for them all? And as for " all the" for " all;"—in English "all" is idiomatically used for " all the" and " all those." If this is antiquated, it is at least as intelligible as "howbeit," or " straightway," or as " save" for " but," or " or" for " ere," or " which" for " who."

20. " From the roots." No article in the Greek.

24. " Have received" = ἐλάβετε. Why not as well present as perfect, and avoid the apparent nonsense? See Matt. iii. 17.

32. " Verily" for " indeed" = ὄντως. (?) " To be a prophet" for " that he was a prophet" = ὅτι προφήτης ἦν.

XII.

1. " A pit for the winepress" for "*a place for* the winefat" = ὑπολήνιον. Now what was dug out was certainly "a place for" the apparatus,—whether it were "a pit" or not; and it was dug for " the wine-*vat*," the bottom of the apparatus, whether it were for " the wine-*press*" or not. So that the A. V. is right, whether the Revisers are or not.

But they are so sure of their point that they have represented "pit," "press" and all, as being *expressed* in the Greek word.

10. " Have ye not read ?" = ἀνέγνωτε; "the stone," "the head," "the corner;"—no articles in Greek.

12. "Spake" for " had spoken." Wrong, and inconsistent; see vi. 17; ix. 34; and especially John ii. 22; iv. 1; ix. 35, etc.

13. "That they might catch him" for "to catch him" = ἵνα, κ.τ.λ. (?) Cf. iv. 21; xv. 15, 20, etc. "In talk." Better, "with talk" (dat. inst.) or " in *his* talk" (A. V.); or "with *their* talk"?

26. "Are raised" for "rise" = ἐγείρονται: see vi. 16.

27. Here the Revisers render "the God" three times where there is no article in their text;—the more wonderful, as the article was in the old text.

33. "His neighbour." Whose neighbour? This is antiquated, and scarcely intelligible. We now say " one's neighbour," in such cases.

36. " Footstool of thy feet" for "thy footstool." This is more antiquated than the oldest English.

38. "Desire to have" is here put for "will have," adding the "have" after all; see Matt. xxvii. 43.

39. "Chief seats" for "the chief seats." Which is the natural idiomatic English? But ah! the Greek article! And yet "at feasts" = ἐν τοῖς, etc.

43. "Superfluity" for "abundance." Superfluous?

XIII.

1. "Behold" for "see = ἴδε. What important distinctions in meaning this ἴδε must embrace, and how the authors of the A. V. are to be pitied for their ignorance in not perceiving them! At Matt. xxv. 20, 22, "lo" is put for "behold" as its translation, and at John xx. 27, "see" is put for "behold."

2. Οὐ μή is twice rendered simply "not," and so at verses 30 and 31; but see ix. 41.

9. "In" = εἰς :—"in synagogues shall ye be beaten."

12. "The brother" (A. V.) here expresses the meaning of the Greek as exactly as "the father" of the Revisers does.

And what right had they to insert " his" (not italicized) before " child," and not before the second " brother"? So far as articles are concerned, surely no faithfulness required any change of the A. V. in this passage.

14. " When ye see" for " when ye shall see" = ἴδητε. But verse 7, " when ye shall hear" = ἀκούσητε. Both after ὅταν and with the imperative.

17. "Woe to them that are with child." Of course the οὐαί cannot be an imprecation here. In some other cases it *might seem* to be; yet the Revisers have given it the same version always. Is this deciding a doubtful sense? Would it not have been true and plainer to have translated this expression in all cases by " alas!" " alas for you!" " alas for them!" etc.—as the A. V. has done in the Revelation, where the Revisers have substituted " woe" for the " alas"?

20. " Would have been" for " should be." This may be defended here, standing as if all were past and finished in the counsel of God. But in St. Matthew the tense is future.

22. " That they may lead astray" for " to deceive" = πρὸς τὸ ἀποπλανᾶν.

30. " Be accomplished" for " be done" = γένηται. See the Lord's Prayer.

34. Why not as well insert "*who*" as " when"? And what great difference after all?

XIV.

5. " They murmured," for the imperfect. Why not " were murmuring"? See verse 18 and Luke ii. 33.

6, 8, 9. " Hath wrought" = εἰργάσατο.

10. " That he might deliver him up" for " to betray him" = ἵνα, κ.τ.λ. (?) Cf. iv. 21; xv. 15, 20. " He that was;" rather " who was" simply, as if ὁ = ὁ ὤν (which they, too, seem to assume); but see their version at xvi. 6; Matt. xxiii. 9; Rom. ix. 5; and in the Lord's Prayer, " which art," etc., etc.

11. For change of construction, compare Matt. ix. 12, 22; xii. 24, etc.

12. " Of unleavened " = τῶν ἀζύμων. At verse 1 they

retain the article, and say "the unleavened." "Make ready" for "prepare," and so, at verse 15, "ready" for "prepared;" but see Luke ii. 31.

18. "*Even* he that eateth" for "which eateth"= ὁ ἐσθίων: and so, verse 20, "he that dippeth" for "that dippeth." But, the verbs being in the singular in English, the exact sense is secured without these cumbrous insertions.

22. "Took bread, and, when he had blessed, he brake" for "took bread and blessed and brake" = λαβὼν ἄρτον εὐλογήσας ἔκλασε. A similar change is made in St. Luke, where the Greek construction is the same. But in St. Matthew the Revisers leave it, "Took bread and blessed and brake." Wherefore, then, this change here in St. Mark? Is it, perchance, because here there is no καί before εὐλογήσας? This is making a very nice distinction, which, if thrust into such a formula as this, should be faithfully adhered to elsewhere. But see xv. 1, where, *without* καί, they say "held, and bound, and carried;" while, at Matt. xxvii. 1, with καί, they say again, "took; and they bound, and led" *for* "took: and, when they had bound, they led." Verily, they are hard to please; or, they find it difficult to keep their split hairs steadily in the focus. In 1 Cor. xi. 23, 24, the construction is different; the καί there connects verbs and not participles. See viii. 33, note.

"Take ye" for "take" = λάβετε. But see xii. 35, where they faithfully put "watch" for "watch ye," because there is no ὑμεῖς in the Greek. Do they recognize that euphony or rhythm has any rights in a translation? Then they must elsewhere be judged accordingly.

28. "Raised up" for "risen" = ἐγερθῆναι. But see vi. 16; Matt. xvi. 2; xxvii. 64, etc., etc., especially in the middle forms.

30. Here they put "thou" just where it stands in their new Greek text, whatever may happen to the English. If there is so much virtue in the Greek order, why did they not faithfully translate: "Thou, before twice a cock crow, thrice shalt deny me"?

31. "Not" *for* "not in any wise" = οὐ μή. But see ix. 41; xvi. 18, etc., etc. Alas for the poor A. V.! How it

infallibly blunders, whichever way it turns! If it says " not in any wise," it should be " not;" and if it says " not," it should be "in no wise."

33. "Sore troubled" for " very heavy" = ἀδημονεῖν. (?) Cf. John xi. 33; xii. 27.

36. "Howbeit" for " nevertheless" = ἀλλά: elsewhere for πλήν :—better, simply " but' ' or " yet.' '

54. "Had followed" for " followed" = ἠκολούθησεν. Note that this is direct narrative. Cf. John xviii. 24.

56, 57. " Bare false witness," twice, for the imperfect.

64. "Ye have heard" = ἠκούσατε.

67. " The Nazarene, *even* Jesus," for "Jesus of Nazareth ;"—harsh and unnecessary; see " daily bread."

72. " The second time" = ἐκ δευτέρου. But see "a second," " a third," at Matt. xxvi. 42, 44.

XV.

4. " Again" is here faithfully transposed into the Greek order ; but it is (unfaithfully?) left at verse 13 in the English order, contrary to the Greek. Who can measure the unspeakable faithfulness which required the substitution of " Pilate again answered him" for " Pilate answered him again"?

5. "Insomuch that" for " so that ;" see iv. 37, note.

15. " Wishing" for "willing" = βουλόμενος. (?) And see a similar change for θέλων at Acts xxiv. 27.

19. Imperfects disregarded. But see the pains the Revisers took at Matt. iii. 14. Might they not have succeeded with as little circumlocution here? These imperfects are immediately preceded and followed by aorists, and ought they not to be distinguished? See John xvii.; and see Mark xvi. 3 ; Luke i. 22.

37. " Gave up the ghost" = ἐξέπνευσεν. At Matt. xxvii. 50 they have "yielded up his spirit" for "yielded up the ghost' ' = ἀφῆκεν τὸ πνεῦμα. How can "ghost" be got out of ἐξέπνευσε, if it is not found in πνεῦμα ?

40. "Beholding" for "looking on" = θεωροῦσαι. (?)

43. "Of honorable estate" for "honorable" = εὐσχήμων. (?)

44. They say "were dead" for τέθνηκε, and "had been dead" for ἀπέθανε. Note the tenses.
47. "Was laid" = τέθειται.

XVI.

4. "Exceeding" for "very" = σφόδρα (not περισσῶς). Exceeding nice.
5. "Arrayed" for "clothed" = περιβεβλημένον : cf. Matt. xxv. 35; "robe" for "garment" = στολήν. How exquisitely faithful! Cf. John xix. 2, 5.
11 and 16. "Disbelieve" for "believe not" = ἀπιστέω. But see Rom. iii. 3, where the sense given is merely privative; and Matt. xiii. 58, where ἀπιστίαν = not "disbelief," but "unbelief."
18. "In no wise" for "not" = οὐ μή. But see xiv. 31.

ST. LUKE.

I.

1. "Have been fulfilled" for "are most surely believed." Have not the Revisers here yielded too easily to the authority of the Vulgate? And would they not have done better to interchange the text and the margin? Does πληροφορέω ever thus mean *exactly the same* as πληρόω? They have given the same rendering also at 2 Tim. iv. 5, having the old marginal reading to support them. But elsewhere, as at 2 Tim. iv. 17; Rom. iv. 21; xiv. 5, they have retained the idea of full assurance—not the mere completion of fact, but the complete confirmation of evidence. At Col. iv. 12 they have corrected the A. V., putting "fully assured" for "complete," the text being changed from πεπληρωμένοι to πεπληροφορημένοι. This verb "to be fully assured of" may be compared with the verb "to be entrusted with." A person *is entrusted* with a thing, or the thing *is entrusted* to the person; so a person *is fully assured* of a thing, or the thing *is fully assured* to the person, and so *is surely believed* by him.
13. "Because" for "for;" —why? "supplication" for "prayer;"—consequential. "Is heard" is for an aorist.

17. Note the omission of the Greek articles here, and throughout these prophecies and hymns; also the use of the aorist for the perfect. Yet at verse 19 they put "was sent" for "am sent;" but see verses 30 and 47-55.

22. "Continued making signs" for "beckoned" = ἦν διανεύων. But see i. 14; xv. 16, etc.; Mark i. 22, etc.

35. Here one can only wonder that the suggestion of the American Revisers was not followed.

44. "Behold" for "lo" = ἰδού. "When" for "as soon as" = ὡς. (?)

46-55. Aorists rendered perfects all through, and articles inserted without any in the Greek.

59. "Would have called" = ἐκάλουν. This seems to imply an "if" following. Would it not have been better if they had said, "were disposed, or minded, to call"?

62. "What" for "how." Very nice. Perhaps they would correct the French also, and put "que (for "comment") s'appelle-t-il"?

68-79. Aorists and articles as at 46-55. At 72, if the article is supplied it will give the old translation and a more consistent sense.

76. "Make ready" for "prepare" = ἑτοιμάσαι: but see ii. 31.

II.

2. "The first" for "first;"—no article in the Greek. See Matt. xxii. 39. They translate as if they thought that, in the phrase "was the first made," etc., the "was made" could be the translation of ἐγένετο: but it is plain the phrase must mean "was the first which was made," and yet they have not marked "made" as an insertion. In the "was first made" of the A. V., "was made" = ἐγένετο, and that without any trouble.

6, 21, 22. "Fulfilled" for "accomplished;"—consequential.

8. "By night over their flock" for "over their flock by night." See also verse 41. Theirs is the Greek order, but the A. V. has the English and the logical order; and besides, our ears are used to it. But see ii. 11; Matt. xii. 40, note; 2 Pet. ii. 3, etc.

9. "An angel," "the glory;"— no article in the Greek for either. See also "the city of David," verse 11, and "the Holy Ghost," verse 25.

10. "Be not afraid" for "fear not;" but see ix. 34.

29. "According to thy word, in peace." One cannot but wish that the servile faithfulness of the Revision had sometimes improved the English or cleared the sense; but for the most part it does just the contrary. See note at verse 8. The Revisers are after-all inconsistent with themselves.

31. Here they render ἡτοίμασας "hast prepared" and not "hast made ready." They probably adopted some recondite distinction, but as it was purely arbitrary, nobody can thank them for it.

"Were marvelling" (imperfect); but see Mark xiv. 5, etc., etc.

34. "Rising up" for "the rising again" = ἀνάστασιν : it should be "the rising again," if it is "the falling;" there is no article in the Greek with either; but if they are referred to different parties, the second requires the article in English as well as the first. "Which is" for "which shall be." The latter is certainly more consistent with the context, but neither need be inserted.

35. "Thoughts of many hearts" for "the thoughts," etc. Why omit the article here, and yet insert it so often, where the Greek has none? See verse 38, "the redemption" for "redemption." (?)

43. "As they were returning" for "as they returned" = ἐν τῷ ὑποστρέφειν αὐτούς : (?)—" on their return."

48. "Sought thee" for "have sought thee." "Sought thee," when? The A. V. is surely right.

52. "Advanced" for "increased." This, as an intransitive verb, is a new word in the English Version. Is it necessary to faithfulness?

III.

2. "In the high-priesthood of Annas and Caiaphas" for "Annas and Caiaphas being high priests." This comes from the singular ἀρχιερέως being substituted in the text for the plural ἀρχιερέων. But after all it has left the sense

the same; and if a change in the expression must be made to conform to the new Greek, it would be simpler to say: "Annas being high priest and Caiaphas."

4. "Make ready" for "prepare." But see ii. 31, and xii. 20.

7. "Warned" for "hath warned." (?)

13. "Extort" for "exact" = $\pi\rho\acute{a}\sigma\sigma\varepsilon\tau\varepsilon$. Does the Greek mean "work out of" or "twist out of"?

14. "Exact anything wrongfully" for "accuse *any* falsely" = $\sigma\upsilon\kappa o\phi\alpha\nu\tau\acute{\eta}\sigma\eta\tau\varepsilon$. (?)

16. "With water." The American Revisers suggest "in water." On what ground, when there is no preposition in the Greek, and it is an instrumental dative? They are to translate each Gospel independently. But the preposition $\dot{\varepsilon}\nu$ means "with" or "by" in cases innumerable.

23, etc. The articles here belong to the names and not to "son" understood. "The" should be in italics, therefore, as well as "son." See Matt. xxii. 42.

IV.

2. "Completed" for "ended." This is better than putting "fulfilled" for "accomplished" at ii. 6, 21, 22.

11. "And," separated from the quotation. Right; but they should have been as careful elsewhere, as, *e.g.*, at Heb. x. 38.

16. An awkward change of construction to suit the arrangement of the Greek. Faithfulness could not require it for that purpose; and whether the sense required it, any intelligent reader can judge.

18. "Anointed" for "hath anointed," aorist; but it is manifestily coördinated, not contrasted, with a perfect. Cf. Acts xxi. 21, 24; xxv. 10, 11, etc.

21. "Hath been fulfilled" for "is fulfilled;" but see "it is written," "it is finished," etc., etc.

26, 27. "But only" for "save" and "saving" = $\varepsilon\dot{\iota}\ \mu\acute{\eta}$. This is very well; though the "only" is really added. It is not in the Greek here, as it is at vi. 4; where, curiously enough, the Revisers have (for consistency's sake?) put "save" for "but" = $\varepsilon\dot{\iota}\ \mu\acute{\eta}$: as here "but" for "save."

And yet (for still greater consistency's sake?) at the perfectly parallel passage, Matt. xii. 4, they have retained the "but" of the A. V. ; while again at the parallel passage in St. Mark they have changed the "but" to " save." Indeed this εἰ μή seems to have been made a sort of football in the Revision. The translation is changed from "but" to "save,"—with no better and no more consistent reasons than in the foregoing instances,—at Matt. xi. 27 ; Mark ix. 29, where "nothing but" is changed to "nothing save" (while at Mark xi. 13 and Matt. v. 13 "nothing but" is left); x. 18; Rom. xiii. 8; 1 Cor. ii. 11 ; 2 Cor. xii. 5 ; Rev. xiv. 3. On the other hand "save" is changed to "but," not only here in St. Luke, but at Rev. ii. 17, "no man saving" changed to "no one but," while at xiii. 17 and xiv. 3, "no man save" is retained. At Rom. vii. 7, "but" is changed to "except," while, in per-. fectly similar constructions, at Matt. xii. 24 ; xv. 24 ; John x. 10 and xiv. 6, the "but" is retained. Similar cases of *consequential* changes in the translation of ἐὰν μή will appear hereafter.

28. Here the change of construction is either needless or nonsensical. What sort of wrath is "wrath in the synagogue"?

34. "Ah" for "let alone" = ἔα. (?) "Art thou come" = ἦλθες (aorist).

38. "Holden" for "taken" = συνεχομένη. This may be faithful, but it is harsh in English. Would not "seized" be better? see its legal sense.—Or "afflicted"?

V.

9. "Amazed" for "astonished." (?) Scarcely consequential even.

10. "Sons" for "the sons ;"—the less natural English.

17. "One of those days" for "a certain day" = μιᾷ τῶν ἡμερῶν. But this is not literal after all, for τῶν is not "those."

19, 20. Change of construction needless; and see Mark ix. 33 ; Acts xxi. 2, 3, 4.

27. "Beheld" for "saw" = ἐθεάσατο : but see Matt. xi. 7, note.

ST. LUKE. 63

VI.

1. "Was going" for "went;" but "plucked" and "did eat" are equally for imperfects; why not "went on plucking and eating"?

35. "Sons" for "the children." But we have a right to insert the article with the predicate, if it makes more natural English; and we often use "children" for υἱοί, as "the children of Israel."

38. "Guide" for "lead;" what is gained?

48, 49. "Brake" for "beat vehemently" = προσέρρηξεν. (?)

VII.

4. "And they, when they" for "and when they, they." A familiar piece of hypercriticism; but see ix. 47; xxiii. 6, 8; Mark xv. 39; Matt. ix. 12; xi. 2; xii. 24, etc., etc. "Worthy that for him" for "worthy for whom" = ἄξιος ᾧ.

5. "Built" for "hath built." (?) In such cases, only let the intelligent reader consider which is the most natural tense in the connection; and remember that the decision does not depend at all upon the form of the Greek.

12. "One that was dead" for "a dead man" = τεθνηκώς. "The only son," no article in Greek; why not "an only son"? See v. 20, etc. "*Was* a widow," why insert "was"?

20. "Cometh" for "should come" = ὁ ἐρχόμενος = "is to come" or "is coming" or "shall come." See xviii. 20; John xviii. 4; xvi. 13; Acts xix. 4, etc. And see Matt. xi. 3, note.

22. The article is here inserted six times, and yet "the Gospel" is changed to "good tidings." How did the Revisers ascertain that the *verb* εὐαγγελίζομαι must mean to preach "good tidings" (a gospel) and not "the Gospel"? Certainly not from the Greek article.

24. "Behold" for "see." See Matt. xii. 7, note.

30. "For themselves" for "against themselves" = εἰς. What does this mean? Is not εἰς connected with βουλήν,

meaning, if not "against," "towards" or "in regard to"? But cf. Heb. xii. 3.

38. "Wet" for "wash" = βρέχειν: and so, at verse 44, "wetted" for "washed." This certainly does not *sound* well in English, though it may be the exact sense. It is too perfunctory, too menial. We must consult the English idiom, and ask what we should say in the circumstances. If we may not say "wash," is not the natural English expression "bathe"?

39. "That" for "for" = ὅτι. (?)

42. "Not wherewith" for "nothing." (?) In the connection the A. V. leaves no ambiguity.

48. "Her sins, which are many, are forgiven" = ἀφέωνται αἱ ἁμαρτίαι αὐτῆς αἱ πολλαί. If they had been as zealous for the Greek arrangement here as in some other cases, they would have translated: "Her sins are forgiven (or Forgiven are her sins), which are many, for" etc.; and would thus have given us what the preceding parable and the immediately subsequent clause show to be the true sense of the original, viz., that the woman's great love showed, not only that her sins were forgiven, but that her sins forgiven were many, "for to whom little is forgiven the same loveth little."

49. "Who is this that even forgiveth sins?" for "who is this that forgiveth sins also?" By this minute change how entirely the majestic movement and cadence of the English is ruined! And as for the sense, or faithfulness to the Greek, see their own translation at Matt. v. 40; John xi. 52; James iii. 2, 3, etc. If they say that the other things to which the "also" makes an addition are expressed in those other cases and not in this, we answer, the distinction is purely arbitrary; it is enough that the other things are implied, that they are in the mind of the hearer or reader, whether they are expressed or not.

VIII.

25. "Marvelled" for "wondered." Shall we call this a "marvellous" or a "wonderful" piece of faithfulness? But see Matt. xv. 31; Luke ii. 18; iv. 22; xxiv. 41; Acts

vii. 31; xiii. 41, etc., where it seems that this word $\vartheta\alpha\nu\mu\alpha'\zeta\omega$ may mean *to wonder* as well as *to marvel*.

31, 32. "Intreated" for "besought" = $\pi\alpha\rho\varepsilon\varkappa\alpha'\lambda o\upsilon\nu$. What is the faithful difference? They have rendered this word by "besought" at Matt. viii. 5, 31, 34; xiv. 36; xviii. 29, and in almost innumerable other cases; and, to cap the climax, they have so rendered it at Mark v. 10, 12, the passage which is directly *parallel* with this. Yet here they go out of their way to *correct* the A. V.! Is it faithfulness? Is it wantonness? Nothing but their *consequential* rule could be pretended as a justification of the change here; and yet they violate that rule on the spot.

34. "Had come to pass" for "was done" = $\gamma\varepsilon\gamma o\nu o';$. As for the tense, these are both forms of the pluperfect, and often so recognized by the Revisers. And for the signification of the word, see verse 56, " had been done;" Matt. xviii. 31, "was done;" xxiv. 21, "hath been;" Mark ii. 21, " is made;" Luke xxii. 42, "be done;" xxiii. 47, 48, "was done," "were done."

37. "Holden" for "taken" = $\sigma\upsilon\nu\varepsilon i\chi o\nu\tau o$. Why not "seized (*i.e.* possessed) with great fear"?

39. "Publishing" for "and published."(?)

45. Change of construction unnecessary, and for the worse in English. The Greek has not unfrequently a singular verb before several connected subjects.

48. "Go in peace." Gr. εiς rendered "in;" not "into."

56. "Amazed" for "astonished." Consequential. See ix. 43.

IX.

9. "Sought" for "desired" = $\dot{\varepsilon}\zeta\dot{\eta}\tau\varepsilon\iota$. (?)

23, 24. "Would" for "will," again. See Matt. xvi. 24, 25, note.

34. "Said these things" for "thus spake" = $\tau\alpha\tilde{\upsilon}\tau\alpha$ $\lambda\dot{\varepsilon}\gamma o\nu\tau o;$. But see xix. 28; John ix. 6. "They feared" = $\dot{\varepsilon}\varphi o\beta\dot{\eta}\vartheta\eta\sigma\alpha\nu$,—not "were afraid," as see ii. 10.

"This is my Son, my chosen." For construction, compare Matt. xvii. 5; Mark ix. 7.

43. "Astonished" for "amazed" = $\dot{\varepsilon}\xi\varepsilon\pi\lambda\dot{\eta}\sigma\sigma o\nu\tau o$. Consequential, and amazingly important! Cf. viii. 56.

47. "But when Jesus saw the reasoning" for "And Jesus perceiving the thought." We let pass the idea of "seeing a reasoning;" and merely observe that the Revisers have here adopted a construction which they have corrected in the A. V. in unnumbered instances, substituting for it the construction "but Jesus, when he saw," etc. = ὁ δὲ Ἰησοῦς ἰδών, κ.τ.λ.: and that they substitute in this case the Latin circumlocution for the participial construction whose use they had promised to enlarge. That ἰδών might mean "perceiving" appears from their own translation at Matt. xiii. 14; and Mark iv. 12, where ἴδητε = "perceive." "Thoughts" is their translation of διαλογισμοί at Matt. xv. 19; Mark vii. 21; Luke ii. 35; vi. 8. Truly they are hard to please. See vii. 4, note.

X.

5. "Shall enter" for "enter;" but see John iv. 14.
11, 20. "Howbeit" for "notwithstanding" = πλήν.
14. "Howbeit" for "but" = πλήν. This "howbeit" is evidently a faithful favorite. See Matt. xxvi. 64, note.
18. "Beheld falling" for "beheld fall,"—πεσόντα. But compare Mark ii. 16; vii. 2; ix. 38.
21. "Didst hide" and "didst reveal" for "hast," etc. (?)
22. "Have been delivered" for "are delivered;" but see at verse 20, "are written." "Willeth to reveal" for "will reveal;"—note, they do not here say, "desireth to reveal."
30. "Made answer, and" for "answering" = ὑπολαβών. What of using more participial constructions?
35. "I, when I;"—stiff in English, and needless. "Back again" for "again." Either word might be used, but what need of both? The Greek does not refer to a second return, nor does it at all require this reduplication.
40. "Did leave" for "hath left;" and yet at verse 42, "hath chosen" = ἐξελέξατο. (!) At verse 39 why did they not render the imperfect by "was hearing" (ἤκουε)?

XI.

8. "Arise" for "rise" = ἐγερθείς:—a petty distinction being made between ἀναστάς and ἐγερθείς: and yet the latter is elsewhere freely translated by the word "rise."

ST. LUKE. 67

14. "Marvelled for "wondered" = ἐθαύμασαν. See viii. 25, note.

18, 19, 20. " Devils'' = τὰ δαιμόνια (not "the devils'').

24. "When he is gone out" = ὅταν ἐξέλθῃ. But see Matt. v. 11 ; Mark xii. 25, for the tense. And for the construction, see Matt. xii. 43, note. "Turn back unto" for "return" = ὑποστρέψω. (?) See Matt. xii. 44.

33. "In a cellar" for "in a secret place" = κρύπτην. The A. V. is right, whether the Revision is or not. "Crypt"— cellar—is a later usage.

35. If, to be very faithful, the μή is here to be rendered "whether," ought not the ἐστίν to be rendered " is" and not "be"?

40. "Foolish ones" for "fools" = ἄφρονες. (?)

41. "Howbeit" for "but rather" πλήν: and see also at xii. 31. See Matt. xxvi. 64, note.

42. The article is here again omitted before "mint" and "rue," but see "the weeping and gnashing."

XII.

5, 7. Three times φοβηθῆτε is rendered by "fear," but at verse 4, being followed by ἀπό, by "be afraid." See ii. 10, where it is "be afraid" for "fear," without the ἀπό.

15. "Keep yourselves from" for " beware of" = φυλάσσεσθε, i.e. "be on your guard against." Is not the A. V. right?

20. " Hast prepared " for "hast provided" = ἡτοίμασας, not "made ready." See iii. 4, etc.

26. That which is least" = ἐλάχιστον. It is not τὸ ἐλάχιστον: so that the Revisers recognize that the absence of the article may not differ much from the use of the generic article. See conversely "the sower," "the virgin," etc.

33. "Draweth near" for "approacheth;"—how faithfully necessary!

39. "Know this" for "this know" = τοῦτο δὲ γινώσκετε. Who can fathom the depths of revisional faithfulness? " Have left" for "have suffered" = ἀφῆκε: where

the sense must be the same, unless they suppose the man *went away* from his house, to go to sleep.

45. "Shall say" for "say" = εἴπῃ. What is the difference in the sense? It is subjunctive aorist, it is true; but see xiv. 34; xvi. 30, 31; John viii. 51, where we have "go," "rise," "have lost," and "keep," in the same construction.

48. "Is given" = ἐδόθη. "Commit" for have committed" = παρέθεντο. (?) Both are to be regarded as perfects.

53. Here the sense is the same, whether with or without the articles. If used, they are generic or indefinite; they do not refer to any particular object already definitely in the mind.

59. "Have paid" for "hast paid" = ἀποδῷς. But see verse 50, "be accomplished;" John xiii. 38, "hast denied;" 2 Pet. i. 19, "dawn;" Matt. xviii. 30, "should pay;" Mark xii. 36, "make," etc.

XIII.

2, 4. "Were sinners,"—ἐγένοντο.

4. "That dwell" for "that dwelt." If we say "dwellers," which of the two would be understood in this connection? That will test the two translations.

3, 5. The ὡσαύτως and ὁμοίως of these two verses,—which are both rendered "likewise" in the A. V.,—have been interchanged in the new text; and, to show the exquisite nicety of their faithfulness, the Revisers have rendered one of them "in like manner"! While they were about it, why did they not render, ὁμοίως "likewise," and ὡσαύτως "just so," and thus transfer in full the Greek etymologies?

6. They insert "man" (without italics) instead of their ordinary "one."

7, 8. "Also" = καί,—not "even;" see vii. 49. "Doth cumber" for "cumbereth." What, in the Greek or in English, requires the change?

14. "Day of the sabbath" for "Sabbath day." The English reader will now know exactly what day is meant. At xiv. 5, however, they put "sabbath day" for the same Greek. What *can* we say?

22. "On unto" for "toward" = εἰς. See John xx. 3, where we have "toward" for "to" = εἰς. "That be saved" = οἱ σωζόμενοι. They retain the "be" for "are," and they do not say "be being saved;" but see Acts ii. 47.

25. "Is risen up and hath shut," for the aorist subjunctive with ἄν.

31. "Would fain" for "will" = θέλει. Why not "seeketh or is minded (to kill thee)"? This would be as consequential as "would fain," which is so soon after, at xv. 16, used for ἐπεθύμει.

XIV.

1, 5. "A sabbath" for "the Sabbath day." Here is an instance of the Revisers' articular precision. But if faithfulness required such minute punctiliousness here, it surely required them to be consistent with themselves elsewhere. Yet at Matt. xii. 2; John vii.22, 23, they render ἐν σαββάτῳ (no art.) "on or upon the sabbath." At Mark vi. 2, γενομένου σαββάτου, and at Mark xvi. 1, διαγενομένου σαββάτου, are rendered "when the sabbath was," etc. At Luke xxiii. 54 σάββατον (no art.) is rendered "the sabbath" (drew on).

8, 10. "Art bidden" = κληθῆς—not "shalt be," but see xvii. 10; Mark xiii. 7; and compare with these last Matt. xxiv. 15 and Mark xiii. 14.

13, 21. In the 13th verse we have "the poor, the maimed, the lame, the blind,"—all without any article in the Greek; —and, in verse 21, we have "the poor and maimed and blind and lame,"—with the article in the Greek before "poor" only. Now if, in English, the article is understood before the latter members of the enumeration after being expressed before the first, in verse 21, we cannot comprehend why it could not have been understood in like manner in verse 13; for to insert "and," if necessary, before the last would be cheaper than to insert "the" three times. But if it is not so understood in verse 21, then we do not see why it should have been inserted at all in verse 13. But we humbly beg pardon for our obtuseness.

28. "Desiring" for "intending" = θέλων. Is not the

A. V. right here; and, in general, does not θέλω refer more to effective purpose or volition, and less to mere idle desire, than the Revisers are accustomed to recognize?

XV.

1. "Were drawing near" for "drew near."—Harsh.
4. "And having lost one" for "if he lose one." See verse 8, showing that the sense is really the same; and then compare Heb. vi. 6.
5, 6. "When he hath found" = εὑρών: and "when he cometh" = ἐλθών: both with the indicative present.
9. "I have found" = εὗρον. "I had lost" = ἀπώλεσα: but see Mark xii. 12.
18, 21. I "have sinned" = ἥμαρτον,—not "I sinned;" see Rom. v. 12.
24. "Is alive again" = ἀνέζησεν. "Is found" = εὑρέθη.
30. "Came" for "is come," and "killedst" for "hast killed." Aorists, as before at verses 5, 6, 9, 18, 21, 24, also at 32; where they are rendered perfects.

XVI.

2. "Canst" = δυνήσῃ, future; see Mark iii. 17.
4. "Each" for "every." But see Matt. xxvi. 22.
6, 7. "Bond" for "bill" = τὰ γράμματα:—writings or scrip. (?)
8. "His lord" for "the lord" = ὁ κύριος. It means "his lord" no doubt, but see at verse 1, "the disciples" put for "his disciples." Is there any doubt that they were "his disciples"? The construction following (with the A. V.) departs from the order of the Greek, which puts "their generation" after "wiser;" but compare other passages where the Revisers so servilely follow the Greek construction. "The light" for "light" = τοῦ φωτός. Here the generic article is not necessary in the English idiom; see Rom. xiii. 12; Eph. v. 11.
9. "That they may receive you." Why not "that ye may be received"? See xii. 20.
13. The omission of the article before the second "one,"

in English, makes the "or else" utterly unmeaning. We say nothing about the change of the Greek text; but cf. Acts i. 24.

16. "Entereth violently" for "presseth" = βιάζεται: —why not say "forceth his way"?

21. "Yea, even" for "moreover" = ἀλλὰ καί. But see xxiv. 22.

25. "Son," retained for τέκνον. This would better suit the English ear in many other cases also; and in like manner "children" for υἱοί. But the Revision commonly grecizes.

30, 31. "Go," "rise,"—not "shall go," "shall rise"—for "went," "rose." But after all is the A. V. here so very far from right; considering that "went" and "rose," after "if," used often to mean, and still may mean, "should go" and "should rise"? In fact, if the revised translation at John viii. 55 is correct, then the A. V. in this pasgage,—much as it has been criticised and condemned,—is right after all. For the question is not whether "went" and "rose" may mean "should go" and "should rise,"—of this there can be no doubt, as, *e.g.*, "if you went you would not find him,"— but the real question is whether such a conditional tense as "should go" or "should say" can grammatically be joined with a future. But it is so joined at John viii. 55,—"If I should say . . . . I shall be;" and that in the Revision, and that deliberately, for it is a passage where the Revisers have made one of their characterstic emendations of the A. V., putting "shall be like unto you, a liar," for "shall be a liar like unto you." See also 2 Cor. x. 8 and xii. 6. Also John vi. 62 may be an analogous case, where the Revisers put "if ye should see" for "if ye shall see;" while at Luke xii. 45, they correct the A. V. by putting "if he shall say," for "if he say;" and then here, "if one go" and "if one rise"!

XVII.

2. "Were well" = λυσίτελει: "were hanged" = περίκειται: "were thrown" = ἔρριπται (perf.). So English idiom counts for something.

6. "Would have obeyed" = ὑπήκουσεν. What a jumble

of tenses and of ideas *in English;*— "if ye have faith, ye would say, and it would have obeyed"! Cf. verses 2, 9, 10.

8. "Have eaten and drunken." Compare xv. 4, 8,—to show that the Greek tenses are somewhat flexible.

9, 10. Here, the tenses, following the A. V., are conformed to the requirements of the sense; cf. verse 6.

20. "Cometh" for "should come." It should be either (orat. rect.) "when cometh the kingdom of God?" or (orat. obl.), "when the kingdom of God should come;" as in the A. V. See xviii. 9,—"were" for εἰσί.

24. "When it lighteneth" for "that lighteneth;" because the text is changed by omitting the article before the participle. Is this required by faithfulness, or is it the precision of pedantry? Cf. John iv. 39 and v. 44, note.

33. "Gain" for "save" = περιποιήσασθαι (new text for σῶσαι). Do they mean, "gain his livelihood"? At Heb. x. 39, they retain "saving" for περιποίησις.

XVIII.

5. "Wear out" for "weary" = ὑπωπιάζῃ. (?)

7. "Cry to him day and night" for "cry day and night unto him." How punctilious the faithfulness!

19. "*Even*" for "*that is.*" Is this for better English, or is it for greater faithfulness to the Greek?

30. "World to come" = τῷ ἐρχομένῳ. See vii. 20.

37. "That" should have been omitted, as elsewhere by the Revisers, or else the tense changed. See xix. 7, 11, etc.

XIX.

8. "Have wrongfully exacted" for "have taken by false accusation" = ἐσυκοφάντησα. (?)

14. "We will not that" for "we will not have." Which is the better English? Cf. Acts. xvi. 3; 1 Cor. x. 1; Col. ii. 1.

17. "Wast found" for "hast been" = ἐγένου. (?) For tense see verse 8.

22. "That I am" for "that I was." But see verses 7 and 11.

23. "Then wherefore" for "wherefore then"?

ST. LUKE.

27. " Howbeit" for " but" = $\pi\lambda\acute{\eta}\nu$. " But" is retained at xxii. 21, 22; xxiii. 28; Matt. xviii. 7, etc. Howbeit—
42. " Are hid" = $\dot{\varepsilon}\varkappa\rho\acute{\upsilon}\beta\eta$.
43. " Bank" for " trench" (" embankment" ?) = $\chi\acute{\alpha}\rho\alpha\varkappa\alpha$.
47. " Chief of" changed to " principal men of" = $\pi\rho\tilde{\omega}\tau o\iota$. How important! how exquisitely exact! or, how considerate of the English ear!
48. " Listening" = $\dot{\alpha}\varkappa o\acute{\upsilon}\omega\nu$. But " listening" is too strong. Why not say "as they heard him," and be consistent with xvii. 24?

XX.

1. " There came" for " came" encumbers and enfeebles the English without being a whit more faithful to the sense of the original.
17. " Was made" for " is become," = $\dot{\varepsilon}\gamma\varepsilon\nu\acute{\eta}\vartheta\eta$. (?)
20. " Righteous" for " just men." A frequent change—bad, here, and rarely necessary.
25. " Then render" for " render therefore." Does a change in the order of the Greek require a change in the order of the English?
33. " In the resurrection therefore" for " therefore in the resurrection." Greek order again. But is this for better English, or is it for a different sense? Which?
36. " Sons" for " the children"= $\upsilon\acute{\iota}o\acute{\iota}$. As for the article, this is a predicate; and as for the noun, what is the difference? and see " the children of Israel."
43. " Footstool of thy feet," again. For this un-English reduplication, the Revisers, as we ought to acknowledge, have the authority of the Rhemish version. But the Vulgate was not deformed with such a verbal jingle, reading " scabellum pedum tuorum;" which Wyclif imitated well with his "stool of thi feet." The case is similar also with the original Hebrew text. In the Greek the alliteration may have been a beauty or a necessity. There may have been no good word for *stool*, which was not " footstool."

XXI.

1. If " the " belongs to " rich men," here, what occasion for inserting " that were" before " casting"? And notice

that though the order in the Greek text has been changed so as to bring "treasury" before "gifts," the Revisers have not felt bound in faithfulness to change the order in the English, and say "casting into the treasury their gifts." This is sensible; but see xx. 25, etc.

12. "Bringing" for "being brought" = ἀπαγομένους. Which is more faithful to the original?

13. "Unto" for "to," with dative. How exquisitely, how unspeakably nice the sense which found this change required by faithfulness! At xviii. 7, they substitute "to" for "unto," their text having substituted the dative for πρός with accusative!

15. "Withstand" for "resist." Why?

19. "Win" for "possess." Good; but would not "gain" be better?

XXII.

1, 7. "Of unleavened bread," τῶν ἀζύμων. But the article?

10. "Whereinto he goeth" for "where he entereth in" = οὗ εἰσπορεύεται = "where he goeth in."

17, 19. Change of construction entirely indefensible. See Mark xiv. 22; note.

18. "Until shall come" = ἔλθῃ. But see xii. 59.

24. "Is accounted" for "should be accounted." Better, "was accounted" (orat. obl.), *i.e.*, rightfully, as A. V. means?

31, 32, 33. "Asked" for "hath desired;" "made supplication" for "have prayed." (?) In all their other changes in these three verses the Revisers are inconsistent with themselves, except in putting "stablish" for "strengthen," and this was scarcely necessary. For "thou," etc., see xxiii. 6, 8.

37. "Fulfilled" for "accomplished" = τελεσθῆναι. But see John xix. 28, 30. So "fulfillment" for "end" = τέλος.

42, 43, 44. "Be done" = γινέσθω: "being" = γενόμενος: "became" for "was" = ἐγένετο. But one of the pet ideas of the Revisers seems to have been to correct the A. V. in its variations of the rendering of the same word in a given connection. See Acts xxvi. 24, 25.

46. "That not" for "lest" = ἵνα μή. But see John v. 14; xii. 40, etc. What is their nice distinction?

56. "In the light *of the fire*" for "by the fire" = πρὸς τὸ φῶς = "at" or "by the light," not "in." (The Portuguese uses "lume" for "fire.") The change of construction is needless. "Looking steadfastly" for "earnestly looked" = ἀτενίσασα: but at Acts vi. 15 they have actually changed the "looking steadfastly" of the A. V. to "fastening their eyes," although there are in the Greek no more "eyes" there than here!

57. In their text the order of the Greek is changed from γύναι, οὐκ οἶδα αὐτόν to οὐκ οἶδα αὐτὸν, γύναι: and yet they have left "woman" as it stood in the A.V. But see xx. 25; see also Matt. xxvi. 22, 25, etc.

64. The change of construction here is unnecessary, and destroys a pleasing variety.

XXIII.

1. "Brought" = ἤγαγον: but at xxii. 54 it is rendered "led away." In the A. V. it is "led" in both cases. At xxii. 54, εἰσήγαγον, "brought," immediately follows. Which translation is most faithful to the original?

6, 8. "When Pilate heard," "when Herod saw." For the construction see vii. 4, note.

14, 15. These aorists would be more naturally translated as English perfects, with the A. V. See verses 22 and 41.

19. The insertion of "one" before "who" (for ὅστις) is not necessary, as they themselves show elsewhere. "Was cast into" = ἦν βληθεὶς ἐν τῇ. Here ἐν τῇ φυλακῇ—a new reading—is rendered just as εἰς φυλακήν is at verse 25 —preposition and article to the contrary notwithstanding.

20. The "again" is not put in the Greek order; but see the faithful corrections at Mark iv. 1; viii. 13, 25; xiv. 70, etc.

44. "Now" = ἤδη. But see Matt. xiv. 15, where "now" is changed to "already." "A darkness" for "darkness" = σκότος. But see Matt. xxvii. 45, and Mark xv. 33, where they say "darkness." Was this petty insertion of "a," then, required by faithfulness here and not there?

47. "Certainly this was a righteous man." In St. Matthew the centurion "and they that were with him" said, "Truly this was the Son [not 'a son'] of God," Matt. xxvii. 54. The centurion had probably heard at the trial of Jesus—and must have heard from the taunts of those who mocked him upon the cross—that he *claimed* to be "the Son of God." He now cries out, "Certainly this was a righteous man,"—a man who would be guilty of no falsehood or fraud; he must therefore be *what he claimed to be*,—he must be, "*he was, the Son of God.*" Whether the centurion himself used the various expressions, or whether they are to be ascribed partly to the centurion and partly to "them that were with him," is a matter of no consequence. We should say of Achilles, "He was the son [not 'a son'] of a goddess;" and of Hercules, "He was the son of Jupiter."

49. "Seeing" for "beholding" = ὁρῶσαι. Now if this were an original translation we should be far from finding any fault. But was there any need of the change? The lexicons give to ὁράω and εἶδον the meaning "behold." The Revisers translate ἰδού in the next verse "behold." The connection shows that ὁρῶσαι in this verse means the same as θεωρήσαντες in the 48th verse; and we have already seen (and shall further find) that the Revisers have been constrained to allow "see" as a translation of θεωρέω, as well as of ὁράω. See John viii. 51, etc.

54. "The day," "the sabbath." No article in the Greek.

56. The μέν is here ignored. The answering δέ is in the next verse (xxiv. 1).

XXIV.

6 and 34. "Is risen" = ἠγέρθη :—not "was raised;" but see 1 Cor. xv., etc.

13. "Were going" for "went." But this might mean, "were intending, or about, to go."

26. "Behoved it not" for "ought not." Why not say "must not," as at Mark xiv. 31?

30. "When" for "as" = ἐν τῷ = while.

34. "Is risen" = ἠγέρθη : "hath appeared" = ὤφθη. See John ii. 22.

39. "Behold me having" for "see me have;"—Greek for English.

41. "Disbelieved for joy"! A strange state of mind; but see Mark xvi. 14, and Rom. iii. 3 and iv. 20. Unbelief, or want of faith, and positive disbelief are two things.

51. "He parted" for "he was parted" = διέστη. The verb may mean either "to stand apart" or "to be parted."

50. "Over against" for "to" = πρός. Here πρός is a new reading for εἰς, and of course must be respected. But it is rendered "to" or "unto" by the Revisers fifty times to once of "against," and we do not find another instance of "over against."

ST. JOHN.

I.

3 and 10. "Were made" = ἐγένετο.

6. "Came" for "was" = ἐγένετο.

7. "Came" = ἦλθεν. "Might believe through him" for "through him might believe." Did faithfulness require this conformity to the Greek order just here and not at Matt. x. 32, etc., etc.?

7, 8. "That he might," "that they might," for "to" = ἵνα. But cf. verse 19; iii. 17, etc.

9. "There" for "that" spoils the sense; and what need of inserting "even the light"? unless, indeed, the text is to mean the same as the margin; and, if so, the margin is certainly the clearer and better translation.

11. Here the Revisers have only half done their work. They have shown that the second "his own" are persons (masculine); they fail to show that the first "his own" are things (neuter). It would be difficult fully to bring out the distinction in English. If we might change the number of the first "his own," we might say, "he came to what was his own, and they that were his own received him not;" or, retaining the number, "he came to his own possessions, and his own people received him not." At Matt. xix. 21, τὰ ὑπάρχοντα (plural) is rendered "that thou hast." But what trifling! Everybody knew before that the second

"his own" meant persons, and the first, though neuter in the Greek, must mean substantially the same.

12. "Children" for "the sons," and "the right" for "power." No article in Greek with either; and yet "children" is a predicate, while "right" is not.

14. "We beheld his glory, glory," etc. Surely the last "glory" should have either "the" or "a;" for by the foregoing "his" it has already been individualized. The marginal reading is curious on articles.

15. Here "is become" for "is preferred" is scarcely intelligible. Why not say, "is put"?

18. A perfect and an aorist are coördinated; and ὁ ὤν is rendered "which is," and not "even he which is."

27. Cf. "*even* he that" with "which" at verse 29; and "one whom" with ὁ σπείρων.

32 and 38. "Have beheld" for "saw" = τεθέαμαι, and "beheld" for "saw" = θεασάμενος. But see vi. 5; Mark xvi. 14; Acts xxi. 27; Rom. xv. 24, etc. And are not τεθέαμαι and ἔμεινεν in fact coördinated in time? Cf. iii. 32; Phil. iv. 11, 12, etc.

36. Here the A. V. follows the Greek in the participial construction, which the Revision changes.

41. "Findeth first" for "first findeth." Well?

42. "Unto" for "to" = πρός. Happily it is not "over against." But see Matt. ii. 12; iii. 14, etc., etc., where all along πρός is rendered by "to." Just think of this ineffable faithfulness.

43. "Was minded to" for "would;" much better than "desired to," as elsewhere.

45, 46. Why not follow the Greek order,—"Jesus, son of Joseph, even him from Nazareth"? Compare Heb. ii. 9; and for "son" without the article compare Mark iii. 17.

II.

3. "The wine" for "wine" (gen. abs.), no article in Greek. Faithfulness;—see Matt. xxvi. 27, etc.

9. "Now become" for "which was made,"—marg. "that it had become," = γεγενημένον. How they wrestle with their articular purism!

ST. JOHN. 79

10. "Have drunk freely" for "have well drunk" = μεϑυσϑῶσιν. Is either right? The Greek word has no relation to *drinking*, except in connection with *drunkenness*.

13. "Passover of the Jews" for "the Jews' Passover." (?) See verse 6.

15. "He made" for "when he had made" = ποιήσας.(?)

16. If faithfulness required the order to be changed here, why did they not also say at verse 15, "the tables he overthrew," thus being consistent?

20. "Was in building" = ᾠκοδομήϑη—aorist rendered as imperfect, for continued action.

22. "Was raised" for "was risen" = ἠγέρϑη, again. See Luke xxiv. 34, etc.

III.

3. "Anew" for "again" = ἄνωϑεν. (?) The A. V., margin, "from above."

4. "A second time" for "the second time" = δεύτερον. (See Mark xii. 31 and xiv. 72); and then "of water and the Spirit,"—no article in Greek with either.

6. "That which is born," not "has been born." See verses 18, 21, and 27.

12. "If I told" for "if I have told" = ἐὰν εἴπω: not "shall tell." See their correction at Luke xii. 45; and for the "have" see Luke xiv. 34, etc. Cf. John viii. 55.

13. "Out of heaven" = ἐκ τοῦ οὐρανοῦ. But see verse 31. "Which is" = ὁ ὤν: not "even he which is." But see James iv. 12.

15. Text and margin, interchange?

16. "His only begotten Son," not "his Son, the only begotten," or "even him who was his only begotten," to conform to the Greek.

18. "Judged" for "condemned;"—but the judgment must here imply condemnation, and yet it is not the idiomatic or natural English word for that purpose. "Doom" and "condemn" would be the exact etymological correspondents to κρίνω and κατακρίνω.

21, 27. "Have been wrought," "have been given," for "are wrought" and "be given;" but see "it is written," and verse 6; and see at verse

24. "Was (not yet) cast" = ἦν βεβλημένος = "had been cast."

32. Ἑώρακεν and ἤκουσεν are coördinated, and are rendered together as perfects. Cf. xvii.

33, 34. Aorists continue to be rendered as perfects right through; and here we have "hath sent" for ἀπέστειλεν, which elsewhere is rendered "sent." Cf. xvii.

IV.

3. "Departed" = ἀπῆλθεν. But see v. 15 and Acts xvi. 39, 40.

4. "Must needs" = ἔδει. But see Acts i. 16; xvii. 3; and compare Luke xxii. 7 and Heb. ix. 26.

8. "Were gone," not "had gone" for the pluperfect.

9. "Therefore" for "then," and order changed. This is the οὖν of sequence, not of consequence? "Samaritan woman" for "woman of Samaria,"—faithfulness!

10. "Knewest;" should it not be "hadst known," as it is followed by "wouldest have asked"?

17. "Saidst" for "hast said" = εἶπας. (?)

18. "Hast had" = ἔσχες.

19. "Perceive" = θεωρῶ. But see xii. 19.

25. "Declare" for "tell" = ἀναγγελεῖ = announce, report. "Tell" is nearer than "declare"?

27. "Speak" for "talk" = λαλέω. (?)

31. "Prayed" (not "asked") = ἠρώτων : note.

33. "The disciples therefore said" for "therefore said the disciples." How strikingly necessary! "Hath brought'" = ἤνεγκεν.

35. "Look on" (not "behold") = θεάσασθε. Cf. 1 John i. 1, where they change "looked upon" to "beheld."

39. "Who testified." No article with the participle; but see Heb. i. 1, and Luke xvii. 24.

45. "So" for "then." The οὖν of sequence. And so, often; but what of it?

46. But here "so" is changed to "therefore." Compare verses 52 and 53.

47. "When he heard .. he;" not "he, when he heard" = οὗτος ἀκούσας.

V.

54. "Having come" for "when he was come." See Mark xiv. 45 and Acts xx. 2.

2. "In" for "at :"—faithfulness.
3, 5, 7. "Impotent" changed to "sick" = ἀσθενούντων: but "infirmity" retained for ἀσθενεία.
6. "Wouldst" for "wilt ;" but see verses 21, 40.
8. "Arise" for "rise." (!)
9. "Was made [not 'became'] whole" = ἐγένετο.
10. "So" for "therefore" = οὖν :—wherefore? Cf. iv. 46.
14. "Lest" = ἵνα μή : but see xii. 35, 40. "Befall" for "come unto" = γένηται. (?)
15. "Went away" for "departed;" see iv. 3.
16. "For this cause" for "therefore" = διὰ τοῦτο, followed by "because," also at verse 18; and so at vi. 65, and 1 John iii. 1. But cf. Matt. xiii. 13; xxiv. 44; Luke xii. 22, etc.
19. "But" = ἐὰν μή. Compare Gal. ii. 16. Note the τι, rendered "what," equivalent to "that which," like ἅ afterwards.
26, 27. "Gave" for "hath given;" (?) "a son of man" should be "the son of a man," if any change. "Shall come forth" (not "go") = ἐκπορεύσονται.
29. "Done [or practised] ill," for "done evil" = τὰ φαῦλα πράξαντες.
34. Literally: "but I not from man receive the testimony." "May be "saved" for might be saved" = σωθῆτε. (?)
35. Better, "the burning and shining lamp" than "the lamp that burneth and shineth." (?)
44. "Which receive" = λαμβάνοντες,—not οἱ λαμβ. : see also iv. 39 ; but compare Luke xvii. 24; Heb. i. 1, etc.

VI.

2. "Sick" for "diseased;" but see Acts xxviii. 9.
5. "Seeing" = θεασάμενος : but see i. 32, etc., etc.

6. "Are to" for "shall." The subjunctive does not require the change.

11. "Having given thanks" for "when he had given thanks." If faithfulness required this change here, why not also at Mark xiv. 22, 23; Luke xxii. 17, 19? and compare Matt. xxvi. 26, 27.

12. "Broken pieces" for "fragments." (?)

13. "So" for "therefore" = οὖν. How nice! See verse 19 and iv. 46.

14. "When, therefore, the people saw the sign . . . they said," for "then those [the] men, when they had seen the miracle, said," = οἱ οὖν ἄνθρωποι ἰδόντες σημεῖον. See Luke xxiii. 8, where σημεῖον = "miracle;" see verse 11 for the tense of ἰδόντες: and ἄνθρωποι commonly means "men." As for the change of construction it is directly the reverse of the Revisers' ordinary correction,—see Luke vii. 4, note. "Cometh" for "should come" = ὁ ἐρχόμενος. See Matt. xi. 3 and Luke vii. 20, notes.

15. "Were about to" for "would" = μέλλουσι: but see verse 6, "would" = ἔμελλε, and verse 71.

17. "Was" = ἐγεγόνει, why not "was [or 'had'] grown." "Had come" = ἐληλύθει for "was come;" but see xi. 30; xvi. 28, 32; xvii. 1, etc., etc. Consistency, faithfulness, "straightway." "Unto" for "toward" = εἰς: but see xx. 3, where they put "toward" for "to;" and they have frequently changed "to" to "for" = εἰς,—see Acts xxvii. 1, 6—to which "toward" would here correspond; per contra, Acts xxvii. 2. The intelligent English reader can decide questions like these as well as the profoundest Greek scholar.

19. "When therefore" for "so when" = οὖν after part. perf. See verse 13.

21. "They were willing, therefore, to receive him," for "Then they willingly received him" = ἤθελον οὖν λαβεῖν. Which is the sense?

25. "When they found" for "when they had found" = εὑρόντες. See verse 11, note, and Acts xxi. 2, 3, 4. "Camest" = γέγονας, not "hast come;" see also Gal. iii. 17; 2 Cor. ii. 13; Heb. xi. 28. How durst they render a

perfect thus? Cf. i. 3; Matt. xix. 8; xxiv. 21; xxv. 6; Mark v. 33, etc., etc.; especially Mark ix. 21.

27. "For him the Father, *even* God, hath sealed" = τοῦτον γὰρ ὁ πατὴρ ἐσφάγισεν, ὁ Θεός. What a jolt in the English! And why change at all? or, if they must change, why not adhere strictly to the Greek, and say: "for him did the Father seal, *even* God"?

28. "What must we do?" for "What shall we do?" = τί ποιῶμεν; (?) What shall we say?

29. "Hath sent," marg. "Sent" = ἀπέστειλεν. Wondrous nicety.

30. "What workest thou?" for "What dost thou work?" Revisional faithfulness.

31. "Ate" for "did eat." But see verse 49, where "did eat" remains. They could not hold the split hair steady. "Out of heaven" for "from heaven." But see iii. 31; Rev. x. 4, etc.

32, 34. "Jesus therefore" for "then Jesus," = οὖν. (?)

37, 39. "All that which" for "all that" = πᾶν ὅ. (?)

40. "Beholdeth" for "seeth" = θεωρῶν. (?)

44. "In" for "at" (the last day) = ἐν. But they retain "at" at 39, 40, 54, etc.

49, 58. "Died" for "are dead." But see viii. 52, etc.

41, 53, etc., etc. "Therefore" for "then" = οὖν. This change is so frequent in St. John's Gospel that we need refer to it no more in particular. The question is, does the οὖν express narrative sequence or logical consequence? The Revisers differ in judgment here from the forty-seven translators of the A. V., assuming a logical consequence much more frequently than their predecessors. This can be supposed and imagined in many cases, where it is by no means necessary to presume it. Let intelligent readers judge.

56. "Abideth" for "dwelleth" = μένει. So the indwelling of Christ, or of the Holy Spirit in us, is henceforth to be an "in-abiding."

65. "For this cause" for "therefore" = διὰ τοῦτο. See ix. 16; Acts xxviii. 20; Rev. xii. 12; and notes at v. 16, and 1 John iii. 1. "Be given" for "were given" (have been given).

66. "Upon this" for "from that time" = ἐκ τούτου.
67. "Would (for " will") ye also go away" = θέλετε; but see v. 40.
70. "Did choose" for "have chosen." (?)
71. "Should" = ἤμελλεν: not "was about to." See verse 15 and vii. 39.

VII.

3. "Behold" for "see" = θεωρέω. The particular cases of this pet alteration need not be further noticed. Is it required by faithfulness? Again, let English readers judge.
4. "Manifest" for "show." (?)
10. "Were gone up" = ἀνέβησαν: "went up" = ἀνέβη. Cf. xvii.
16, 17. "Teaching" for "doctrine" = διδαχή. The Revisers seem to have assumed that διδαχή means the act of teaching (δίδαξις) exclusively, and διδασκαλία the thing taught or doctrine. But is not this an arbitrary distinction? Does not διδαχή in this very case mean the thing taught, the doctrine, and not the act of teaching? "Willeth" = θέλῃ:—not "desireth." "From myself" for "of myself." "To speak of myself" might be ambiguous, but "to speak from myself" is hardly English. See 28 and xi. 51.
21. "Did" for "have done" = ἐποίησα. It is followed by "marvel" and not "marvelled." So at verses 23 and 29; compare verse 31.
23. Change of order needless, and it enfeebles the English. "Wroth" for "angry" = χολᾶτε—equally needless.
24. "Appearance" for "the appearance" = κατ' ὄψιν: a phrase,—compare "in town," "in the city," and the French "à vue d'oeil." But is their phrase a settled English idiom?
26, 27. "Know" = ἔγνωσαν and οἴδαμεν. Why not say "What!" for μή, as at verse 41, and be consistent? See Acts xxvi. 24, 25.
31. "Hath done" = ἐποίησε. This refers to the σημεῖα, one of which is spoken of in verses 21, 23. "When the Christ shall come" for . . . "cometh." But see xvi. 13, and cf. viii. 28.
38. "Hath said" = εἶπεν.
39. "Were to" for "should" = ἔμελλον. So vi. 15 and

Acts xxii. 29 ("were about to"); but see vi. 71 and Gal. iii. 23. Πνεῦμα = "the Spirit" (no art.).
40. "This is of a truth" for "of a truth this is"!
45. "Did bring" for "have brought." (?)
51. "A man" = τὸν ἄνθρωπον,—the generic article. See Matt. i. 23; ὁ σπείρων, etc.

VIII.

9. "Where she was" = οὖσα. There is nothing at all for "where." Is this translation or paraphrase? They might have said "being," or omitted οὖσα altogether; but they would have been quite as near the original, even in their new text, if they had retained the "standing" of the A. V.
14. "Even if" for "though" = κἄν. But see x. 38.
16. "Yea and if" for "and yet if" = καὶ ἐάν . . . δέ = "but even if."
17. "Yea and" for "also" = καί . . . δέ = "but also," or "but even."
25. "Even that which I have also spoken unto you," for "Even the same that I said unto you" = ὅ τι καὶ λαλῶ ὑμῖν,—("what I am also speaking to you [from the beginning" = τὴν ἀρχήν]).
26. "Heard" for "have heard" = ἤκουσα. (?)
27. "Perceived" for "understood" = ἔγνωσαν. But see verse 43 and x. 6; see also iii. 10, "understand" for "know." "Spake" = ἔλεγεν : just above "speak" always stands for λαλέω.
28. "Have lifted up" = ὑψώσητε. Cf. vii. 31.
29. "That are pleasing to" for "that please" = τὰ ἀρεστά. Faithfulness.
31. "Truly" for "indeed" = ἀληθῶς. See vi. 55; but surely ἀληθῶς corresponds as well to the adverb "indeed" as ἀληθής did.
33. "We be" = ἔσμεν : is this the English of the present day? "Shall be made" = γενήσεσθε, —not "shall become." Why not? Elsewhere they struggle hard to get in something besides "made," see ii. 9, etc.
34. "Bond-servant" for "servant" = δοῦλος. Elsewhere in text, "servant."

36. "If therefore the Son" for "if the Son therefore,"—exquisite faithfulness. "Shall make," see Luke xvi. 30, 31, etc., etc.

39. "Our father is Abraham" for "Abraham is our father." Oh! wondrous faithfulness! The subject has the article in Greek; but does not a proper name make some difference? Cf. Acts xviii. 5; 1 John ii. 22; v. 1.

40. "Heard" for "have heard" = ἤκουσα. (?)

41. "Works" for "deeds" = ἔργα. The Revisers allow ἔργον to mean "deed," in the singular number, as at Luke xxiv. 19, etc., etc.; but not in the plural to mean "deeds," as cf. Acts vii. 22. But this is an arbitrary distinction; and their vigilance has failed them in one instance, 2 Pet. ii. 8. What would be unobjectionable in an independent translation may be unjustifiable as a correction of a former version.

42. "Have come" for "am come" = ἐλήλυθα. See xvi. 28, and vi. 17, note.

44. "A lie" = τὸ ψεῦδος. In margin, ὅταν λαλῇ = "when *one* speaketh;" cf. Heb. x. 28.

45, 46. "The truth" = τὴν ἀλήθειαν and ἀλήθειαν alike.

47. "The words of God" for "God's words;" why? "For this cause" for "therefore" = διὰ τοῦτο: but see ix. 23, etc., etc., and notes at v. 16 and 1 John iii. 1.

50. "One that seeketh" = ὁ ζητῶν: see "the sower," ὁ σπείρων. If the absolute ἔστι, "there is," is appealed to as making a difference in this and similar cases (as at v. 45), then cf. "there shall be the weeping and gnashing," and Rom. xv. 12.

51. "Word" for "saying" = λόγον. (?) "See" = θεωρήσῃ: also at ix. 8. How happened they to forget "behold"?

52. "If a man keep" = ἐάν τις τηρήσῃ,—not "shall keep," and so at x. 9; but see Matt. xxiv. 48, and Luke xii. 38, 45, etc., where they carefully insert "shall."

54. "Glory" for "honour" = δόξα.

55. "If I should say" = ἐὰν εἴπω,—"I shall be." But see Luke xvi. 30, 31, etc.

IX.

5. "I am the light"=φῶς εἰμι τοῦ κόσμου. See 1 Tim. vi. 10.

6. "Thus spoken"= ταῦτα εἰπών. So also xi. 43; but cf. xi. 28, and Luke ix. 34.

8. "Which saw" for "which had seen"= θεωροῦντες,— not "beheld." The pluperfect is not wrong.

10. "They said therefore" for "therefore said they." So also at verse 16. What of it?

15. "Received" for "had received." But see verse 18. Can one explain why that should be pluperfect and not this?

17, 21. "In that" for "that"= ὅτι: "how" for "by what means"= πῶς. In the last case the A. V. is plainly right; and perhaps "because" would be better in the other. "Opened" for "hath opened." (?)

23. "Therefore"= διὰ τοῦτο. So x. 17; cf. viii. 47, etc.

24. "A second time" for "again"= ἐκ δευτέρου: but does not it mean "again" if it means "a second time"? And ἐκ δευτέρου they commonly render "the second time."

27. "Told even now" for "have told already"= ἤδη. (?) See Matt. xiv. 15.

30. "The marvel" for "a marvellous thing"= θαυμαστόν!!

31, 32. "Any man," "any one"= τις.

35. "Finding" for "when he had found"= εὑρών. See vi. 11 (note); xi. 28, 43, and Luke xv. 5; Acts xxi. 2, 3, 4, etc.

37. "Speaketh" for "talketh"= λαλῶν.

38. "Lord, I believe"= πιστεύω, κύριε. Cf. Matt. xxvi. 25, "Is it I? Rabbi."

39. "May see" for "might see" (present); "may be made" (not "may become") for "might be made" (aorist).

X.

1. "Fold of the sheep" for "sheepfold."

4. "Hath put" for "putteth"= ὅταν ἐκβάλῃ. But the Revisers sometimes render this construction of the aorist

subjunctive by the indicative present, as at Matt. xxiv. 32, 33, and Mark xiii. 28, 29, and Heb. i. 6, etc.

6. Understood = ἔγνωσαν. See viii. 27.

9. "Shall go in and go out and shall find," for "shall go in and out and find." Why not "shall go out," and finish it? Which is the English idiom? Do we not say "go in and out" rather than "'go in and go out"?

10. "That he may steal," etc., for "to steal," etc. = ἵνα κλέψῃ. But see verse 31 and iv. 34; v. 36, etc.

12. "A shepherd" for "the shepherd." But ποίμην is a predicate, and the hireling was probably "*a* shepherd," though not "*the* shepherd." "Snatcheth" for "catcheth;" which does a wolf do most naturally?

19. "Words" for "sayings" = λόγους.

21. "Sayings" for "words" = ῥήματα, and so at xii. 47, 48,—arbitrary faithfulness. They freely render ῥῆμα "word," as at Matt. iv. 4; 1 Pet. i. 24, 25, and here in John at iii. 34; v. 47; vi. 63, 68; viii. 20, 47; xiv. 10; xv. 7; xvii. 8,

24. "Hold us in suspense" for "make us to doubt" = ψυχὴν ἡμῶν αἴρεις. This is from the margin of the A. V.; but which is the simpler and better translation? We confess our judgment follows that of the forty-seven.

28. Is "pluck" any more antiquated or unintelligible here than "we be" is at viii. 33?

32. "Have I showed" = ἔδειξα: but

36. "Sanctified" for "hath sanctified." "*The* Son of God;" why italicize "*the*" just here? See Matt. iv. 3, 6, etc., etc., etc. They print "Son" with a capital.

38. "Though" = κἄν: changed to "even if" at viii. 14.

39. "Went forth" for "escaped"—out of their hand.

XI.

3. "The sisters therefore" for "therefore his sisters." "The sisters" means "his sisters," and "therefore" means the same in one place as in the other. But again,

6. "When therefore he heard" for "when he had heard therefore" = ὡς οὖν ἤκουσεν (he abode).

ST. JOHN.

7, 8. "The" for "his" (disciples); but see 41, etc., etc. "But now" for "of late" = νῦν : *i.e.* "just now." We may as well insert "just" as "but," and make current English,—if we *must* change.

12. "Will recover" for "shall do well" = σωθήσεται ("will get well"—colloquial).

14. "Is dead" = ἀπέθανε.

19. "Console" for "comfort" = παραμυθήσωνται. But see verse 31. Why change here? "Straightway"!

20. "When" for "as soon as" = ὡς. "Still sat" for "sat *still*" = ἐκαθέζετο. Cf. Acts xvii. 14.

22. "Even now I know that" for "I know that even now." Is not the true sense more plainly expressed by the latter?

26. "Whosoever" = πᾶς ὁ, also at xvi. 2; elsewhere rendered "every one who," and the A. V. corrected accordingly. Cf. Matt. v. 22, 28; Luke vi. 47, etc.

27. "Even he that cometh" for "which should come" = ὁ ἐρχόμενος. See Acts xix. 4. Why did they not render in this last case "that came" or "was coming"?

28. "Said this" for "so said" = τοῦτο εἰποῦσα: but cf. ix. 6; xi. 43, etc.

29. "Went" for "came" = ἤρχετο. But Jesus and not Mary is the centre of our thoughts.

42. "Heardest" for "hast heard." "Around" for "by." "Didst send" for "hast sent." (?)

43. "Loud" = μεγάλῃ : but see Rev. v. 12, note.

44. "Hand and foot" = τοὺς πόδας καὶ τὰς χεῖρας. So idiom goes for something; but see "the footstool of his feet," and "two witnesses or three," etc.

46. "The things which" for "what things." "Had done" = ἐποίησεν.

50. "Take account" for "consider." Well?

51. "Should die" (not "was about to die") = ἔμελλεν. But see vi. 15.

52. "Also," out of place. In Greek it adds "the children" rather than the "gathering."

53. "That they might" for "to" = ἵνα, etc., and so x. 10; but see verse 55 and iv. 34; v. 36; x. 32; xi. 19, 55, etc.

In the modern Greek νά (for ἵνα) is the distinctive sign of the infinitive mood,—or of the substitute for it.

XII.

3. "Precious" for "costly" = πολυτίμου. The same sense, one in Latin, the other in Anglo-Saxon.

4. The order changed so that, in the English, "which," that should refer to Judas, may by the ear be referred to the disciples;—note their punctilious carefulness at xi. 20.

7. The margin, or the old text, to be preferred. The "anointing for the burial" was that in Bethany;—see the other Gospels.

14. "Having found" for "when he had found" = εὑρών, —(not "finding" as at ix. 35). The construction of the A. V. here is the same as the Revisers have elsewhere *substituted* for another, see Acts xxi. 20, 32, etc., etc.

16. They, with the A. V., render a pluperfect by "were written," and an aorist by "had done."

19. "Behold" for "perceive" = θεωρεῖτε: but see iv. 19, where θεωρέω is rendered "perceive." And then here ἴδε is rendered "lo" for "behold," although "behold" is, even with the Revisers, its customary meaning. "Is gone" = ἀπῆλθεν,—not "went away" or "departed."

21. "These therefore came" for "the same came therefore" = οὗτοι οὖν. But at John i. 2, 7, and vii. 8, οὗτος is rendered "the same." "Asked" for "desired" = ἠρώτων. Cf. Luke vii. 36, where they say "desired."

27. "Is troubled" = τετάρακται.

35. "That . . . not" for "lest" = ἵνα μή: and so at Col. iii. 21, ii. 4; Phil. ii. 27; Heb. xi. 28. But they render "lest" at verse 40 and Matt. xvii. 27, xxvi. 5; 1 Tim. iii. 7; Rev. xvi. 15, etc. What is the clew?

40. "Perceive" for "understand" = νοήσωσιν. (?)

42. "Even" for "also" = καί. See Luke vii. 49 (note.)

47, 48, 49. "Sayings" for "words" = ῥήματα; and "spake" for "have spoken." (?)

XIII.

2. "Already" for "now" = ἤδη: cf. ix. 27.
11. " That should betray him" = τὸν παραδιδόντα.
14. " The Lord and the Master" for "*your* Lord and Master." Surely this is harsh English; and if faithfulness to the Greek article required it here, why did not they say also in verse 13, "ye call me the Master and the Lord"? The Greek article is there also; but English idiom seems to have prevailed.

1, 3, 12, 14, 15. "Had given" = ὅτι δέδωκεν: "had washed," etc. = ὅτε ἔνιψεν: "have washed" = εἰ ἔνιψα: "have done" = πεποίηκα and ἐποίησα: and "have given" = ἔδωκα. Cf. ch. xvii.

17. "Blessed" for "happy" = μακάριος. (?)
18. "Lifted" for "hath lifted." (??) "Have chosen" = ἐξελεξάμην.

22, 29. "Spake" and "said" = λέγει.
27. "That thou doest" retained for ὃ ποιεῖς: but see vi. 37.

31. "Is glorified" = ἐδοξάσθη. "When therefore he" for "therefore when he." But the Revisers often begin a clause with "therefore;" and it is a matter of English and not of Greek construction.

38. "The cock" (no art.). Why not "no cock shall crow"

XIV.

2, 3. "A place for you" = τόπον ὑμῖν, and ὑμῖν τόπον. Elsewhere such a change in the Greek is a great mystery.

18. "Come" for "will come" = ἔρχομαι. But is not the meaning "will come"? and if "come" means *the same* in English, what sort of faithfulness required the change?

9. "Have been" = εἰμί.
10. "From" for "of" (myself); cf. vii. 28 and xi. 51.

7, 12, 19, and of. xv. 20. "My Father also," "he do also," "ye shall live also," "they will also persecute you." According to what appears to have been the punctilious rule of the Revisers for the construction of "also," the first (in verse 7) is right: but should not the others be "he also," "ye also," and "you also" (will they persecute)?

21. "He it is *that*" = ἐκεῖνός ἐστιν ὁ: and so at v. 39; ix. 37; and at xiii. 26, ἐκεῖνός ἐστιν ᾧ: cf. Matt. i. 21. Here we have the true use of the formula: "it is he that." It furnishes a subject common to two predicates. Thus, if you would know who shall betray me, it is he that receiveth the sop; if you would know who loveth me, it is he that keepeth my commandments; who is the Son of God? it is he that speaketh with thee. But it is abundantly evident that no such reference can be attached to the αὐτός in the angelic interpretation of the name Jesus in St. Matthew. The question, "Who shall save his people from their sins?" the angel could not suppose to be present in the mind of Mary or of Joseph, nor the question "What else shall he do?" And he could not have intended by his interpretation to answer any such inquiries. He must plainly have intended to furnish, not a subject to any given predicate at all, but a predicate to the given subject. The question was, "What shall this child be or do?" And the answer was, "He himself (αὐτός, not ἐκεῖνός ἐστὶν ὁ) shall save his people from their sins;" *i. e.*, "he shall save them, and that by his own inherent and sufficient power." So that the rendering, "it is he that shall save his people from their sins," is illogical as well as paraphrastical. See also i. 30 and Phil. ii. 12.

22. "What is come to pass?" for "how is it?" = τί γέγονεν; ("how is it come to pass?" or, "how is it done?" or, "how does it happen?" or, "how is it?")

23. "Our abode" = μονήν. Cf. Matt. xxvi. 27 and 1 Cor. xv. 38.

26. "Said" for "have said" = εἶπον: as at Matt. xxviii. 20. Surely the A. V. is right. Did our Lord refer to sayings in some indefinite past? Did he not include all down to the moment when he was speaking? The other changes in this verse are entirely unnecessary.

27. "Fearful" for "afraid" = δειλιάτω. "Give I;" the order of the Greek is departed from.

28. "Heard" for "have heard." (?) The repetition of

"I" in this verse and the insertion of "he" in verse 30 have no authority in the Greek, and how they are required by faithfulness it is hard to see. They seem to be the result of a kind of sublimated hypercriticism.

XV.

2. "That beareth" = φέρον and τὸ φέρον alike.

4. "Except" = ἐὰν μή:—an ellipsis must be presumed, as, "neither can it bear fruit at all;" for the meaning cannot be that, if it abide in me it can bear fruit *of itself*.

6. Two aorists are rendered as present. "A branch" = τὸ κλῆμα.

9. Two aorists are rendered as perfect. "Abide" for "continue." (?)

15. "No longer" for "henceforth not" = οὐκέτι, *i.e.* "not now" or "not now nor in future." Had he been accustomed to call them servants before? "Heard" for "have heard" = ἤκουσα. But is it to be presumed that he had heard nothing from the Father since a certain indefinite moment in the past? The Revisers cannot have inferred this from the mere aorist form of the verb. for they immediately add: "Have made known" = ἐγνώρισα.

17. "May love" for "love." But is it not the substance rather than the end of the commandment that is referred to? If. ἵνα is appealed to, then say "should love," and not "may love;" for it is a *commandment*.

19. "Chose" for "have chosen ;" cf. xiii. 18.

20. "A" for "the" (servant). Generic and aphoristic, therefore no article in Greek. It may have either article in English, as we cannot use it without any; but "the" is the better.

XVI.

4. "Is come" for "shall come" = ἔλθῃ: and so the A. V. at verse 13. But cf. Matt. ix. 15; xix. 28; xxi. 40; xxv. 31; and Mark ii. 20.

7. "Go" for "depart." There is a different word in the Greek for this "go" and for the two preceding (go away); there ἀπέλθω, here πορευθῶ. Would not "depart," therefore, be better, for one or the other?

11. "Hath been judged" for "is judged." Cf. "It is written," and see xii. 27.

13. "All the truth," for "all truth;" why not then, "the Spirit of the truth," as well? "The things that are to come" = τὰ ἐρχόμενα: and so Rev. i. 4, 8, not "the things that come." Cf. vi. 14 and xi. 27. "Is come" = ὅταν ἔλθῃ, and future following; but see vii. 31; Matt. xxi. 40, etc.

21. "A woman" = ἡ γυνή: "is born" = ἐγεννήθη, so A. V.

22. "And ye therefore now" for "and ye now therefore." Revising faithfulness.

28. "Am come" = ἐλήλυθα: elsewhere changed to "have come," see vi. 17; viii. 42, etc. And cf. "is come" at verse 13. "Every man" = ἕκαστος. In such cases they generally put "one" for "man," and "each" for "every."

XVII.

3. "Him whom thou didst send, even Jesus Christ." The change of tense and construction in this classical passage is entirely uncalled for. We have seen that the Revisers have familiarly rendered the Greek aorists by the English perfect, and this very ἀπέστειλα among the rest. But here, at verse 4, they put "glorified" for "have glorified;" at 6, "manifested" for "have manifested;" at 8, "received," "knew," "believed," for "have," etc.; at 12, "perished" for "is lost;" at 14, "hated" for "hath hated;" at 25, "knew" three times, for "have known;" and at 26, "made" for "have made;" thus throwing all these acts out of connection with the (then) present into the indefinite past, as historical events which had taken place at some particular though indeterminate time, —as dead historical facts. Now the Revisers cannot, consistently with their own translation elsewhere, appeal to the mere form of the Greek aorist as settling the question in their favor. Neither can they appeal to the intermingling of Greek perfects with Greek aorists in this passage; for at Acts xxv. 10, 11, "I have done" is for a Greek aorist, and "I have committed" for a Greek perfect, in im-

mediate succession; and at Acts xxi. 21–24, and Rev. xviii. 2, 3, the aorist and perfect of the very same verb are both rendered by the English perfect. At Phil. iii. 12; iv. 11, 12, they have rendered an aorist and a perfect by the perfect. And even in this very gospel at xiii. 14, 15, they render "have washed" for an aorist, and "have given" for a perfect. Also at Matt. xxvi. 12, 13, the aorist of the same verb is rendered first preterite and then perfect. The question here between the Authorized Version and the Revision must be settled by that sort of judgment of the context and of the nature of the case which any intelligent English reader is as well qualified to exercise as an equally intelligent Greek scholar. And we may add that the Revisers have against them the whole English Hexapla, Luther's German, De Sacy's French, Diodati's Italian, and almost all, if not all of the former translations from the Greek; and let it not be forgotten that no appeal will lie here to any modern discoveries in Greek grammar or to any mysteries recently laid open in regard to the Greek aorist tense. Cf. further, Mark v. 19; Heb. xii. 4, 5, etc.

21, 23. "May all" for "all may;" "perfected" for "made perfect." Revising faithfulness.

24. Even the change of text will scarcely justify the mangling of this verse, which is made so harsh and discordant to the English ear,—and to the English mind.

XVIII.

4. "Were coming" for "should come" $= \grave{\epsilon}\rho\chi\acute{o}\mu\epsilon\nu\alpha$. Why did they not say "came"? See vi. 14 and cf. xvi. 13; also vi. 15 and 71.

6. "When therefore" for "as soon then as" $= \acute{\omega}\varsigma\ o\grave{\tilde{\upsilon}}\nu$: "said" for "had said." (?)

9. "Lost" for "have lost." (?)

10. "Struck" for "smote." Faithfulness. Cf. Luke xxii. 50, etc.

13. "High priest" for "the high priest"—a predicate; and what's the difference? but, "faithfulness"! The A. V., forsooth, was ignorant of the use of the Greek article. Cf. xix. 7, Acts x. 42, etc.

20. "Synagogues" for "the synagogue." Their own text has συναγωγῇ: but what is a question of *number* to that of the *article*?

30. "Evil-doer" for "malefactor" = κακοποιός. Plainly the word is here to be understood in its legal, or criminal, sense. Cf. Luke xxiii. 32, 33, where they render κακοῦργοι "malefactors."

31. "Yourselves" for "ye" = ὑμεῖς: and so at xix. 6. Who is most "faithful"?

35. "Delivered" for "have delivered;" but immediately "hast thou done" renders an aorist.

38. "Crime" for " fault" = αἰτία: and at xix. 4, 6.

XIX.

2, 5. "Garment" for "robe" = ἱμάτιον—with "purple." (?)

4, 5. "Out" for "forth" = ἐξῆλθεν: and so at verses 13, 17, and xxi. 3. But cf. Acts ii. 17.

6. "When therefore the chief priests and the officers" for "when the chief priests, therefore, and officers." How momentous these changes!

10, 11. Power = ἐξουσία—not "authority." "Greater sin" for "the greater sin;" but, at verse 8, "the more" = μᾶλλον,—no art.

12. "Release" for "let go." But cf. Acts iv. 23.

18. "Others" for "other." But cf. xxi. 2; Acts xvii. 18.

19. "There was written" for "the writing was" = ἦν γεγραμμένον. Now the simple reader will not only understand the meaning, but will know how the Greek says it.

31. "On" for "upon," and "upon" for "on;" and "the day of that sabbath" for "that Sabbath day." Exquisite and untiring faithfulness! Think of each of these being solemnly put to a two thirds vote! "Asked" for "besought" = ἠρώτησαν: and so, verse 38; but cf. xvi. 26.

39. "He who" for "which" = ὁ (ἐλθών); cf. iii. 13; Matt. vi. 4, etc., etc.

40. "Custom" for "manner." (?)

42. A needless and bungling rearrangement, spoiling the flow and cadence without improving or even altering the sense of the passage. Compare this faithfulness with that *e.g.* at Acts xx. 25, 31. If the Revisers *would* make these changes they were bound to be consistent, and to give us the Greek construction always.

XX.

3. "Went toward" for "came to" = ἤρχοντο εἰς: but cf. Acts xxviii. 14. And why did they not say "were going," as at vi. 17?

5. "Stooping, he" for "He, stooping." (?)

5, 6, 8. "Entered in" for "went in" = εἰσῆλθεν. But cf. Acts xxi. 26, "went into" = εἰσῄει. Does not ἔρχομαι signify "go," as well as εἶμι? The Revisers do not hesitate so to render it, and to correct the A. V. at the same time; see verse 3, and xi. 29.

6, 7, 12, 14. By comparing these verses it will appear that θεωρέω means the same as βλέπω or εἶδον, and no more.
"When she had said" = εἰποῦσα.

23. "Forgive" for "remit" = ἀφῆτε. Well?

27. "See" for "behold" = ἴδε. "Behold" can take an accusative in English as well as "see;" and it does not appear that ἴδε changes its meaning according to the case following. But faithfulness—to θεωρέω, "behold"!

XXI.

1. "He manifested himself on this wise" for "on this wise showed he himself." (?)

2. "Two other" = ἄλλοι δύο. Cf. xix. 18.

3. "Come" for "go" = ἔρχομαι. Cf. xx. 3. "Took" for "caught" = ἐπίασαν: so at verse 10.

4. "Beach" for "shore" = αἰγιαλόν. It was certainly a "shore," whether it was properly a "beach" or not.

8. "Of fishes" = τῶν ἰχθύων: but see "the weeping and gnashing."

9. "Got out upon the land," for "were come to land" = ἀπέβησαν εἰς τὴν γῆν—simply they "landed," or "had landed."

12. "Break your fast," for "dine" = ἀριστήσατε, *i.e.* "dine" or "breakfast;" and the same at verse 15. The Revisers translate ἄριστον, "dinner," at Matt. xxii. 4 ; Luke xi. 38, and xiv. 12 ; and, at Luke xi. 37, they translate ἀριστήσῃ, "dine." Indeed, ἄριστον has no more to do with "breaking a fast" than every meal must have, from the nature of the case ; and our very word "dine," from "*dîner*," "*disner*," is not unlikely of the same origin as "*déjeûner*," to breakfast. As to the time of the day at which this meal was taken, we cannot say exactly at what time it was. It seems likely it was early. But we cannot make much account of the proper hour of "dining," when a London dinner may be taken at from eight to twelve o'clock at night.

12, 24. "Inquire" for "ask" = ἐξετάσαι : "beareth witness" for "testifieth;" "witness" for "testimony." Consequential.

ACTS.

I.

2, 11, 22. "Received up" for "taken up" = ἀνελήφθη : and so the A. V. at Mark xvi. 19. The word may be rendered either way. From the Latin it is "*assumption*"— a taking up or taking to one's self. At verse 9 they had better have said "lifted up" for "taken up" = ἐπήρθη. Cf. Matt. xvii. 8 ; where they so render.

3. "Proofs" for "infallible proofs" = τεκμήρια. Lex., "sure signs or tokens," "demonstrative proofs."

4. "Charged" for "commanded" = παρήγγειλεν. So also at iv. 18; v. 28, 40; xvi. 18, etc., etc. But cf. xvii. 30; Mark viii. 6; Luke ix. 21; viii. 29 (and compare this last with Acts xvi. 18), etc., etc. Faithfulness illustrated.

6. "They therefore, when they were come together, asked," for "when they therefore were come together, they asked." But cf. again Matt. viii. 12; ix. 12; xi. 2; xii. 24; Luke ix. 47; xxiii. 6, 8; John xxvi. 14, etc. See Luke vii. 4 (note).

11. "Which was received up" for "which is taken up" = ὁ ἀναληφθείς. But cf. Matt. ii. 2, ὁ τεχθείς = "he that is born," etc., etc.

12. Why did they not say "a mountain, *even the mountain* which"? Cf. Gal. ii. 20.

14, 19. Order changed contrary to the Greek.

16. "It was needful that . . . . should be" for "must needs have been" = ἔδει. But cf. John iv. 4; Heb. ix. 26, etc.—"must needs," "must."

17. "His portion" = τὸν κλῆρον. Elsewhere, in similar cases, they often carefully put "the" for "his."

18. "Received" for "obtained" = ἔλαχε (not ἔλαβε). "Obtained" for "purchased" = ἐκτήσατο. (?)

19. The order is here changed without need and contrary to the original. Truly these Revisers are hard to please. If the A. V. departs from the order of the Greek they change it; if it follows the order of the Greek they change it,—and always from sheer "faithfulness."

"Akeldama" for "Aceldama." Anywhere else one would call this pedantry; here it is only "faithfulness." The English has become accustomed to the Latin spelling of such names; and what is gained by change? Besides, one who changes is bound to be consistent. Why then did they not say "Kephas"?

21. "Of the men therefore . . . . of these" for "wherefore of these men." The A. V. gives the simple English construction, and that quite as near the Greek as the Revision is. And how much does "wherefore" differ from "therefore"? In the original there is for "these" only an article; and yet the Revisers by their dislocation render it emphatic. "Went in and went out" for "went in and out;" which is the English for the repeated or customary action?

23. "Put forward" for "appointed" = ἔστησαν. Cf. xix. 33; also Matt. xxvi. 15.

24. "The one" = ἕνα. Cf. Matt. vi. 24; Luke xvi. 13.

25. "The place in this ministry and apostleship, from which," for "part of this ministry and apostleship, from which" = τὸν τόπον (old text κλῆρον) τῆς διακονίας ταύτης καὶ ἀποστολῆς ἀφ' (old text ἐξ) ἧς. Here "min-

istry," etc., is in the genitive (not "in," therefore, but " of"), and "from which" should refer not to "the place," but to "ministry," etc.; so that the new version would be misunderstood, for it grammatically means "the place which." This is the effect in English of the article introduced from their new text before "place."

II.

2. "Of the rushing of a mighty wind," for "of a rushing mighty wind" = φερομένης πνοῆς βιαίας. Here the A. V. is literally exact to a hair's breadth. What is the key to the Revisers' "faithfulness"?

3. "Parting asunder" for "cloven" = διαμεριζόμεναι. Here the sense remains substantially the same. The only question is, whether the participle is to be conceived of as middle or passive. The Revisers take the former and the A. V. the latter; but the Revisers have themselves rendered it as passive at Luke xi. 17, 18; xii. 52, 53. The Septuagint use it as middle; but its active form and use are found both in the classical and N. T. Greek; see verse 45.

6, 8. Why did they not say, after the Greek, "they, every man," "how do we, every man," and so avoid the ambiguity in the latter verse? That might have been an object worthy of their revisional faithfulness.

11. "Mighty works" for "wonderful works" = μεγαλεῖα (= "grand or magnificent things"). But greatness is no more nearly related to *might* than to *wonder*. Cf. δυνάμεις, "mighty works."

12. "Perplexed" for "in doubt" = διηπόρουν. Which is the simpler and the more strictly, and even etymologically, correct? So at v. 24 and x. 17.

14. "Spoke forth, *saying*," for "said" = ἀπεφθέγξατο (= "said plainly").

17. "Pour forth" for "pour out"= ἐκχεῶ. But see x. 45 and cf. John ii. 15; xix. 4, 5, etc.

26. "My heart was glad and my tongue rejoiced" for "my heart did rejoice and my tongue was glad." How wondrous nice!

28. "Gladness" for "joy" = εὐφροσύνη. "Madest" for "hast made." (?)

32. "Did raise up" for "hath raised up." (?)

36. "Let all the house of Israel therefore" for "therefore let," etc. Πᾶς οἶκος = "all the house;" cf. Eph. iii. 13.

46. "At home" for "from house to house" = κατ' οἶκον (so, marg. of A. V.); but just above and below, "day by day" = καθ' ἡμέραν = A. V. "daily."

47. "Those that were being saved" for " such as should be saved" = τοὺς σωζομένους = "those that were saved" or "that should be saved." So also they render at 1 Cor. i. 18; 2 Cor. ii. 15. But cf. Luke xiii. 23, "they that be saved;" also, John xiii. 11, "him that should betray him" = τὸν παραδιδόντα.

III.

6. "That" = τοῦτο—not "this."

12. "Fasten ye your eyes" for "look ye so earnestly" = ἀτενίζετε. But cf. i. 10; xxiii. 1—"looking stedfastly."

13. "Release" for "let go." Cf. iv. 23.

14. "Asked for" for "desired" = ᾐτήσασθε. Cf. Luke vii. 36.

16. "Hath made strong;" "hath given;" both for aorists.

18. "Foreshowed" for "before had shewed" = προκατήγγειλε. "Fulfilled" for "hath fulfilled"—aorist. (?)

21. "Spake" for "hath spoken"—aorist.

22, 23. "To him shall ye hearken" for "him shall ye hear" = ἀκούσεσθε. If there is any ambiguity in the A. V., there is the same in the Greek. "Speak" for "say" = λαλήσῃ. (?)

24. "Them that followed after" for "those that follow after" = τῶν καθεξῆς. The distinction is not in the Greek at all events—either that of the tense, or of the "them" and "those." "Told" for "have (fore) told." (?)

IV.

2. "Sore troubled" for "grieved" = διαπονούμενοι. (?) "Proclaimed" for "preached" = καταγγέλλειν. (?)

12. "And in none other is there salvation" for "neither is there salvation in any other." "Neither is there any other name" for "there is none other name." In the last their text is οὐδέ for οὔτε.

13. "Had perceived" for "perceived" = καταλαβόμενοι. Cf. the reverse change at John ix. 35, etc., etc. Cf. λαβών at Matt. xxv. 20.

14. "Seeing" for "beholding" = βλέποντες (= "looking at"). Cf. Matt. vii. 3; Luke vi. 41; 1 Cor. x. 18; Col. ii. 5; Rev. xvii. 8, in all which they render "behold;" also Rev. xi. 9; xviii. 9, where they put "look upon" for "see;" and 1 Cor. i. 26, where they put "behold" for "see"!

16, 22. "Miracle" = σημεῖον. It is difficult to dispense with the received English words when one is making an English translation;—"Si furcâ expellas."

18. "Charged" for "commanded." See i. 4 (note); and 1 Tim. i. 3 (note).

20. "Saw and heard" for "have seen and heard." (?) "Was wrought" for "was showed" = ἐγεγόνει (= "had been done," see verse 30).

23. "Being let go" = ἀπολυθέντες (= "having been let go"). But see iii. 13 and John xix. 12 ("released"); and see verse 13 for the tense.

24. "And they, when they heard it," for "and when they heard it, they." See i. 6 (note). "The heaven and the earth, the sea," for "heaven and earth, the sea." See Rev. ix. 1; Matt. xxiv. 35, etc.

28. "Foreordained" for "determined before" = προώρισε. Which is the more faithful to the very etymology of the Greek word? "To come to pass" for "to be done" = γενέσθαι. Cf. verse 30, where they render γίνεσθαι "to be done." Does the tense change the sense?

29. "Look upon" for "behold" = ἔπιδε. What's the difference? But the Revisers have a consequential reverence for θεωρέω before their eyes.

30. "While thou stretchest forth" for "by stretching forth" = ἐν τῷ, κ.τ.λ. Why not say, "in stretching forth"?

35. "Each" for "every man" = ἑκάστῳ. Cf. John xvi. 28.

36. "Son" for "the son." But what's the difference in a title? See their own usage at i. 19; Matt. iii. 3; John xix. 19, etc. Would they not have done better to have retained "consolation" in the text, and relegated "exhortation" to the margin? But this is a question, not of Greek authority, but of private judgment. The decision suggested has the A. V. to sustain it.

V.

17. "Jealousy" for "indignation" = ζήλου.
18. "Public ward" for "the common prison" = τηρήσει δημοσίᾳ. This is nearer the Greek etymology, but less intelligible in English.
20. "Go ye and stand" for "go stand." No ὑμεῖς (ye) and no καί (and) in the Greek; for the καί in the text connects "speak" and not "stand" with "go." Faithfulness?
31. "Did exalt" for "hath exalted." (?)
33. "They, when they heard," for "when they heard, they." See i. 6 (note).
42. "At home" = κατ' οἶκον, for "in every house." But κατ' οἴκους they render "from house to house," Acts xx. 20; and ἐν οἴκῳ they render "at home," 1 Cor. xi. 34, and xiv. 35.

VI.

"Therefore" for "wherefore"—needless change. "May appoint" = καταστήσομεν (future).
4. Why this change? Προσκαρτερήσομεν may as well mean "we will give ourselves continually to," as "we will continue stedfastly in."
7. "Exceedingly" for "greatly" = σφόδρα. Exceeding faithful!
15. "Fastening their eyes" for "looking stedfastly" = ἀτενίσαντες. But see vii. 55 and xxiii. 1, where they render "looking stedfastly"! And whence the "eyes"?

VII.

4. "Wherein" = εἰς ἥν, not "whereinto."
5. "In possession" for "for a possession" = εἰς κατάσχεσιν. (?) See verse 45 and the Septuagint.

20. "Three months in his father's house" for "in his father's house three months." The English naturally puts the designation of place before that of time; but the Revisers are apt to follow the Greek.

22. What need of inserting "he"?

28. The "wilt" and the "didst" of the A. V. are idiomatic English. For the former see John v. 21, 40.

35. Why did they not say here "an angel's hand, *even the angel* that appeared"? There is no article in the Greek till we come to the participle. Cf. 2 Tim. ii. 24, and particularly Gal. ii. 20; also cf. Rev. viii. 4, and x. 8, 10, for the articles.

44. "Appointed" for "had appointed." Cf. 2 Cor. viii. 5.

VIII.

5. "Proclaimed" for "preached" = ἐκήρυσσεν: so also at ix. 20. But cf. xv. 21; 1 Cor. i. 23; Phil. i. 15, etc.

23. "Art in" = εἰς ὄντα: and note articles.

39. "When they came" for "when they were come." Whether in English we should use the preterite or the pluperfect in such cases is not determined by the Greek tense, but depends upon whether we conceive the two actions compared to be synchronous or consecutive. It is not Greek scholarship therefore, whether ancient or modern, that is to decide the question, but good common sense. Cf. the translation of the Revisers at xi. 2, "was come" (but see Gal. ii. 11, 12); Mark vii. 17, "was entered;" Luke xxii. 14, "was come" (but see John iv. 45, "came"); John xiii. 3, "was gone;" xxi. 15, "had broken;" Rev. v. 8, "had taken."

IX.

3. "Out of heaven" = ἐκ τοῦ οὐρανοῦ. "The earth" immediately follows. For the article cf. iv. 24; vii. 49; x. 11, etc.; and for the preposition cf. xi. 5; Matt. xvi. 1; xxviii. 2; John iii. 31; Rev. viii. 10, ix. 1; x. 4, 8; xi. 12; xiv. 2, 13, etc.

7. "Beholding" for "seeing" = θεωροῦντες. But it is here opposed to "hearing;" and cf. xix. 26 and xxi. 20, where they render the same verb by "see."

11. "To the street" for "into" = ἐπί, *i.e.* "upon" or "along." "Into" is nearer than "to."
13. "Did" for "hath done." (?)
14. "Upon" for "on ;" but cf. verse 21. Who can keep up with the versatilities and niceties of revisional "faithfulness"?
15. Why did they not say, " Gentiles and kings," etc. ? There is no article in the Greek.
18. "As it were" for "as it had been" = ὡσεί. So also at x. 11 ; but cf. vi. 15, where they render "as it had been."
20. The order needlessly changed. "Proclaimed" for "preached" = ἐκήρυσσεν. See viii. 5 (note).
27. Order changed. What trifling! Cf. xv. 2, xx. 25, etc.
31. "Being edified" for "and was (were) edified." (?)
34. "Healeth" for "maketh whole." Cf. xiv. 9. What is the logical, or etymological, or practical difference between "healing" and "making whole"?
41. For the change of construction compare this and x. 8, 17 with xxvi. 31, etc., etc.

X.

1. "By name" for "called" = ὀνόματι : also viii. 9. But this is not adhered to elsewhere. Better say "named," as the Revisers do at Luke i. 5, v. 27, x. 38, xvi. 20, xxiii. 50 ; Acts v. 1, 34, ix. 12, xxiii. 36, etc., etc.
4. Construction changed without improvement. The *seeing* was the *cause* of the *fearing.*
5. "Fetch" for "call for" = μετάπεμψαι : but see verses 22, 29, xxiv. 26, and cf. xvi. 37. To "send for" and to "fetch" are commonly different things ; and after "send," already used, repetition was unnecessary, and "call for" is near enough to the sense.
8. "Rehearsed" for "declared" = ἐξηγησάμενος. (?)
10. "Hungry" for "very hungry" = πρόσπεινος. (?) "Desired to eat" for "would have eaten." But cf. xiv. 13, where they render "would have."
11. "The heaven" for "heaven ;" but cf. verse 16 and xi. 5, 9, 10, where "heaven" is rendered without the article which is in the Greek.

30. 'Apparel" for "clothing" = ἐσθῆτι. (!)
33. "Have been" for "are" (commanded). But see "it is written," etc., etc., and especially John xii. 27.
42. "To be the judge;" no article in the Greek. Cf. John xviii. 13.
45. "Poured out;" but cf. ii. 17, where they correct the A. V. and render "pour forth."

XI.

5, 6. "From heaven" and "of the heaven" = τοῦ οὐρανοῦ: and "fowls" for their "birds" elsewhere. 9. "A voice out of heaven," and so at Matt. iii. 17; Mark i. 11; Luke iii. 22; but at Rev. x. 4, 8, xi. 12, xiv. 2, 13, they say "a voice from heaven."
14. The *repetition* of "thou" here and at xvi. 31 is neither required nor authorized by its being *expressed* in the Greek. We cannot follow the Greek construction, but, if we would bring out the number of the Greek verb, we might say, "thou shalt be saved and all thy house."

XII.

10. "The first" = πρώτην: "the second" = δευτέραν. Cf. Matt. xxii. 39.—No article.
21. Construction changed for the worse, and not required by the slight change in the text. "The throne" for "his throne" is an inconsistency.
22. "The voice of a God" = Θεοῦ φωνή. Cf. Matt. xxvii. 54, margin (note); say "the son of a God."

XIII.

12. "Teaching" for "doctrine" = διδαχῇ,—here liable to be misunderstood.
19, 20. The text which the Revisers have adopted here is difficult to reconcile with accepted facts.
36. The margin is better: "served his generation." There ought to be very cogent reasons for abolishing the Scripture authority for this phrase. The antiquated "fell on sleep" is retained. May not unlearned readers stumble over it?

46. "Spake out boldly and said" for "waxed bold and said" = παρρησιασάμενοι εἶπον. But cf. 1 Thess. ii. 2, where they say "waxed bold."

XIV.

3. "Bare witness" for "gave testimony" = μαρτυροῦντι —consequential. "To be done" = γίνεσθαι.
5. "Onset" for "assault" = ὁρμή. . This is a new word; is it needed? "Treat shamefully" for "use despitefully" = ὑβρίσαι. The A. V. is the more accurate. There is no "shame" in the word at all. Cf. Luke xx. 11, where "handle shamefully" is for ἀτιμήσαντες, and rightly.
6. The change of construction makes the sense ambiguous, for Lycaonia might be supposed to be the name of a city as well as Derbe and Lystra. The Revisers do not always follow the Greek; as cf. Acts xx. 25.
9. "Fastening his eyes upon" for "stedfastly beholding" = ἀτενίσας. Cf. vii. 55, xxiii. 1; 2 Cor. iii. 7, 13.
13. "Whose *temple*" for "which" = τοῦ. This is a paraphrase instead of a translation, and, besides, it expresses what, from the text, is at least uncertain as a matter of fact. They should have said, "the priest of the Jupiter which was," etc. It may have been a statue and not a temple of Jupiter which was before the gate?
15. "The heaven," etc. See iv. 24, (note).
19. Construction of "thither"? Did faithfulness require the omission of "*certain*"? It was confessedly not expressed in the original.
26. "Had fulfilled" for "fulfilled" = ἐπλήρωσαν. (?) In verse 23 the change of "believed" to "had believed" is right.

XV.

2. "Certain other of them." Cf. Luke x. 1. "Should go up" is not in the order of the Greek; cf. ix. 27.
10. "That ye should put" for "to put." The latter is literal from the Greek, and is idiomatic English as well as quite intelligible here. Cf. Heb. vi. 10. The Revisers often put the infinitive instead of the construction with ἵνα (*that*) in the original, as at John iv. 34; v. 36; xi. 19, 55.

11. Here the construction is changed, though the A. V. follows the order of the Greek.
16. What need of the extra "I"?
21. "Preach him" = κηρύσσω αὐτόν. Cf. viii. 5.
22. "Seemed good" for "it pleased." (?)
22, 25. "To choose men" for "chosen men" = ἐκλεξαμένους ἄνδρας. The A. V. "faithfully" follows the Greek construction, and if there is any ambiguity in the English there is the same in the Greek.
23. It should be (à la grecque), "The apostles and the elders, brethren." For "apostles and elders," cf. verses 2 and 22, and xvi. 4.
20 and 29. Compare these verses for the use of the article in Greek.
36. "Proclaimed" for "preached." (?) "How they fare" for "how they do" = πῶς ἔχουσι. (?)

XVI.

3. "Would have" = ἠθέλησεν, and so at xiv. 13. But cf. Luke xix. 14.
12. Construction bungling. The A. V. is nearer the Greek after all, only putting "that" for τῆς. They make "the first" = πρώτη: and so, marg. of A. V.
37. "Men that are Romans" for "being Romans" = Ῥωμαίους ὑπάρχοντες. "Cast out" for "thrust out;" "bring" for "fetch." (?)
39. "Asked them to go away from the city" for "desired them to depart from the city." (The text for "depart" is changed from ἐξελθεῖν to ἀπελθεῖν ἀπό.) What a wondrous elevation and vigor of style;—"asked them to go away from the city"! At the end of the chapter they say they "departed;" and at John xii. 36, they render ἀπελθών "departed."

XVII.

2. "Sabbath days" = Σάββατα. Elsewhere they have omitted the "day."
3. "It behoved" for "must needs have" = ἔδει. So Luke xxiv. 26; but cf. Mark xiv. 31; John iv. 4; Heb. ix. 36, etc., etc. "The Christ" for "Christ." (?)

5. "Rabble" = ἀγοραῖοι = "hangers on about the market." For the change of construction, compare Matt. xxvi. 26, 27, etc. They have no more right, in faithfulness, to consult variety in rendering the same constructions, than in rendering the same words.

13. "Proclaimed" for "preached." (?)

16. "Full of idols" for "given to idolatry" = κατείδωλον. So the A. V. in margin. Whose judgment is to be preferred?

18. "Would" for "will" = θέλει. (?) "Other some"—archaism retained, instead of simply saying, "others" = οἱ δέ.

22. "Somewhat superstitious" for "too superstitious" = δεισιδαιμονεστέρους. Is this the sense of the comparative absolute—softened even below the simple positive? Cf. 2 Pet. i. 19; Heb. xiii. 19, 23; John xiii. 27; 2 Cor. viii. 17.

23. "An unknown God" for "The unknown God." Cf. Luke xxiii. 33; John xix. 17; Acts i. 19; Heb. xii. 22, and names and titles generally. Did the Athenians dedicate their altar to *any* one among the "unknown gods," or rather to some definite, particular, though as yet "unknown, God"—one of whom they had a sort of presentiment?

XVIII.

15. "Am not minded to be" for "will be no." The A. V. gives the sense of the Greek simply, accurately, and without ambiguity.

20. "Asked" for "desired" = ἐρωτώντων. At Luke vii. 36, they render the word "desired."

24. Order changed for the Greek; but the A. V. has the logic.

25. "Carefully" for "diligently" = ἀκριβῶς: and 26, for "perfectly." Should these not be "clearly" in verse 25, and "more accurately" in the 26th?

XIX.

4. "That should come" = τὸν ἐρχόμενον—not "that came." Cf. Luke vii. 20, etc.

22. "While" for "season" = χρόνον. (?)

26. "See"= θεωρεῖτε, with "hear;" but cf. ix. 7, where they render "behold."

29. The Greek order here is no improvement to the English, and makes no change in the sense. "Was minded to" for "would have"= βουλόμενος with aorist. (?)

32. "In confusion" for "confused"= συγκεχυμένη: pluperfect passive; for which, "was confused" may stand, but "was in confusion" may not. The Revisers, it seems, feel at liberty to depart from the strict Greek construction when they think they can correct the A. V. in so doing. But note their scrupulosity at verse 29 and at xviii. 24. "Were come" = ἐληλύθεισαν: elsewhere, we have seen, they render "had come." Did faithfulness require this diversification?

35. "Temple keeper" for "worshipper" = νεωκόρον. This is from the margin of the A. V., and, but for a spice of pedantry, might have been left there.

38. "That" for "which." Did faithfulness require the change?

39. "The regular" for "a lawful" = τῇ ἐννόμῳ. (?) What is a substantive or an adjective to an article?

40. "And as touching it"= περὶ οὗ. But "it" must refer to "riot" = στάσεως, above, which is feminine. Both the text and their translation of this verse are very confused.

XX.

2. "Gone through" for "gone over." (?)

3. "Determined" for "purposed"= ἐγένετο γνώμη— "was minded"?

9. "Borne down" and "being borne down"= καταφερόμενος and κατενεχθείς.

18. "Set foot in" for "came into"= ἐπέβην εἰς. So also at xxi. 4; but cf. xxv. 1.

19. "Lowliness" for "humility." (?)

24. The text is changed. "I hold not my life of any account as dear unto myself." Is it not rather, "the life *which is* dear unto myself I hold of no account"?

27. "The whole counsel" for "all the counsel"= πᾶσαν τὴν βουλήν. But the Revisers have not only rendered πᾶς

ὁ and πᾶσα ἡ by "all the" in innumerable cases, but they have put "all the city" *for* "the whole city" at Matt. viii. 34. (Cf. Acts xiii. 44, where they say "the whole city"); "all the multitude" *for* "the whole multitude" ["stood"— "were on"] at Matt. xiii. 2 and Mark iv. 1; "all the multitude" *for* "the whole multitude" ["sought"] at Luke vi. 19 (cf. Luke i. 10, "The whole multitude were praying," and Acts vi. 5, "The saying pleased the whole multitude"); and "all the earth" *for* "the whole earth," at Luke xxi. 35.

34. "Ye yourselves know" = αὐτοὶ γινώσκετε. And so the A. V., and so right. But cf. verse 18, where they put "ye yourselves" for "ye" = ὑμεῖς ἐπίστασθε. "Ministered" for "have ministered;" but in verse 28, "hath made" (aorist), while most of the aorists in this connection are rendered by the simple preterite.

XXI.

1. "The next day" for "the day following" = τῇ ἑξῆς. Cf. iii. 24.

2, 4. "Having found" for "finding" = εὑρόντες, followed by an aorist verb; cf. John ix. 35.

3. "Leaving it, we" for "we left it and" = καταλιπόντες, also followed by an aorist verb.

5. "Kneeling, we" for "we kneeled and,"—an aorist participle again, followed by an aorist verb, as at verses 2, 3, and 4. Also at verse 8, "entering, we" for "we entered and;" and at verse 11, "coming, and taking, he" for "when he was come, he took and." Compare all these with the correction at verses 2 and 4.

9. "Now this man" for "and the same man" = τούτῳ δέ. But cf. John i. 2, 7, etc.

21. "They have been informed" for "they are informed." This is the translation of the aorist κατηχήθησαν, but even if it had been of a perfect, the change would have been uncalled for (cf. "it is written"). And it is striking that the Revisers have given the very same translation for the aorist here, which, at verse 24, they have given for the perfect of this same verb, κατήχηνται: see also Rev. xviii. 2, 3. "Telling" for "saying" = λέγων. The construction of

the A. V. is nearer the Greek; "telling them" would require αὐτούς to be αὐτοῖς. For "saying that they ought not," in the A. V., cf. Gal. v. 7; Heb. iv. 6; and especially Rev. x. 9, where they give us "saying unto him that he should give" = λέγων αὐτῷ δοῦναι — thus retaining "saying" even though the dative follows, and the accusative with the infinitive has to be supplied. Why did they not say "telling him to give"? Of that text, that would have been the simple and direct translation. But that *text* was new, and so they had no opportunity to snub the A. V. with one of their faithful improvements in the English translation.

23. "Wrote" for "have written." (?)
26. "Went into" for "entered into" = εἰσῄει εἰς. Cf. Matt. x. 12; Luke xi. 33, etc. Is there any reason why εἴσειμι should not mean "enter" as well as εἰσέρχομαι and εἰσπορεύομαι, both which are also freely translated "come" and "go" as well as "enter"? Also at verse 18.
24. "Moreover" for "further." (?) "Defiled" for "polluted." (?)
32. "And they, when they" for "when they ... they." And so at verse 20; but see Luke vii. 4, note, and Acts i. 6, note.
34, 35. "Crowd" for "multitude" = ὄχλος. (?)
36. "Multitude" = πλῆθος: but at verse 27, ὄχλος is "multitude;" and at xxiii. 7, they have "assembly" *for* "multitude" = πλῆθος.

XXII.

3. "Instructed" for "taught." Faithfulness. "For God" for "toward God" = τοῦ θεοῦ.
5. "Journeyed to" for "went to" = ἐπορευόμην εἰς: but cf. verse 10, and xxviii. 14.
9. "Beheld" for "saw" = ἐθεάσαντο. But see xxi. 27, where we have "saw" = θεασάμενοι.
12. "Well reported of by" for "having a good report of" = μαρτυρούμενος. Which is the better English, — "of by"?
13. Why did they not say "Saul, brother" for "brother,

Saul," and follow the Greek as they have done at Gal. vi. 18, etc.? "That very hour" for "the same hour,"— what is the faithful difference? "Up on" for "up upon;" but this is liable to be misheard, and see Matt. xiv. 25, where they give us "upon" for "on,"—out of their marvellous faithfulness.

14. "A voice" for "the voice." (?)
15. "Hast seen and heard" = ἑώρακας καὶ ἤκουσας.
18. "Of thee testimony" for "thy testimony." Elsewhere they faithfully put "witness" for "testimony," as at John iii. 32, 33; v. 34; viii. 17; xxi. 24, etc., etc. Their zeal about the article (which is omitted before μαρτυρίαν) has led to their rendering σοῦ as if it were παρά σου, or were governed by παραδέξονται. (?) Cf. Rom. ix. 7.
21. "Unto the Gentiles" = εἰς ἔθνη.
23. "Threw" for "cast" = ῥιπτούντων. "Cast" for "threw" = βαλλόντων. What an unspeakable improvement is here!
24. "For what cause they so shouted" for "wherefore they so cried." There are three words for one, and "shouted" for "cried;" and, after all, we are where we were before.
25. "When they had tied him up" for "as they bound him" = ὡς δὲ προέτειναν. But cf. xxv. 14, where they actually correct the A. V. by putting "as they tarried there many days" for "when they had been there many days" = ὡς δὲ διέτριβον, κ.τ.λ., followed as here by another aorist.
29. Here they change the construction of the English, although the A. V. gives the same sense, and follows the Greek construction, with the exception of οὖν, which here means "thereupon," and may as well come first as second in the English order.

XXIII.

1. "Looking stedfastly on" for "earnestly beholding." Cf. iii. 12. "Before God, in all good conscience," for "in all good conscience, before God." The A. V. has the words in the Greek order.

5. "A ruler" for "the ruler." Can it be doubted that here the A. V. is right? And so, in verse 6, "a son," in apposition and with an anarthrous genitive. Cf. verse 8, where they say "the Sadducees" and "the Pharisees," though there is no article in the Greek. 9. "Clamor" for "cry" = κραυγή: but see verse 6, "he cried" = ἔκραξεν.

12, 14. "Bound," and so on until "have killed,"—all aorists indicative and subjunctive, and variously rendered in the preterite, perfect, and pluperfect.

15. "Or ever he come near,"—retained. "As though ye would judge more exactly" for "as though ye would enquire something more perfectly" = ὡς μέλλοντας διαγινώσκειν ἀκριβέστερον.

18. "Took, and" = παραλαβών = "took along, and." "To say" = λαλῆσαι. Cf. iii. 22 (xxvi. 22, "say"); John viii. 25, 26 (xvi. 18, "say"); xviii. 20, 21, etc., where "speak" is substituted for "say."

20. "Have agreed" = an aorist. "To bring down" for "that thou wouldst bring down" = ὅπως καταγάγῃς,—also verse 23. But cf. John xi. 53.

27. "Slay" for "kill" = ἀναιρεῖσθαι,—and so in verse 21 = ἀνέλωσιν: but "kill" for "slay" in verses 12 and 14 = ἀποκτείνω. Cf. xxv. 3, where ἀνελεῖν is rendered "kill," not "slay."

32. "To go" = ἀπέρχεσθαι,—not "come off."

33. "And they, when they came," for "who, when they came" = οἵτινες. Cf. Matt. vii. 15; Heb. xii. 7; Tit. i. 11; 2 Tim. ii. 18; 2 Thess. i. 9; Eph. iv. 19; Rom. iv. 18, etc.; where they render ὅστις "who" or "which;" though in many of those cases faithfulness would require a remodelling as much as here.

35. "Thy cause" for "thee" = σοῦ.

XXIV.

1. "And they" for "who;"—here right, for it prevents an ambiguity in English.

4. "Intreat" for "pray" = παρακαλῶ. (?)

9. "Affirming" for "saying" = φάσκοντες. (?)

10. The construction of the A. V. is nearer the Greek,

and the sense the same. The Revisers would improve the English. Faithfulness?

12. "A crowd" for "the people" = ὄχλου. (?) Why not say "the multitude," their usual rendering? In this construction, in the genitive, the article is not required in Greek. At verse 18, "crowd" for "multitude" spoils the English rhythm, besides introducing the unusual rendering.

22. "Determine" for "know the uttermost of" = διαγνώσομαι. (?)

24. Is not this change of construction for the worse, rendering a subordinate clause coördinate; and, in any event, is it not unnecessary?

26. "Call thee unto me" for "call for thee" = μετακαλέσομαι. Cf. xx. 1, where they have made just the contrary change!

27. "Desiring" for "willing" = θέλων (and so at xxv. 9) = "having a mind to." But Cf. Rom. ix. 22, where, in a precisely similar construction and meaning, they render "willing." "In bonds" for "bound" = δεδεμένον. Is not the sense the same? And which is the more faithful to the Greek?

XXV.

1. "Having come into" for "when he was come into" = ἐπιβάς. But cf. xx. 18; and xxi. 4, where they render ἐπιβαίνω εἰς "set foot in." Their changed order, "to Jerusalem from Cæsarea," is unnatural in English; and, as for faithfully conforming to the Greek, they might as well have rendered the interpretation of Emmanuel, after the Greek: "with us God." 3. "Kill" = ἀνελεῖν. See note xxiii. 27. 4. "Howbeit" for "but" = μὲν οὖν = "whereupon"? And so at xxviii. 5. "Howbeit" seems to be their favorite Jack at a pinch, if one may be allowed the colloquialism.

8. "Have I sinned" for "have I offended" = ἥμαρτον. Note the aorist. The A. V. would reserve the English word "sin" for offending against God. "Desiring" for "willing" = θέλων, see xxiv. 27. "Wilt thou go" = θέλεις,—not "wouldst thou."

10, 11. "Have I done," aorist; "have committed," perfect in the Greek.

17. "When therefore" for "therefore when," and so, habitually. But wherefore is it necessary? May not "therefore" begin a clause in English? And does not the illation here belong logically to the principal rather than to the subordinate clause with "when"? "Next day" for "morrow," but, at verse 6, "morrow" for "next day,"— where the same fact is referred to. Exquisite faithfulness!

22. "Could wish" for "would" = ἐβουλόμην. (?)

23. "In" for "forth." Nothing in the Greek for either.

25 and 21. The marginal "the Augustus" may indeed be Greek, but is it English?

27. "In sending" for "to send." Why change? The sense is the same, and neither follows the Greek. That, literally translated, would be "that one [or 'that I'] sending a prisoner should not also signify," etc.

XXVI.

6. "Stand to be judged" for "stand and am judged" = ἕστηκα κρινόμενος. (?)

7. "By the Jews." No article in the Greek.

8. "If God doth raise" for "that God should raise." Which is English, and which is good reason?

10. "And this" for "which thing" = ὅ. What sort of faithfulness required this change? "Vote" for "voice" = ψῆφον. The difference?

11. Change of construction certainly unnecessary. "Strove to make" for "compelled" = ἠνάγκαζον. If there was any ambiguity it was in the Greek.

16. "Have appeared," an aorist. "To this end" for "for this purpose," and what then? "Wherein" for "in the which." The sense is the same; and one expression is about as antiquated as the other. But "the which" they elsewhere use and multiply.

22 and 23. "Should" = μελλόντων and μέλλει. Also at xii. 28; xix. 27; xx. 38. But cf. verse 2 and xxiii. 27; xxii. 29. They translate by "would" at xxiii. 15, and change it quite at xii. 6 and xvi. 27.

24. "Mad," "madness," "mad." But cf. Matt. xxii. 3. Why not there say "to bid the bidden" or "to call the called"? However it may be in Greek, such repetitions are disagreeable in English. Does faithfulness require them? If so, then it requires them in all cases alike. Cf. also Rev. xii. 15.

28. "With but little persuasion thou wouldst fain make me" for "almost thou persuadest me to be" = ἐν ὀλίγῳ με πείθεις ποιῆσαι [γενέσθαι]. Even if the ἐν ὀλίγῳ cannot mean "almost," the Revisers have certainly given a questionable rendering of the Greek. Would not the most faithful and literal translation be: "In brief thou art persuading me to make me a Christian"? Or, if we would avoid the repetition of "me," say: "thou art using persuasion to make me." For ἐν ὀλίγῳ see Eph. iii. 3.

XXVII.

2. "Sail unto" = πλεῖν εἰς. But see verses 1 and 6, "sailing for."

7. Present and aorist participles co-ordinated in the Greek, and both translated as pluperfects.

23. "The God" for "God." But cf. 24 and 25.

24. "Granted" for "given" = κεχάρισται. (?)

29. "Let go from" for "cast out of" = ῥίψαντες ἐκ. "To cast anchor" is an idiomatic phrase in English; and how often the Revisers substitute "out of" for "from" as a translation of ἐκ we have seen. In the next verse they translate it both ways; and substitute "lay out" for "cast out" (anchors) = ἐκτείνειν = "stretch out." But is "lay out" any more faithful than "cast out"?

34. "Beseech" for "pray" = παρακαλῶ,—not "intreat;" cf. xxiv. 4. "Safety" for "health" = σωτηρία. (?)

43. "Desirous" for "willing" = βουλόμενος = "being disposed, or minded, to." But θέλω more usually means to will with choice or purpose.

XXVIII.

4. "Hath suffered" for "suffereth" = εἴασεν. Why change? Cf. εὐδόκησα.

5. "Howbeit he" for "and he" = ὁ μὲν οὖν: and followed by οἱ δέ.

8. "And it was so" for "and it came to pass" = ἐγένετο δέ. But see the almost frantic efforts elsewhere made to render γίγνομαι differently from εἰμί. "And laying" for "and laid" = ἐπιθείς,—not "having laid;" cf. xxi. 2, 4. Change of construction here unnecessary and inconsistent; cf. Matt. xxvi. 26, 27, etc.

12. "Touching" for "landing" = καταχθέντες. (?) And, here again, not "having touched."

14. "Intreated" for "desired" = παρεκλήθημεν,— not "besought," cf. xxvii. 34. "To Rome" for "toward Rome" = εἰς. Note the connection and cf. John xx. 3.

15. "The brethren, when they," for "when the brethren, . . . they." See notes, Luke vii. 4, and Acts i. 6.

16. "Abide" for "dwell" = μένειν. Consequential.

18. "Desired" for "would have" = ἐβούλοντο. (?)

27. "This people's heart" for "the heart of this people" = ἡ καρδία τοῦ λαοῦ τούτου. As here is the full suite of articles, it is difficult to guess why they made this petty change. But cf. Matt. xii. 40. "They have" for "have they,"—oh! unfathomable faithfulness! "Perceive" for "see" = ἴδωσι. Is this faithfulness? If ἴδωσι is not the simple word for "seeing," "seeing with the eyes," what is that word?

30. "Abode" for "dwelt" (see verse 16); and "dwelling" for "house" = μισθώματι. But is there anything that determines this last to be a "dwelling" rather than a "house"? Not unlikely it was a dwelling-house.

ROMANS.

I.

3, 4. "Jesus Christ, our Lord," is dislocated after the Greek construction, to no purpose but to spoil the English. Cf. 2 Peter iii. 1. "Who was born" for "which was made" = τοῦ γενομένου: and so at Gal. iv. 4. But is this change necessary? The Revisers have elsewhere familiarly rendered γίνομαι " be made;" and it is not to be confounded with γεννάομαι and τίκτομαι.

10. " May be prospered" for " might have a prosperous journey" = εὐοδωθήσομαι. Which is the more faithful to the sense? and note the future form.

12. "That I with you may be comforted in you" = συμπαρακληθῆναι ἐν ὑμῖν = "that [being] among you I with you may be comforted"?

14. If "to Greeks and to barbarians," then say "to wise and to unwise," not "to the wise and to the foolish." But at verse 16 they render "the Jew and the Greek," although there is no article in the text.

17. "A righteousness of God" for "the righteousness of God" = δικαιοσύνη Θεοῦ: and so at iii. 21, 22. But this is a sort of title, a fixed Pauline phrase. "The" is better English than "a;" as the English will scarcely bear no article like the Greek. The Apostle is not thinking of righteousness which might be counted. Cf. iii. 5;—can the accusative in Greek dispense with the article any more readily than the nominative in such a case as this? Cf. also iii. 21, 22.

19. "Manifested" for "hath showed." But this is not a historical aorist,—see "is manifest," just before.

20. "Through" for "by," the instrumental dative; change unnecessary, for "by" leaves the sense no more doubtful in English than it is in Greek.

21. "Knowing God" for "when they knew God" = γνόντες. (?) "Senseless" for "foolish" = ἀσύνετος (better, "stupid"?); elsewhere they have rendered this word "without (or void of) understanding."

II.

5. "For" for "unto" = dative. "In the day," "the righteous judgement." No article; cf. 2 Cor. vi. 2.

7. "In well-doing" = ἔργου ἀγαθοῦ. Why not be faithful, and say "in a good work"? "Incorruption" for "immortality" = ἀφθαρσία,—consequential.

8. "Factious" for "contentious" = ἐξ ἐριθείας: and so

generally, introducing the new word "faction," even to saying, James iii. 14, "having faction in your hearts."

12, 13. "Have sinned" = ἥμαρτον: "under law," "judged by law," "a law" (bis). But is not "law" here "the law,"—"the revealed law"? Can it be any law whatever? Cf. verse 17.

15. "In that they" for "which" = οἵτινες. See note, Acts xxiii. 33 ; and see especially Matt. vii. 15.

16. "By Jesus Christ." Needlessly displaced, and "by" = διά.

21. "Thou therefore that" for "thou therefore which." The A. V. put "which" here to avoid the juxtaposition of three *th*'s, and afterward used "that" when there was no "therefore;" but the Revisers, out of sheer faithfulness to the original Greek, have felt obliged to put "that" in all the clauses alike, as far as to verse 23, where they say "who" for "that." But "thou that" having been used four times, why is it then changed to "thou who"? Is this an effect of faithfulness also? 22. "Idols" = τὰ εἴδωλα.

25. "Be a doer" = πράσσῃς. Elsewhere they change "do" to "practise" for this verb.

27. "With" for "by" = διά, *cum gen.*

29. "In the spirit," "in the letter;"—no article in the Greek.

III.

1. "Circumcision." Why not "the circumcision" = τῆς περιτομῆς?

3. "Were without faith" = ἠπίστησαν. At Mark xvi. 16, and Luke xxiv. 11, 41, they render "disbelieve;" but are "want of faith" and "disbelief" the same? At iv. 20, they render ἀπιστία "unbelief," not "disbelief."

4. "Be found" for "be" = γινέσθω: but see margin just before. "When thou comest into judgement" for "when thou art judged" = ἐν τῷ κρίνεσθαί σε. Wherefore?

7. "Through my lie,"—ἐν.

8. "Evil" = τὰ κακά: "good" = τὰ ἀγαθά.

9. "Are we in worse case?" for "are we better?" = προεχόμεθα. Οὐ πάντως = "in no wise." Cf. 1 Cor. ix. 10.

12. Aorists coördinated with presents, and rendered by perfects.
19. "Under" = ἐν(τῷ νόμῳ).
20. "The knowledge of sin" = ἐπίγνωσις :—no article.
21. "The law," "a righteousness ;"—no article with either. "Hath been" for "is (manifested);" but see "it is written."
22. "Even the righteousness'" = δικαιοσύνη δέ. Cf. i. 17.
23. "All have sinned" = πάντες ἥμαρτον : and so at ii. 12. Here coördinate with a present. Cf. v. 12.
25. "To show" = εἰς τὴν ἔνδειξιν, "for the showing" = πρὸς τὴν ἔνδειξιν. Very nice!
26. "The justifier" = δικαιοῦντα.—No art.
27. Aorist = "it is excluded." "A law" for "the law (of faith)." But cf. next verse, "the works of the law" = ἔργων νόμου.
30. "And he" for "who" = ὅς. Why not say, "the God is one, who shall," etc. Cf. Acts xxvii. 23.

IV.

1. "What then shall we say?" for "what shall we say, then?" = τί οὖν ἐροῦμεν; But cf. vi. 1; viii. 31; ix. 14.
6. "Pronounceth blessing upon" for "describeth the blessedness of" = λέγει τὸν μακαρισμὸν τοῦ. But what of articles?
7. "Are forgiven," "are covered,"—aorists.
9. "Is pronounced" for "*cometh*," is inserted without italics.
11. "The sign" = σημεῖον : "the father" = πατέρα, and "righteousness" = τὴν δικαιοσύνην : at verse 12, "circumcision" and "the circumcision," no article with either; at 13, "the world," "the righteousness," no article; at 14, "of the law" = ἐκ νόμου : "faith" = ἡ πίστις, "the promise" = ἡ ἐπαγγελία : and at 16, "of the law" = ἐκ τοῦ νόμου : "of the faith" = ἐκ πίστεως. And why did they forget to say, "of Abraham's faith"?
18. "Who in hope believed against hope" for "who

against hope believed in hope"= ὃς παρ' ἐλπίδα ἐπ' ἐλπίδι ἐπίστευσεν. Which is the more faithful?

20. "Yea looking" is inserted without italics.

V.

1. "Being therefore" for "therefore being."* But the A. V. is good English, good logic, and the true sense.

5. "Which was given" for "which is given"= τοῦ δοθέντος: and so at xii. 3, but cf. verse 1, and Matt. ii. 1, etc.

6. "While we were weak" for "when we were without strength"= ὄντων ἀσθενῶν. (?)

11. Νῦν ἐλάβομεν, *must* be rendered perfect.

12. "Sinned" for "have sinned"= ἥμαρτον. But we have already seen several cases in this very epistle where they have rendered this very word "have sinned." The subject "all" brings it down to the present time, as also at iii. 23. They might, with reason, have changed "passed" to "hath passed;" but, at all events, ἥμαρτον is not related as a pluperfect to διῆλθεν,—the "sinning" and the "passing" went (or have gone) on together. See ii. 12, 13; Acts xxv. 8, etc.

14. "Who is a figure of him that was to come,"—τοῦ μέλλοντος:—not "who was a figure," etc., nor "that is to come." Cf. Matt. xi. 14.

VI.

2. "Died" for "are dead," and order changed. (?) Manifestly a present condition of "death to sin" is referred to.

3. "All we who were baptized" for "so many of us as were" = ὅσοι ἐβαπτίσθημεν. Why not say: "that we, so many as were," etc.?

4. "We were buried therefore" for "therefore we are buried;"—they do not say, "we therefore," cf. v. 1. And, for the tense, see γεγόναμεν in verse 5. It is an ancient Christian idea that, by continual mortifying our corrupt affections, we *are buried* with Christ; thus carrying into effect what is signified in baptism.

6. "Was crucified" for "is crucified" (*i.e.*, "has been");

it reaches to the present result. Cf. Gal. v. 24, where, in the Revision, ἐσταύρωσαν = "have crucified."

7. "He that hath died" for "he that is dead" = ὁ ἀποθανών. But this is only one form of the English *perfect* for another; and so they break down at last in their substitution of the preterite for the perfect in translating ἀπέθανον:—they did not venture to say "he that died." At 1 Thess. v. 10, they render the same participle, referring to Christ, "who died,"—and rightly; but at Heb. xi. 4, they render it, referring to Abel, "being dead," not "having died," and still less "who died." Cf. Matt. ii. 1, where they render ὁ τεχθείς "he that is born;" and Heb. vi. 4–6 "who were enlightened." Cf. also 1 Thess. iv. 14, where "Jesus died" = ἀπέθανε, and "them that are fallen asleep" = τοὺς κοιμηθέντας,—not "that fell asleep." The change to "died" in verse 8 is a palpable incongruity, and, in general, their occasional and arbitrary substitution of *have* for *be* with *die, come, go,* etc., is uncalled for, and strange after "Our Father which."

8. "Died" for "be dead" = ἀπεθάνομεν. This is a present condition, as appears from verse 11, where an unequivocal expression is used in a perfectly parallel case. Cf. vii. 6.

17. "Became obedient to" for "have obeyed" = ὑπηκούσατε. Above they rendered the same verb "obey," and not "become obedient." Why change here? What has become of their painful consequential faithfulness? Cf. "enter in, enter in, enter;" "mad, madness, mad;" "subjection, subjection, subject, subjected, subjected, subject;" Matt. xxiii. 13; Acts xxv. 24, 25; 1 Cor. xv. 27, 28.—The "whereas" here is not in the original. The A. V. and the margin give the proper rendering and the simple meaning of the text, unless it is proposed to paraphrase.

VII.

1. "A man" = τοῦ ἀνθρώπου.

2. "Discharged from" for "loosed from" (opposed to "bound") = κατήργηται. And so they often say, for "delivered," "freed," "loosed," etc. Is the change required by faithfulness? Is it even any improvement? There is

nothing in the original word about a "charge" or a "load" of any kind, whether literally or figuratively.

3. "Joined" for "married" = γένηται. (?)

4. "Were made dead" for "are become dead," and "was raised" for "is raised" (aorists). The old versions, with the Rhemish, all agree with the A. V. here, as in all the parallel cases.

6. "We have been discharged" for "we are delivered" (*i.e.*, "have been"),—aorist. "Having died" for "being dead;"—at Heb. xi. 4, they render the same participle "being dead."—Here they render in both cases the aorist by the perfect, for our deliverance from the law and our death with Christ; and close the verse with referring it to a present state. Why not translate consistently with this elsewhere?

7. "Except" for "but" = εἰ μή. The change is unnecessary here. It is not consistently adhered to elsewhere; for they not only render εἰ μή by "but," but often substitute "but" for some other word in the A. V. The following "except" is in a different construction.

8. "(Sin) finding occasion" for "taking occasion" = ἀφορμὴν λαβοῦσα. Which is most faithful to the Greek? The syntax of διὰ τῆς ἐντολῆς is open to question: whether the commandment was used as an occasion or as a means of the working of sin? From what follows in verse 11, the Revisers would seem more likely to be right.

15. "Know not" for "allow not" (*i.e.*, "approve not"). But what sense is thus made? Is not the true sense: "what I do, I do, not recognizing it to be right, *i.e.*, not approving it"? And will not γινώσκω bear this sense?

17, 20, etc. "Sin which dwelleth" for "sin that dwelleth;" but at verse 2, "the woman that hath" for "which hath." What infinitesimal nicety of faithfulness! And yet "our Father which art"! In the Greek the "sin" is as definite as the "woman," being in the very same form of construction; and is not "Our Father" *the* Father of us?

25. Why not say, "a law of God," "a law of sin," at least in the margin, = νόμῳ Θεοῦ, νόμῳ ἁμαρτίας? Cf. viii. 14, 16, and Matt. xxvii. 54, marg. In fact "the law," "law," "a law" are very much mixed up between the text

and the margin; and the presence or absence of the article in the Greek by no means determines the translation. Not special Greek scholarship, but good English common-sense, with a study of the context, a consideration of the nature of the case, and an apprehension of the Apostle's doctrinal drift, must be appealed to and must be relied upon for that purpose. But neither common-sense, nor the context, nor the nature of the case, nor the Apostle's drift, are any special discoveries " of to-day," or since the translation of 1611.

VIII.

2. " Made" for " hath made;" but see the *νῦν* just before.

9. " The" four times;—no article in Greek.

11. They have not got " also" into the right place after all. It should be "your mortal bodies also,"—if they have any rule for its position.

14, 16. " Are sons of God" for " are the sons of God;" "children" for " the children." These are both predicates and genitive constructions; and, besides, cf. verse 23, " our adoption."

19–23. " Creation" for " creature" = *ἡ κτίσις*. Would it not have been better to have substituted " creature" for "creation" at verse 22, and thus have harmonized the whole? They have broken down with their " creation" at verse 39 and rendered " creature." The word *κτίσις* does not stand here for the act of making, but for what is made; and *πᾶσα ἡ κτίσις*, at verse 22, whether rendered " the whole creation," or " all the creatures," or " every creature," does not mean literally all created things,—" the whole creation" absolutely,—unless the Gospel is to be preached, and has been preached, to all created things, including beasts, birds, fishes (St. Anthony?), trees, stones, winds and waves, sun and moon, stars and comets. See Mark xvi. 15; Col. i. 23. " The whole creation" or " every creature" is, simply, " all mankind" or " every man,"—and that too in a general, not in an absolute sense.

28. The English is stiffened by a Greek construction,—making an awkward " *even*" necessary. Cf. 2 Peter iii. 1.

29. "The first-born" = πρωτότοκον. No article. But see verses 14 and 16;—all predicates.

31. "What then shall we say?" for "what shall we then say?" τί οὖν ἐροῦμεν; And so at iv. 1. For this same formula, at vi. 1 and ix. 14, they content themselves with following the A. V. and saying: "What shall we say then?" What hair are they splitting? Who can fathom the depths of this kind of faithfulness? If they had simply conformed the rendering of the A. V. here to that at vi. 1, and elsewhere, they might have had some pretext for the change,—but, even then, how very, very slight!

36. "We were accounted" for "we are accounted," aorist; meaning "we have been," for it is co-ordinate with a present. Cf. iii. 12.

38, 39. The transposition of "powers" following a change of text is unfortunate for the English; and the rhythm of a magnificent passage is brought to utter confusion. And what is gained thereby? Cf. 2 Peter iii. 1.

IX.

8. "Children" for "the children," "a seed" for "the seed," predicates. This may be "a sense," but is it "the sense"? At verse 7, "thy seed" has no article, though in the nominative case. Why did they not there say, "a seed to thee"?

9. "A word of promise" for "the word." Does the apostle mean that the form of expression which he quotes is of the nature of a promise? That surely is jejune enough. Does he not rather plainly mean that "this is the very promise" which was made to Abraham? Where the Greek predicate noun is in the singular number without the article the English is, *à priori*, more likely to require "the" than "a," if it must have some article;—unless "the" would refer to some specific object definitely expressed or implied in the immediate context.

19. "Still" for "yet,"—to what purpose? Cf. 1 Cor. xv. 17.

22. "Willing to show" = θέλων ἐνδείξασθαι,—not "desiring" or "wishing." Cf. Acts xxiv. 27; xxv. 9.

27. "If" for "though" = ἐάν. But what is here expressed is not a condition but a concession.

X.

3. "Did not subject" for "have not submitted." In verse 2 we read "they have a zeal for God;" the case is, therefore, a present one. Otherwise, on what occasion was it that "they did not subject themselves," etc.?

11. "Shall not be put to shame" for "shall not be ashamed" = καταισχυνθήσεται. If the verb be treated as passive, they are right; if as middle, the A. V. is right. But what of it?

12. "The same *Lord* is Lord of all, and is rich," for "the same Lord over all is rich" = ὁ αὐτὸς Κύριος πάντων, πλουτῶν, etc. There is no "and" in the original; cf. i. 3, 4.

14. "Have not believed" and "have not heard," for Greek aorists.

19. "Did Israel not know?" for "did not Israel know?" = μὴ Ἰσραὴλ οὐκ ἔγνω; Now we shall all understand the Word of God.

XI.

1, 2. "Did God cast off his people?" for " hath God cast away his people?" When do they suppose the historical fact to have taken place? If the A. V. had said "cast off," we might have expected the Revisers to substitute "cast away."

3. Aorists rendered by perfects. Compare the foregoing verses, and the 7th, 8th and 11th.

7. "Obtained" for "hath obtained" (bis).

8. "Gave" for "hath given,"—"unto this day"!

11. "Did they stumble?" for "have they stumbled?"— and then, "salvation is come"!

31. "Mercy shown to you" for "your mercy" = τῷ ὑμετέρῳ. Which is translation? If the A. V. is obscure or ambiguous, it is no more so than the original.

32 and 34. Aorists as perfects—again. Cf. verses 1, 2, 7, 8, 11.

33. "The wisdom and the knowledge of God,"—no Greek article.

XII.

3. "That was given" for "given" or "that is given"= τῆς δοθείσης:—and so at verse 6; v. 5, and xv. 15;—but cf. Matt. ii. 2, etc. "So to think as to think soberly" for "to think soberly"= φρονεῖν εἰς τὸ σωφρονεῖν ="to think unto sober thinking," or "to think unto soberness of mind," or "to think unto soberness," or "to think soberly," or "so to think as to be soberminded." "Hath dealt," aorist. "A measure of faith" for "the measure of faith." Cf. Rev. xxi. 17. But surely it is, "according to the measure (not a measure) of faith which God hath dealt to every man." Is "each man" any better English?

10. "In love of the brethren" for "with brotherly love" = τῇ φιλαδελφίᾳ. What authority have they for putting the article with "brethren" and not with "love;" or for using "in" instead of "with" for the mere dative case? And which is, after all, the consistent sense? We might say: "with the brotherly love (*i.e.* which characterizes Christians) be kindly affectioned," etc.; or, more briefly, as the A. V. Compare "the weeping and gnashing."

19. "Vengeance belongeth unto me" for "vengeance is mine" = ἐμοὶ ἐκδίκησις. Cf. Matt. v. 3; xix. 14, etc.

XIII.

1. "Power" = ἐξουσία,—elsewhere usually changed to "authority" or "right." But here "authority" would be more in place than in many of the other cases.

8. "Save" for "but" = εἰ μή: so also at 1 Cor. i. 14. But what necessity for the change? Elsewhere they substitute "but" for "save," see Luke iv. 26, 27.

10. "His neighbour" = τῷ πλησίον = "the neighbour" or "one's neighbour." "His" was right with the A. V., but is not right in the language "of to-day." It is quite as likely to be misunderstood as the "I will have mercy" at Matt. ix. 13.

XIV.

14. "Save that" for "but" = εἰ μή. Cf. Gal. ii. 16, where they make the same change under ἐὰν μή. "But only" would be better in both cases, as at Luke iv. 26, 27, where the Revisers substitute it for "save." The εἰ μή makes an *exception* to a more general clause understood; thus: "nor is anything at all unclean but (or except, or save) to him that reckoneth," etc. But if the exception is directly applied to the clause expressed it becomes nonsense. Unless the ellipsis is supplied, "but" (or "but only") is altogether better than "save that;" and, if the ellipsis were supplied, it would do quite as well as the other.

20. "Overthrow" for "destroy" = κατάλυε. (?)

XV.

9. "Give praise" for "confess" = ἐξομολογήσομαι. In verse 11, "praise" = αἰνεῖτε. Might not the unlearned reader be led to think that the original words were the same?

11. "Let all the peoples praise" for "laud him, all ye people" = ἐπαινεσάτωσαν.

12. "The Gentiles" (bis),—no article in Greek.

15. "I write" for "I have written,"—an aorist.

18. "Wrought" for "hath wrought." (?) The two versions of this verse complement each other; but the A. V. is nearest the Greek.

21. The A. V. is more literal, and equally intelligible.

22. "These many times" for "much" = τὰ πολλά (cf. John iii. 23). There is no "these" in the text. Why not say "often," and have done with it?

30. "By" for "for the sake of" (not "through") = διά with genitive.

XVI.

2. "Hath been"—an aorist. Καὶ γάρ = "for ... also;" cf. Matt. xxv. 73; 1 Cor. viii. 5, etc., where, no "also."

18. "Smooth and fair speech" for "good words and fair speeches" = χρηστολογίας καὶ εὐλογίας. If the A. V.

had given *their* translation can there be any doubt that the faithfulness of the Revisers would have substituted that of the A. V. ? or else, " smooth speech and fair speech"? Just look at the Greek ; and remember their " go in and go out" for "go in and out," etc., etc.

22. " Who write" for "who wrote" = ὁ γράψας : — it should be "who have written."

I. CORINTHIANS.

I.

2. If the Revisers had a right to insert " Lord" in order to make the sense clear, the A. V. had a right to change the order of the words for the same purpose, and so dispense with the insertion.

4, 5, 6. *All* the aorists had better be rendered perfects (as the A. V. in 4 and 5),—as appears by the present tense in verse 7.

9. " Through" for " by" = διά, referring to God. Is that a better translation in such a case?

11. "Hath been signified" for "hath been declared" = ἐδηλώθη. There is no "sign" in the word,—it is not σημαίνω, it is from δῆλον, and means "made clear," "manifested." Cf. Rev. i. 1.

12. "Mean" for "say" = λέγω. It is not their business to gloss, but to translate.

18. "Are perishing" for " perish" = ἀπολλυμένοις. But all to whom the Gospel is brought "are perishing." " Are being saved" for "are saved" = σωζομένοις. But this is questionable English, and a harshness quite unnecessary. So at Acts ii. 47 ; 2 Cor. ii. 15 ; but cf. Luke xiii. 23.

19. " Reject" for "bring to nothing" = ἀθετήσω. But they have rendered this word "to make void" at Gal. ii. 21 and iii. 15 ; and "to set at nought" at Heb. x. 28 and Jude 8.

26. " Behold" for "see" = βλέπετε. They render βλέπω "see," ten to one ; and at Acts iv. 14 they correct the A. V. and substitute "see" for "behold." What a subtlety of faithfulness!

27. "Choose" (three times) for "hath chosen." (?)
30. "Was made" for "is made." (? ?)

II.

6. "A wisdom" for "the wisdom (of this world);" yet at verse 5 they say "the wisdom of men," equally without the article in the Greek; and at verse 7 they say "God's wisdom," which must be "the wisdom of God," though the Greek has no article.

8. "Knoweth" for "knew" = ἔγνωκεν = "hath known." This perfect is often used for the present, but not always; and here the perfect seems more suitable to the context, since it is immediately added: "for had they known," etc. —not "if they knew," etc.

9. "Things which eye saw not," etc.—a strange version indeed, which eye hath not before seen nor ear heard; and all not so much from a change of text as from a change of tense in the translation.

10. "Revealed" for "hath revealed." (?)

11. "Save" for "but" = εἰ μή : but see again Luke iv. 26, 27, and Rev. ix. 4; xix. 12; xxi. 27, etc. "Things of a man," "spirit of the man,"—τοῦ ἀνθρώπου alike in both cases.

12. "Received" for "have received." But immediately afterwards, "are given" = χαρισθέντα. This is right with "have received," but with "received" one would have expected "were given," as at iii. 10, and at Rom. v. 5; xii. 3, 6; xv. 15, etc. But the Revisers' faithfulness seems to have been at fault just when it might have led them to be consistent, at least, if not right.

14, 15. "The natural man" = ψυχικὸς ἄνθρωπος,—no article; and then "he that is spiritual" (i.e., "the spiritual man") = ὁ πνευματικός. Why did they not say "a natural man"? As the article is omitted with ψυχικός and inserted with πνευματικός, the distinction in translation would seem to have been forced upon their articular faithfulness; and yet one can hardly suspect them of slavishly following the A. V. This phenomenon must therefore remain a mystery; but "aliquando bonus dormitat Homerus." In verse 15, "and" for "yet." The A. V. is right, for the apodosis.

III.

10. "Was given" for "is given" = $\delta o\vartheta\varepsilon\tilde{\iota}\sigma\alpha\nu$. Here they have changed "have laid" to "laid" (needlessly, even though the Greek text is changed from perfect to aorist), and so they are consistent; cf. ii. 12. "A" for "the (foundation);" but English idiom requires "the" for the true sense.

13. "Each" for "every" = $\H{\varepsilon}\kappa\alpha\sigma\tau o\varsigma$: and so usually, but not always. At verses 5 and 8 the change is well, as but two only are compared. Here the case is different.

16. "A" for "the (temple of God)." Temple is a predicate and with a genitive; and see the next verse. The A. V. is plainly right, and the Revisers are inconsistent with themselves.

IV.

8. Here is a perfect (or a present with a perfect participle) coördinated with aorists, which latter are (rightly) rendered as perfects or presents,—one of them being conjoined with $\H{\eta}\delta\eta$. So also at verses 9 and 13.

15, 17. Aorist rendered first as preterite then as perfect,— "I begat" and then "I have sent." "Should have" for "have." Cf. Luke xvi. 31.

V.

1. "Actually" for "commonly" = $\H{o}\lambda\omega\varsigma$. (.,

2. Aorist, coördinated with perfect or present, is rendered preterite; but cf. iv. 8. Better render in the perfect (with the A. V.); and render $\dot{o}$ $\pi o\iota\eta\sigma\alpha\varsigma$, afterwards, by "who did," and neither (with the Revisers) "had done" nor (with the A. V.) "hath done."

7. "Hath been sacrificed" for "is sacrificed" = $\dot{\varepsilon}\tau\upsilon\vartheta\eta$. Why did they not say, as they are apt to do in similar connections, "was sacrificed"?

9. "I wrote unto you" (so also the A. V.) = $\H{\varepsilon}\gamma\rho\alpha\psi\alpha$.

Why not "I write" or "I have written (in my epistle)"?
Cf. verse 11, "I write" = ἔγραψα.

VI.

2. "The smallest" = ἐλαχίστων: no article. See also Luke xii. 26, "that which is least" = ἐλάχιστον: but cf. Luke xvi. 10, where they put " a very little" for "the least," so as to be faithful in it ; and, while in the two other cases they had a simple genitive and an accusative to translate, in this last they have the preposition ἐν.

5. "Cannot be found" for "is not among" = οὐκ ἔνι ἐν. Which is the more exact?

11. Aorists rendered preterite (A. V. present or perfect). Is not the perfect better: "Ye have been washed, ye have been sanctified," etc.? The state, the effects, continue; and the apostle is not conceiving them as historical facts in some distant past.

12. "Not all things are" for "all things are not" = οὐ πάντα. Right, but it seems to have been by chance; for at x. 23 they render precisely the same formula "all things are not ;" see also 2 Thess. iii. 2 ; 1 Cor. xv. 51, etc. At 1 John ii. 19, with the margin, they seem to hold to both constructions.

16. "A harlot" = τῇ πόρνῃ. Cf. Matt. ii. 23.

19. "A temple" for "the temple." Cf. Gal. ii. 8, where "the apostleship of the circumcision" = ἀποστολὴν τῆς περιτομῆς. Here, Canon Westcott thinks, "the temple" spoils the logic, but he does not make it logically clear. ("Gospel of the Resurrection," chap. iii. 20).

20. "Were brought" for "are brought." (?) And so at vii. 23.

VII.

11. "But and if" = ἐὰν δὲ καί, also at verse 28 ; and so, for εἰ δὲ καί, 2 Cor. iv. 3 ; 1 Pet. iii. 14. Did the Revisers suppose that, in retaining the old translation in such cases, they were rendering every one of the Greek particles? It is not unlikely that, in the old English, "but and if" was

a corruption of the pleonastic "but an if." Shakespeare often uses "an if" or "and if" for simple "if."

28. "And I would spare you" for "but I spare you" = ἐγω δὲ ὑμῶν φείδομαι. Which is faithful?

32. "I would have you" = θέλω ὑμᾶς. And so the A. V.;—very good.

34. "In body" and "in spirit" = τῷ σώματι and τῷ πνεύματι. But see "the weeping and gnashing."

40. "I think that I also have the Spirit of God" for "I think also that I have" = δοκῶ δὲ κἀγὼ ἔχειν. The "I also" is the immediate subject of "think," and not of "have."

VIII.

5. "No God but one." Elsewhere they have often substituted "save" for "but" = εἰ μή: as at Mark x. 8. "No idol is (anything)" for "an idol is nothing;"—Greek purism. What is the difference? If "anything" must be inserted after "no," how much does it differ from "nothing" after all? Did faithfulness to God's word require this exhibition of a knowledge of the niceties of Greek construction?

7. "That knowledge" = ἡ γνῶσις. "Of a thing sacrificed to" for "as a thing offered unto." Why translate the accusative as a genitive. Did faithfulness either to God's word or to the Greek construction require it?

10. "To eat things sacrificed to idols" for "to eat those things which are offered to idols" = τὰ εἰδωλόθυτα. But what of the Greek article, and faithfulness besides? Suppose the A. V. had had the Revisers' rendering, with what articular faithfulness they would have changed it! "Sacrificed" for "offered," throughout here, is consequential, but is it necessary?

11. "Through" = ἐν.

IX.

10. "Altogether" = πάντως. This word here should have been translated "by all means," as at verse 22. The apostle does not mean to say that, in that precept of the

law, God had no regard at all to the protection of oxen; but that, in it, there is *by all means* contained a principle of far higher and wider application.

12. "Did not use" for "have not used;"—here in immediate correlation with present tenses.

15. "Write" for "have written,"—an aorist. (?) "May be so done" for "should (or might) be so done"= γένηται. "Than that any man should make void"= ἢ οὐδεὶς κενώσει. This is their text, negative, future, and all.

X.

1. "I would not have you" for "I would not that ye should be"= θέλω ὑμᾶς: and so at xiv. 5. But see Luke xix. 14, and 1 Tim. ii. 4, *corrected contrariwise!* "Were all" for "all were"= πάντες ἦσαν.

2. "Baptized unto,"—εἰs: "into," in margin. Why? Not so elsewhere. See Matt. xxviii. 19.

13. "Such as man can bear" for "such as is common to man"= ἀνθρώπινος = "human," "which is incident to the condition of humanity," "which pertains to the common lot of man." Anything more is not derived from the word itself, but is imported into it.

15. "A communion" for "the communion,"—in the predicate. (?)

18. "Have communion" for "are partakers"= κοινωνοὶ εἰσί.

23. "All are not"= οὐ πάντα. But see the logically correct rendering of the same phrase at vi. 12; and cf. Wiclif.

XI.

1. "Imitators" for "followers." A question of simple English idiom and usage.

11, 12. "The woman and the man;" twice without the article, and twice with the article (in Greek). Consequential?

13. "Judge ye" for "judge"= κρίνατε.

14. The Revisers have done well to retain here (with the A. V.) the word "nature" for φύσις. According to the usage of Aristotle, the teaching of "nature" (φύσις) might

mean, in the Greek of any period, "the best sentiment," the teaching of "the highest civilization," of that period. Arist. Polit. (Sir Alexander Grant).

20. "The Lord's Supper;"—no article in the Greek, but cf. x. 4, "a spiritual rock," and with this Heb. xii. 22.

21. Here the Oxford edition of the Revisers' Greek text has ἐκ for ἐν; translated "in" (your eating).

29. "If he discern not"= μὴ διακρίνων: but cf. Heb. vi. 6.

XII.

13. "Were baptized" for "are (have been) baptized;" "were made" for "have been made;" (?) "of one spirit" = ἓν πνεῦμα,—no "of."

15, 16. "The hand"= χείρ:—why not "a hand"?

18. "Hath set"= ἔθετο: and then "pleased" for "hath pleased"= ἠθέλησεν. (?)

24. "Tempered" for "hath tempered." (?)

XIII.

5. "Evil" = τὸ κακόν: "taketh account of" = λογίζεται,—not "reckoneth."

11. "Now that"= ὅτε ("When I am become"). "Felt" = ἐφρόνουν. (?)

12. "In a mirror"= δι' ἐσόπτρου = "through (or by means of) a mirror;" cf. "through the prophets."

XIV.

1. "Yet" for "and"= δέ. Why?

8. "War" for "battle"= πόλεμον. The trumpet was usually sounded for battle and not for war; and will not πόλεμος bear that sense? In Homer and Hesiod the signification "battle" prevails; in the later, and in the Attic Greek especially, that of "war;" but not so that it ever became obsolete in the former sense.

11. "If then" for "therefore if," in the protasis. What is the logic of the difference?

19. "Howbeit" for "yet"= ἀλλά. At our wits' end, we

humbly ask, can it be that "faithfulness" required this change?

21. "By" for "with"= ἐν. (?) And why did they not say "in," by way of consequence?

35. "Would learn" for "will learn"= θέλουσιν.

36. "What?"= ἥ. But cf. x. 22; vi. 9, 16, 19; Rom. ix. 21; vi. 3, etc.

37. "The commandment" = ἐντολή.

XV.

6. "Of whom the greater part"= οἱ πλείους: but cf. x. 5, where they render "most of them." "Are fallen asleep,"—an aorist.

15, 16, etc. "Are raised" for "rise"= ἐγείρονται. The old story come again; but see Matt. xxviii. 6, 7, etc., etc.

17. "Yet"= ἔτι: why not change it to "still," as so often elsewhere? Cf. Rom. ix. 19.

20–26. "The dead," "first-fruits," "the first-fruits," "the resurrection of the dead," "the last enemy,"—all alike anarthrous in the Greek. Why not say "all the enemies," like "all the nations"= πάντας τοὺς ἐχθρούς. They say "all his enemies," but *quaere?*

27. "Put" for "hath put;" but a coördinated perfect form immediately follows, and immediately after that a subjunctive aorist which they themselves render as a perfect (future);—ὑπέταξεν, ὑποτέτακται, ὑποταγῇ. For the repetitions in the English here, cf. Matt. xxii. 3, etc.

31. Why not arrange the clauses after the order of the Greek, instead of inverting, and begin with "I die daily" etc.? Is not the order of the Greek a sacred trust to faithfulness? Cf. Mark v. 15, etc.

33. "Evil company" for "evil communications" = ὁμιλίαι κακαί. Well enough, but what faithfulness required a change from the more to the less literal?

36. "Thou foolish one" for "thou fool" = ἄφρων. "Thou fool" may be too strong, but "thou foolish one" is quite too weak; and, besides, is a phrase which no English writer would employ under such circumstances.

38. "Pleased" for "hath pleased," (?). "Of his own" for

"his own" = ἴδιον. The apostle does not mean simply "a body that shall henceforth belong to it," but "its appropriate body," whereby it is distinguished from all other bodies, or kinds of bodies. And for the matter of the article, see Rom. ix. 7, 2 Cor. vi. 16 (cf. Eph. ii. 10); Col. iv. 15; 1 Thess. ii. 11 (cf. ii. 7); etc.

44. "There is also a spiritual *body*" = ἔστι καὶ πνευματικόν. Is this the faithful place for the "also"?

51. "Not all." But in the Greek the "not" stands after the "all" and is joined with the verb; a construction which, by universal Greek usage (we believe), makes a universal negative. The "we," as appears in the next verse, refers to those who shall be alive and remain at the coming of the Lord. Of such the apostle here declares that none will need to die, but all will be changed.

54. "Is swallowed up" = κατεπόθη,—εἰς νῖκος, *i.e.*, not "victoriously," as in the margin (that would reduce the magnificent figure to mere common-place); but "by victory," or "in victory," or "into victory";—"victory shall swallow up (or swallow down) death;" *i.e.*, "death shall be utterly vanquished."

XVI.

7. "I do not wish" for "I will not;" rather "I do not choose". or "it is not my purpose" = οὐ θέλω.

8. "I will tarry" = ἐπιμενῶ = "I shall tarry."

10. "The brother" for "our brother;" cf. 2 Cor. i. 1.

I. CORINTHIANS.

I.

1. "The whole of" for "all" = ὅλη τῇ. Cf. Matt. iv. 23, 24; and see note Matt. xxii. 40.

4. "Them that" for "them which"; and so at xiii. 2; Rom. viii. 1, xi. 22, xii. 14; but "them which" *for* "them that," Gal. iv. 5. And see "they which," 1 Cor. ix. 13, 14; Rom. ix. 6; Gal. iii. 7, 9, v. 12, 21 (at 24, "they that"), etc., etc.; "they that," 1 Cor. xv. 23, 48; Rom. xvi. 18; Matt. v. 4, etc., etc.; "they who," Rom. xv. 21; "him who,"

Rom. xiv. 14; "her which," and "he that," Gal. iv. 27, 29.; "he which," 2 Cor. iv. 14; "he that" *for* "he which," Gal. i. 23; "them who" *for* "them which," Gal. ii. 2; "them that" *for* "them who," Gal. vi. 10 and Rom. ii. 7; "we which," 2 Cor. iv. 11 and Heb. iv. 3; "us which," 1 Cor. i. 18; "we that," 2 Cor. v. 4; "ye which," Gal. vi. 1; but "you that" *for* "you who," 2 Thess. i. 7; "the things that" *for* "the things which," 1 Cor. i. 27, 28 and 2 Cor. xi. 30; "the things which" *for* "the things that," 1 Cor. xiv. 37, and cf. 2 Cor. iv. 18; "the Spirit which," 1 Cor. ii. 12; "the grace which," iii. 10; "thee which," viii. 10; but "thou that" *for* "thou which," Rom. ii. 21, and "thou who" *for* "thou that" at verse 23.—And so on and on *in infinitum;*—a perfect medley of inconsistencies; at least to our poor, untutored apprehension. In making their corrections the learned Revisers may nave assumed some arbitrary principle of distinction in their use of *who, which* and *that*, but certainly none to which they have themselves adhered throughout; nor, if they had, could any changes in the English have been required at all by differences in the Greek mode of expression which made no difference in the sense. Above, such differences are scarcely found.

12. "We behaved ourselves" for "we have had our conversation" = ἀνεστράφημεν. Cf. Eph. ii. 3, where they render "we lived."

17. "Shew" for "use" = ἐχρησάμην.

23. "Forbare to come" for "came not as yet" = οὐκέτι ἦλθον. Specimens of faithfulness.

II.

13. "I had" = ἔσχηκα,—not "I have had." So at vii. 5; and, at Gal. iii. 17, "which came" = ὁ γεγονώς: Heb. xi. 28, "he kept" = πεποίηκε. But here, at i. 9, they had just carefully substituted "have had" for "had" = ἐσχήκαμεν: and then immediately, "we have set our hope" for "we trust" = ἠλπίκαμεν. But "we have set our hope" is not equivalent to "we have hoped," but rather to "we hope" or "we trust;" so that their elaborate change of

rendering is, after all, only a *semblance* (to use no harsher word) of conformity to the tense of the original.

15. "In them that are being saved" = ἐν τοῖς σωζομένοις. Cf. Luke xiii. 23, etc.

III.

3. "Ministered" = διακονηθεῖσα, "written" = ἐγγεγραμμένη. Here aorist and perfect are co-ordinated and rendered alike.

6. "A new covenant," "the letter," "the spirit." No article in either case.

7. "Look steadfastly upon" for "steadfastly behold" = ἀτενίσαι. Cf. Acts vi. 15, where "looking steadfastly on" is *changed* to "fastening their eyes on." Truly these Revisers are hard to please.

7–11. "With glory" = ἐν δόξῃ and διὰ δόξης: "In glory" = δόξῃ and ἐν δόξῃ.

10. "Surpasseth" for "excelleth." How vastly important!

12. "Such a hope" for "such hope."

11, 13. They render τὸ καταργούμενον "that which passeth away," and then, "that which was passing away" —both alike connected with past tenses.

18. "From the Lord the Spirit" for "by the Spirit of the Lord" = ἀπὸ Κυρίου Πνεύματος. (?) This is the marginal reading of the A. V.

IV.

1. "Therefore seeing we have this ministry." Cf. iii. 12, "having therefore such a hope," and Rom. v. 1, "being therefore justified," etc., etc. It seems therefore that the English is admitted to allow either construction of "therefore;" and it is merely a servile following of the Greek order, if, when we use the same word in English, we put it first when it translates διὰ τοῦτο, and second when it stands for οὖν. The English style is not improved; the English sense is not affected. In an independent translation, this would be servility; and yet, if the translator chose to wear the yoke, we might find no fault with his work. But is it

not more than servility when such meaningless changes are foisted into the revision of a received translation by men who profess to act under the rule of " making as few alterations as possible, consistently with faithfulness" ? "Obtained" for "have received ;"—it is subordinate to a present tense, and is immediately followed by "have renounced" = ἀπειπάμεθα.

4. "Hath blinded" = an aorist; but at verse 6, again, "shined" for "hath shined" = another aorist.

13. "Therefore" = διό (bis). But cf. Rom. ii. 1; iv. 22, etc., etc, where they have carefully changed "therefore" to "wherefore," the sense remaining unchanged in all the cases. Their faithfulness seems to have failed them here.

V.

1. "The earthly house of our tabernacle" for "our earthly house of *this* tabernacle" = ἡ ἐπίγειος ἡμῶν οἰκία τοῦ σκήνους. The "our" belongs (with A. V.) to "house," and not to "tabernacle ;" and had they any business to change its place in order to get rid of the "*this*" inserted in the A. V.? They themselves put "this" oftentimes for the mere article, as immediately below, at verse 4, with this very "tabernacle ;" also at viii. 4, with "grace," where the A. V. has the simple article like the Greek. And when they thus use "this" they do not modestly put it in italics as does the A. V.

5. "Wrought" and "gave" for "have," etc. (?)
7. "By" (twice) = διά.
10. "In" = διά. "Hath done,"—an aorist.
11. "Are made manifest," perfect tense.
12. "To answer" is italicized in the A. V., but not here; although it is not in the text.
13. Aorist and present coördinated, and both translated as present. Cf. John xvii.
14. "All died" for "all were dead" = ἀπέθανον. Should it not be with Tyndal, "all are dead"? The life of those "which live" (in verse 15) is a present life and not a past event, and yet it is as intimately connected with Christ's re-

surrection as our death is with his death. Our death to sin is just as much a present, continuous fact, as our life to righteousness. The former is no more ideally, constructively, or proleptically identified with Christ's death as a historical fact, than the latter is with Christ's resurrection as such a fact. Christ died, we are dead; Christ rose, we live; —cf. *next verse.*

17. "Are passed away" = $παρῆλθεν$, and "are become new" = $γέγονε$: aorist and perfect coördinated and both rendered perfect. The first, the "are passed away," corresponds exactly to the "are dead" ($ἀπέθανον$); and the "are become new" to the new life ($οἱ ζῶντες$).

As regards doctrinal considerations, whether of predestination or of baptismal regeneration, in determining the translation of this and kindred passages (as Rom. vi. 3–11; Col. ii. 11–15, and iii. 3), every man will exercise his own judgment or may be swayed by his own bias; but if, in that connection, *authority* is appealed to,—authority we now mean, not of Greek scholarship, but as to the bearing of dogmatical questions, upon the translation of these passages,—surely the consenting authority of all the old translators, of Luther and De Sacy, of Wiclif and Tyndal, of the Genevan, the Bishops', and, notably, the Rhemish versions, as well as of the the forty-seven translators of 1611, may be boldly held as high as that of the learned authors of the late Revision. The laws of the Greek aorist decide nothing in favor of the Revisers—themselves being witnesses upon the spot—see $παρῆλθεν$; the most diversified shades of theological thought consent in deciding against them. Let this be said once for all.

20. "We are ambassadors, therefore" for "now then we are ambassadors (for Christ)" = ($ὑπὲρ Χριστοῦ$) $οὖν πρεσβεύομεν$. So it seems that when the A. V. puts "then" (= therefore) as a translation for $οὖν$, next the first word of the sentence *à la grecque*, the Revisers can put their "therefore" further on, and where the Greek does not put it; though they have generally been so fastidious in correcting the A. V. elsewhere by putting the "therefore" (for $οὖν$) next after the first word or two, as in the Greek. Why

did they not say,—if they *must* alter the A. V.,—"We are, therefore," etc.? Or, more faithful still, "For Christ, therefore, are we ambassadors"? Cf. Phil. iii. 15, *ad fin.*

VI.

2. "A day of salvation" for "the day," etc. But why change? One thing is clear; the absence of the Greek article does not require the change. Cf. Matt. ii. 1; x. 15; xi. 22, 24; xii. 36: Rom. ii. 5; Eph. iv. 30; Phil. i. 6; 1 Thess. v. 2; Heb. viii. 8, 9; 1 Pet. ii. 12; 2 Pet. ii. 9; iii. 7, etc., etc., where they say "the day" for no Greek article; and see immediately below, where they say "the day of salvation," and no article. In Isaiah, the A. V. has "a day," but surely that cannot control the translation here.

16. "A temple of God" for "the temple," etc. (twice). But, in the first place, the complex expression $ναὸς\ Θεοῦ$, both words being without an article, may mean "the temple of God;" and in the second instance the words are in the predicate; moreover, if the Revisers would be consistent, they should have said "a temple of a living God." Cf. 1 Thess. i. 9.—"My people" $= μου\ λαός$ (no art.). Why did they not say "a people of mine"? Cf. 1 Cor. xv. 38; Rev. iii. 2.

VII.

5. "Had," for a perfect. See Gal. iii. 17, note.
6. "He that comforteth . . . . even God" for "God that comforteth."
7. "By" $= ἐν$ (thrice). Why so?
8. "With" $= ἐν$, and why?
10. "Which bringeth no regret" $= ἀμεταμέλητον =$ "which is not to be regretted," or "repented of."
11. "Concerning you" $= ἐν\ ὑμῖν$. The Revisers seem to claim for themselves no small liberty in translating the Greek prepositions. They are therefore bound to respect an equal liberty in others, even in the A. V.

VIII.

4. "In regard of this grace" $= την\ χάριν$. Would not "for" be better—"beseeching us for the grace and the par-

ticipation in," etc. ? There is nothing in the Greek for their "this" but τήν: cf. v. 1.

5. "Had hoped" for "hoped" = ἠλπίσαμεν. But see Acts vii. 44, where they change "had appointed" to "appointed;" also Matt. xvi. 5; Mark viii. 14, where they change in like manner. Cf. Matt. xxviii. 16; Luke xxii. 13; xxiv. 24,—where the pluperfect is retained, as also in the next verse.

6. "Had made a beginning before" for "had begun" = προενήρξατο:—"in you" = εἰς ἡμᾶς:—"complete" for "finish" = ἐπιτελέσῃ, but the simple "finish" corresponds to "beginning" as "complete" would correspond to "commencement."

10. "Were the first to make a beginning" for "have begun before" = προενήρξασθε. But see their version at verse 6.

12. "A man hath" = ἔχῃ. Thus τις is understood; but see Heb. x. 38.

13. "By equality" = ἐξ ἰσότητος. Is it not "from regard to equality"?

16. "Which putteth" for "which put." Does not the connection here favor the past? Cf. Rev. viii. 9; xix. 19, 21; John xiii. 11.

17. "Our" for "the" = τήν. "Very earnest" = σπουδαιότερος: but cf. Acts xvii. 22.

18. "Have sent,"—an aorist.

20. "That any man" for "that no man" = μή τις = "lest any man." Cf. Acts x. 47.

22. "The great confidence which" = πεποιθήσει πολλῇ τῇ. Cf. their wrestling with a similar construction at Gal. ii. 20.

23. "The messengers of the churches" and "the glory of Christ." No art. in Gr. Cf. 1 Cor. vi. 19; 2 Cor. vi. 16; Mark iii. 17, etc., etc.

IX.

2. "Readiness" for "forwardness of mind" = προθυμία. "Prepared" for "ready" = παρεσκεύασται (so also at verse 3). "Hath stirred up" for "hath provoked" = ἠρέ-

θισε,—an aorist coördinated with a perfect; cf. John xvii.

3. "Have sent,"—an aorist.

5. "I thought it necessary therefore" for "therefore I thought it necessary." But wherefore did the Revisers think the change necessary? " Intreat" for " exhort" = παρακαλέσαι; but for the very same word in the very same sense, at viii. 6, "exhorted" is substituted for "desired." See Phil. iv. 2, note.

9. Aorists = perfects, in poetry.

X.

1. "Intreat" for "beseech;" the difference? See again Phil. iv. 2, note.

4. " Before God" for "through God" = τῷ Θεῷ. (?) The margin of the A. V. suggests "to God."

7. "Consider" = λογίζεσθω,—not "count" nor "reckon." Cf. verse 11, where they have " reckon" for "think."

8. "Abundantly" for "more" = περισσότερον. What then would περισσῶς mean? Cf. 1 Cor. xii. 23, 24; xv. 10; 2 Cor. i. 12; ii. 4, etc. For the tenses here and at xii. 6, cf. Luke xvi. 30, 31 (A. V.)

10. "They say" = φησί ("saith he," the false teacher)? "Strong" for "powerful" = ἰσχυραί: so, at 1 Cor. i. 27 and Rev. x. 1, xviii. 10, 21, they substitute " strong" for "mighty;" at xviii. 2, "mighty" for "strong," and they retain "mighty" at Matt. iii. 11; Mark i. 7; Luke iii. 16; xv. 14; Rev. xix. 6, 18, etc. The nicety of their discriminating faithfulness is worthy of all admiration.

12. "Are without understanding" for "are not wise" = οὐ συνιοῦσιν. (?) That changes the negative construction and thus modifies the sense.

13. "Province" for "rule" = κανόνος. Marg., "Gr. measuring rod."

16. "Parts" for "regions" = ὑπερεκείνα. (?)

XI.

5. Marg., "Those preëminent apostles" = τῶν ὑπερλίαν ἀποστόλων. Whence is the "those" derived?

13. "Fashioning" for "transforming" = μετασχημα-

τιζόμενοι. So at 14 and 15. But what has become of the μετά?

21. "We had been weak" = ἠσθενήκαμεν.

23. "One beside himself" for "a fool" = παραφρονῶν. Elsewhere they have used this same phrase for ἐκστάς (Mark iii. 21); but they have declined to use it (with the A. V.) for μαινόμενος at Acts xxvi. 24.

26. "The Gentiles," ἐξ ἐθνῶν. (No art.) So "the wilderness," "the sea," "the city;" while "rivers," "robbers," "false brethren" are rendered without the article in English.

XII.

2. "Know" for "knew" = οἶδα: but consider the "fourteen years ago." "In the body" = ἐν σώματι: "out of the body" = ἐκτὸς τοῦ σώματος: "the third heaven," no article.

4. "Into Paradise = εἰς τὸν Π. Are not the Revisers still too much under the influence of the Latin idiom? Might not faithfulness revolutionize the English language a little further,—after "the weeping and gnashing,"—and say "into the Paradise"?

5. "Save" for "but" = εἰ μή. Why not "but only," as at Luke iv. 26, 27? "On mine own behalf I will not glory" is absolute. The exception is made to a more general proposition implied, as, "Neither will I glory at all except," etc. The apostle does not mean to say that the only case in which he will glory in his own behalf is when he glories in the cross of Christ; yet this is just what the Revisers make him say. On the other hand the A. V. gives the true sense, as the Revisers have done in St. Luke.

6. "If I should desire I shall not be;"—is that good English? See also x. 8, and cf. Luke xvi. 30, 31.

9. "Power" for "strength" = δύναμις. "Strength" for "power" = δύναμις !!

11. Marg., "Those preëminent apostles" again. What "preëminent apostles"? "Those"?

12. "An apostle" = τοῦ ἀποστόλου. See "the sower."

13. "Except it be" = εἰ μή. Right (with A. V.).

16. "I myself" for "I." Cf. verses 11, 13, 15.

17. "Take any advantage" for "make a gain" = ἐκπλεονέκτησα. (?)

18. "Exhorted" for "desired" = παρεκάλεσα. Cf. ix. 5; x. 1; Phil. iv. 2, note. "The brother" for "a brother;" article in Greek, but not natural in English; see verse 12. "By" for "in;" and then, "in."

19. "Are" inserted for "we do." May not the "are" be stretched too far? Might not some things happen which would not be for their edifying? Remember how carefully they change the place of "still" at John xi. 20.

20. "Should find" for "shall find" = εὕρω: and "should be found," etc. Is this good English in this construction? They themselves often render the subjunctive aorist by a future.

XIII.

1. "Two witnesses or three" for "two or three witnesses." But why not say "and three"? The Greek is καὶ τριῶν. The καί may be of consequence, but the Greek order is not. At all events the καί is there; and their faithfulness must have slept.

4. "Through" = ἐν (thrice).

5. "Or know ye not as to your own selves that Jesus Christ is in you?" for "What! know ye not your own selves how that Jesus Christ is in you?" The A. V. follows the Greek, except the "how" inserted; and they took ἤ for "what!" not "or." Cf. 1 Cor. xiv. 36, note.

GALATIANS.

I.

.8. "Tarried" for "abode" = ἐπέμεινα. But see Phil. i. 24,—"abide" = ἐπιμένειν.

19. "But only" for "save" (marg.) = εἰ μή. Very well.

23. "But they only heard say" for "but they had heard only." Did the apostle mean that all they did was to "hear say," or that none but "they" heard? or rather that

all they had heard about him was, that, etc.? For their construction (in orat. recta) cf. Matt. ii. 23.

II.

1. "After the space of fourteen years" for "fourteen years after" = διὰ (14) ἐτῶν. (?)
5. "In the way of" for "by" (subjection) = τῇ ὑποταγῇ. Say "by way of"?
8. "The apostleship" = ἀποστολὴν τῆς. Why not "an apostleship"? Cf. 1 Cor. vi. 19. There a predicate, here with εἰς. And see Eph. i. 14.
9. Does the utter derangement of this verse, à la grecque, change the sense or improve the expression? If not, what faithfulness required it? Cf. 2 Peter iii. 1. "Should go" ought to continue italicized. Other words might be inserted instead, as "have to do with," or "preach to," or "exercise apostleship towards."
16. "Save through faith in Jesus Christ" for "but by the faith of Jesus Christ = ἐὰν μὴ διὰ πίστεως Ἰησοῦ Χριστοῦ. The Revisers have rendered "the faith *of* Jesus" at Rev. xiv. 12. Their "save" for "but" makes the apostle say that "a man is justified by the works of the law, *only* when he is justified by faith in Jesus Christ and *not* by the works of the law; *for* by the works of the law shall no flesh be justified"! As for the translation of ἐὰν μή in general;—at Matt. xxvi. 42 ("except I drink it") "except" is retained; Mark x. 30 ("but he shall receive") "but" is retained; as also at John v. 19, "the Son can do nothing of himself but what he seeth the Father do." Now this passage in John is perfectly parallel with that here in Galatians, as regards the construction of ἐὰν μή. "The Son can do nothing of himself [this is absolute; 'nor can he do anything at all']; but what he seeth the Father do, that the Son doeth." If in English we put "save" for "but," we must either supply the ellipsis or we come to the absurd statement;—"the Son can do nothing of himself save what he seeth the Father do, *that* the Son doeth of himself;" for the last clause is made an exception out of the first proposition, taken as it stands. This is the same sort of absurdity

as actually follows from their translation here in Galatians—
a translation which is not only at war with itself, but with
the whole context, and with the whole strain of the apostle's
teaching in this epistle. We submit that the meaning of
the apostle is, "A man is not justified by (the) works of
(the) law [this is absolute; 'nor is a man justified at all
save']; but through the faith of Jesus Christ; and by that
we are justified, and not by (the) works of (the) law; for
by (the) works of (the) law shall no flesh be justified." In
both these cases, John v. 19 and Gal. ii. 16, the Vulgate has
nisi for ἐὰν μή. But in both cases, Wiclif, Tyndal, Cranmer,
the Geneva, and even the Rhemish version read "but" (with
our A. V.); and the last cannot be supposed to have been
warped by any predilection for the doctrine of justification
by faith only.

There are several cases of the use of εἰ μή perfectly corresponding to the foregoing cases of ἐὰν μή: *e.g.*, Luke
iv. 26, 27; Rev. xxi. 27; Rom. xiv. 14. It is remarkable
that, in the two instances in St. Luke, while the A. V. has
"save" and "saving," the Revisers have very properly, but
very inconsistently, changed them to "but only." Also in
that in the Revelation they have put "but only" for "but,"
which is well enough, though scarcely necessary. But in
Rom. xiv. 14 they have capped the climax of inconsistency by changing "but" into "save that;" thus making
the apostle say, "Nothing is unclean of itself, save that to
him that accounteth anything to be unclean, to him it is
unclean of itself." Whereas the "but" of the A. V. or
their own "but only" gives the exact sense of the original,
for both the εἰ μή (or the ἐὰν μή) and the ellipsis that is
implied with it are, in English, briefly and idiomatically
expressed by the simple "but" or "but only."

In their corrections of the translation of εἰ μή given in
the A. V., the Revisers are in many instances, as we have
seen (Luke iv. 26, note), grossly inconsistent with themselves, besides making their changes unnecessarily.

16, 17. "Believed" for "have believed" = ἐπιστεύσαμεν. "We sought" for "we seek" = ζητοῦντες. "Were
found" for "are found" = εὑρέθημεν. (?)

19. "Died" for "am dead" = ἀπέθανον: but see "I have been crucified," next after.

20. "In faith, *the faith* which is in the Son of God" for "by the faith of the Son of God" = ἐν πίστει τῇ τοῦ υἱοῦ τοῦ Θεοῦ. As to "in" for "of," cf. Rev. xiv. 12. As to *the faith*, cf. Acts i. 12; 2 Cor. viii. 22; 2 Tim. i. 1; ii. 10; and especially iii. 15, "through faith which is in Christ Jesus" = διὰ πιστέως τῆς ἐν Χριστῷ Ἰησοῦ, not "through faith, *the faith* which is in Christ Jesus."

III.

2, 5. "By" = ἐξ (bis, bis), and so at verse 24, and so all along.

3. "In" = dat. inst., for "by." "Perfected" for "made perfect;"—faithfulness.

6. "For righteousness" = εἰς δικ. This is one of many instances which may be compared with Mark i. 4, where they put "unto" for "for."

7. "Which be" for "which are" = "who are." What faithfulness required this multiplication of obsolete expressions?

11. "By" = ἐν: also at verse 19.

17, 18, 20. "A" for "the" (covenant); "of the law;" no articles. "Which came" = ὁ γεγονώς,—not "has come." Cf. verse 24. See also Heb. xi. 17, 28; 2 Cor. ii. 13; vii. 5; John vi. 25; Matt. xiii. 46; 1 Pet. i. 20; Mark xv. 47 (?); —for perfects rendered as preterites. "A mediator" = ὁ μεσίτης.

22. "Hath shut" = συνέκλεισεν.

23. "Faith" = τὴν πίστιν: "the law" = νόμον: "should be" = "was about to be" (with A. V.).

24. "Hath been" for "was" = γέγονεν: cf. 17.

IV.

3. "Were held" = ἦμεν δεδουλωμένοι, pluperfect.

5. "Born" for "made" = γενόμενον (bis); not γεγεννημένον.

6. "Sent" for "hath sent," aorist, but (?).

9. "Have come to know" for "have known" = γνόντες.

12. "I beseech you, brethren," for " brethren, I beseech you" = ἀδελφοί, δέομαι ὑμῶν. Cf. 2 Thess. iii. 1.

13. "Because of" for "through." But what is the resulting sense? Is not the meaning expressed by "through," or "in," or "notwithstanding;" *i.e.* "though impeded by," or "in spite of"?

23. "Is born" for "was born" = γεγέννηται. This is harsh. Is not the "has been born" here historical, and equivalent to "was born"? Cf. iii. 17.

24. Here "women" may not be needed; for the αὗται ("these") may be feminine by attraction.

29. "He that was born" = ὁ γεννηθείς, it rightly follows the tense of the connection. Cf. Matt. ii. 2.

V.

1. With their new text, would not the most simple and natural translation be: "To freedom—Christ hath made us free—stand fast therefore"? or, better accommodated to the English idiom: "Christ hath made us free; to freedom therefore stand fast"? The οὖν stands after στήκετε instead of ἐλευθερία because it is first suggested by the parenthetical clause.

4. "Ye are severed" = κατηργήθητε. The A. V., with its inversion of subject and object, is nearer the sense of the original. It does not appear that καταργέω ever means properly "to sever," though it may express the consequences of severance. "Would be justified" for "are justified" = δικαιοῦσθε: but is this translation or exposition? "By the" = ἐν.

5. "The Spirit," "the hope;"— no article. By their change of construction, in avoiding one ambiguity they have fallen into another. Why not say: "For we through the Spirit await by faith the hope of righteousness"?

7. They say "should not" for the accusative with the infinitive, and not "did not."

13. "Be servants" = δουλεύετε :—not "bond-servants," as elsewhere; see iv. 1, 8, etc. "Your freedom" = τὴν ἐλευθερίαν. (?) Why not also "your love" for τῆς ἀγάπης?

14. "Is fulfilled" = πεπλήρωται (for πληροῦται). "The

whole law" for "all the law" = ὁ πᾶς νόμος. Cf. Eph. iv. 16—note.

16 and 25. "By the Spirit" for "in the Spirit" = Πνεύματι. But see iii. 3, where they render the same word "in the Spirit." "The" (thrice) for no article, "the Spirit," "the lust of the flesh ;" while, in the next verse the Greek has the articles with all these. Yet no distinction is made.

24. "Have crucified" = ἐσταύρωσαν. Why did they not say "crucified"? Is it not the aorist tense? Cf. Rom. vi. 6, 8; 2 Cor. v. 14; Col. iii. 3. "Thereof,"—better "its (passions and lusts)."

VI.

1. "A spirit" for "the spirit" = ἐν πνεύματι.
11. "Have written," marg., "write,"—aorist.
13. "Keep" = φυλάσσουσιν: cf. Luke xi. 21; John xvii. 12; Acts xii. 4; xxviii. 16; 2 Thess. iii. 3; 1 Tim. vi. 20; 2 Tim. i. 12, 14; 1 John v. 21 and Jude 24 ;—where they render it "guard." Their faithfulness must have exercised the most wonderful discrimination, as will be seen by such cases as 2 Tim., 1 John, and Jude, above cited, and by comparing, say, Acts xxviii. 16 with xxii. 20 and xxiii. 35.— These may be trifles, but they are *changes*, and, if of no importance, are wanton. "The law ;" marg., "a law." Why especially here?

14. "Hath been crucified" for "is crucified" = ἐσταύρωται. Cf. v. 14, etc.

18. For displacement of "brethren" here, cf. 2 Thess. iii. 1.

EPHESIANS.

I.

10. "In the heavens" for "in heaven" = ἐν τοῖς οὐρανοῖς. But see the Lord's Prayer, etc.

11. "Having been foreordained" for "being predestinated" = προορισθέντες, and so at verse 13 ; but see verse 18 and ii. 20, for the tense.

13. "The Holy Spirit" for "that Holy Spirit ;"—the

order of the Greek is, "the Spirit of promise, the Holy." Cf. verse 19.

14. "An earnest" for "the earnest" = ἀρραβὼν τῆς, in predicate. But immediately after they render "the redemption" and "the praise" without Greek article and followed by τῆς. Cf. Gal. ii. 8.

17. "A spirit" for "the spirit," and then "the knowledge," without article.

18. "Having the eyes enlightened" = πεφωτισμένους. Did they suppose, or would they make us think, that this English is also a perfect participle? But cf. iv. 18.

19. "That" for "the" = τήν. But cf. verses 13 and 14, where they put "the" for "that" in a perfectly similar construction and with a similar exposure to ambiguity.

II.

2. "Aforetime" for "in time past." Why?

3. "Lived" for "had our conversation" = ἀνεστράφημεν. Cf. 2 Cor. i. 12. Is "having our conversation" any more obsolete or unintelligible than "or" for "ere"?

8. "Have been saved" for "are saved" = ἐστε σεσωσμένοι. Compare "are being saved" for the present participle. To what, then, shall "are saved" correspond? And see Gal. iv. 3, where they render a pluperfect passive "were held," not "had been held."

12. "Alienated from" for "aliens from" = ἀπηλλοτριωμένοι. Which is the true sense? And they do not say "having been alienated" for the perfect participle, but "(being) alienated." Cf. verse 8.

20. "Being built" = ἐποικοδομηθέντες : but cf. 15 and 16, "having slain," etc., and i. 11.

21. "Each several building" for "all the building" (new reading). What is the probable sense? Christ is the one chief corner-stone on which they are all built, verse 20. Cf. also iii. 15. The several parts of one building or temple are not "several buildings."

III.

15. "Every family" for "the whole family" = $\pi\tilde{\alpha}\sigma\alpha$ $\pi\alpha\tau\rho\iota\acute{\alpha}$. Are we to suppose there are several families (*fatherhoods*) in heaven, as there are here upon earth? One can hardly help thinking that $\pi\tilde{\alpha}\sigma\alpha$ $\pi\alpha\tau\rho\iota\acute{\alpha}$ may here be rendered after the analogy of $\pi\tilde{\alpha}s$ $o\tilde{\iota}\varkappa o s$ $'I\sigma\rho\alpha\acute{\eta}\lambda$, "all the house of Israel;" and that $\dot{\epsilon}\nu$ $o\dot{\upsilon}\rho\alpha\nu o\tilde{\iota}s$ $\varkappa\alpha\grave{\iota}$ $\dot{\epsilon}\pi\grave{\iota}$ $\gamma\tilde{\eta}s$ may be equivalent to a defining genitive. Cf. 1 Pet. v. 1.

16. "Inward man" for "inner man." (?)

IV.

1. "Calling" for "vocation." "Called" immediately follows. Cf. Matt. xxii. 3,—"to call the bidden" and not "to call the called." The Revisers can sometimes study a euphonious variety.

12. "For the" = $\pi\rho\grave{o}s$ $\tau\acute{o}\nu$: "unto the" = $\epsilon\dot{\iota}s$ without article (twice). Why not "a work of ministering" and "a building up of the body of Christ"?

14. "By," "in,"—both = $\dot{\epsilon}\nu$ in coördinate succession: "by sleight," "in craftiness,"—force of idiom.

16. "All the body" for "the whole body" = $\pi\tilde{\alpha}\nu$ $\tau\grave{o}$ $\sigma\tilde{\omega}\mu\alpha$. But see Gal. v. 14, where we have just the reverse change, "the whole law" for "all the law;" and Acts xx. 27, "the whole counsel" for "all the counsel;" and cf. Matt. viii. 32; Luke i. 10; Rom. viii. 22, and Mark xvi. 15.

18. "Being darkened" = $\dot{\epsilon}\sigma\varkappa o\tau\iota\sigma\mu\acute{\epsilon}\nu o\iota$. They construe with $\ddot{o}\nu\tau\epsilon s$, it is true; but that makes no difference; it is still a perfect tense. "Alienated," *i.e.*, "being alienated" = $\dot{\alpha}\pi\eta\lambda\lambda o\tau\rho\iota\omega\mu\acute{\epsilon}\nu o\iota$, immediately follows. Why not, "having been" in both cases? Cf. ii. 8.

24. "Hath been created" for "is created;" both are forms for the perfect, but $\tau\grave{o}\nu$ $\varkappa\tau\iota\sigma\vartheta\acute{\epsilon}\nu\tau\alpha$ = "which was created." Cf. Rom. vi. 6, 8, etc.

32. "Forgave" for "hath forgiven" = $\dot{\epsilon}\chi\alpha\rho\acute{\iota}\sigma\alpha\tau o$. Cf. Phil. i. 29, where they give us "hath been granted" for "is granted" = $\dot{\epsilon}\chi\alpha\rho\acute{\iota}\sigma\vartheta\eta$.

V.

1. "Imitators" for "followers;" "beloved" for "dear." (?)
6. "Empty" for "vain." (?)
7. "Be" = γίνεσθε: not "become." Why?
10. "Well-pleasing" for "acceptable;" but see Rom. xii. 1, 2, where they render "acceptable."
12, 20. Are the inversions here necessary? Are they not rather wanton, and much to the damage of the English? Cf. 2 Peter iii. 1.
25. "For it" = ὑπὲρ αὐτῆς: but cf. vi. 19, "on my behalf" for "for me," etc., etc.
26. "With the word" = ἐν ῥήματι.
32. "In regard of" for "concerning" = εἰς. Would not "as to" or "in relation to" have been better, if we *must* have a change?

VI.

9. "And forbear" for "forbearing" = ἀνιέντες. But see a contrary change at v. 26.
17. "The word of God" = ῥῆμα Θεοῦ, why not "God's word," or "a word of God"? Cf. Acts iv. 36, etc.

PHILIPPIANS.

I.

1. Why not say "with bishops and deacons"?—No article.
4, 5. "On behalf of" for "for" = ὑπέρ. Cf. Eph. v. 25. "For" = ἐπί: and "in furtherance of" = εἰς. Better say "for" for ὑπέρ, "upon" for ἐπί, and "as to" or "unto" for εἰς: cf. verse 12 and Col. iv. 11.
22. "Wot not" = οὐ γνωρίζω: marg., "do not make known;" better "cannot tell."—"Je ne saurais dire."
25. "Abide, yea and abide" for "abide and continue" = μενῶ καὶ παραμενῶ. (?) They render παραμένω "continue," usually;—see Heb. vii. 23; James i. 25; and whence comes "yea"? "In the faith" for "of faith" = τῆς πίστεως.—Render: "for your progress and the joy of your faith"?

29. "It hath been granted" for "it is given" = ἐχαρίσθη. Cf. Eph. iv. 32; and see "it is written."

II.

1. The interchange of "comfort" and "consolation" is consequential; but it is not necessary and is no improvement here.

3. "Faction" for "strife" = ἐριθείαν: and so elsewhere, but is it necessary?

6. "Counted it not a prize to be on an equality with God," etc. Suggestion of the American Revisers better. And observe that aorist participles with aorist verbs are rendered present, just as the present participle is.

9. "Wherefore also God" for "wherefore God also." Is their "also" in its logical position after all? "God also" would be according to their usual rule in relation to the Greek order. But would it not be better, if we *must* make a change, to retain the translation by the perfect, and say: "Wherefore God hath also," etc.?

16. "In the day of Christ" = εἰς ἡμ. Χρ.—"Unto a glorying for me at the day," *i.e.* "when I come to the day," etc. "In vain" = εἰς κενόν.

22. "In furtherance of" for "in" = εἰς:—"unto" or "as to" (the Gospel).

24. "I myself also" for "I also myself" = καὶ αὐτός.

27. "That not" for "lest" = ἵνα μή: cf. 1 Tim. iii. 7, and Rev. xvi. 15, etc.

29. "Joy" for "gladness," and "honor" for "reputation." Such are instances of excruciating faithfulness.

28. "I have sent" for "I sent,"—an aorist! This is an extraordinary correction of an aorist tense; and one is curious to know how they reasoned it out.

30. Here observe that "service" towards *the Apostle* is (with the A. V.) made the rendering of λειτουργία.

III.

12. "Have obtained" = ἔλαβον: and "am made perfect = τετελείωμαι. Cf. John xvii.

15. "Even this shall God reveal" for "God shall reveal even this"! Cf. 2 Cor. v. 20, etc.
16. "Have attained,"—an aorist.
18. "Told often" for "have told often,"—an aorist.
19. "Earthly things" = τὰ ἐπίγεια. (Article.)
20. "A Saviour" for "the Saviour" = Σωτῆρα: in apposition with Κύριον = "the Lord"?
21. "Body of his glory" for "his glorious body." But this is ambiguous; does it mean that his glory has a body? In ordinary English we should scarcely use such an expression in any other sense.

IV.

2. "Exhort" for "beseech" (bis) = παρακαλῶ. So also at 1 Thess. iv. 10; 1 Tim. i. 3; Heb. xiii. 19, 22; and "exhort" for "intreat," 1 Tim. v. 1; but "intreat" for "exhort," 2 Cor. ix. 5, where "exhort" suits as well as here. They have also "exhort" for "desire," 2 Cor. xii. 18; they retain "beseech" at Matt. viii. 5, 31, 34; xiv. 36; Mark i. 40; they put "beseech" where "exhort" might be as well as here, Acts xxi. 12; xxvii. 33, 34; Rom. xii. 1; xvi. 17; Eph. iv. 1; 1 Cor. i. 10; xvi. 12, 15; cf. Heb. xiii. 22, and 1 Peter ii. 11. They put "intreat" for "beseech," Luke viii. 31, 32—cf. Matt. viii. 31, 34; 2 Cor. vi. 1; x. 1, and retain "intreat," Luke xv. 28. They put "intreat" for "desire," Acts ix. 38; xxviii. 14; and "intreat" for "pray," Acts xxiv. 4. They put "beseech" for "desire," Acts viii. 31; xix. 31; and "beseech" for "pray," Acts xvi. 9; Matt. xxvi. 53; Mark v. 18.—Surely if there were "faithful" reasons for all these changes hither and thither, they must be very fine-drawn.

3. "Beseech" for "entreat" = ἐρωτῶ. But they have "ask" for "beseech" at Luke vii. 3; viii. 37; John xix. 31;—"ask" for "desire" at Luke xiv. 32; John xii. 21; Acts xviii. 20; xxiii. 20; and "desire" is retained at Luke vii. 36;—"ask" for "pray" at Acts xxiii. 18, and "pray" is retained at John xvii. 9, 15, 20. At 1 Thess. iv. 1, "beseech" = ἐρωτῶμεν, and "exhort" = παρακαλοῦμεν. This may explain their renderings in these two verses in

Philippians, where the same two words are, not indeed in juxtaposition, but in near proximity to each other. But that could hardly be a sufficient reason for *requiring* a *change* here, considering the great variety of renderings they have given these words elsewhere.

"For they" for "which" = αἵτινες. This they elsewhere render "who" or "which," and the change is not required here,—"whose" (ὧν) immediately following involves the same use of the relative,—while at Matt. vii. 15 such a change would have been very much to the purpose. Cf. Col. ii. 23 and 2 Thess. i. 9, etc.

8. Where did the Revisers get the marginal reading of "gracious" for εὔφημα? The whole question is, whether we should say "of good report" or "of good import," whether the word is to be taken in an active or a passive sense.

10. "Rejoice" for "rejoiced" = ἐχάρην. ("Gr." in marg.) But cf. Mark xi. 24 and xiii. 20. This is another remarkable change in the rendering of an aorist. In the 9th verse the perfects of A. V. were better than their preterites; as in the 10th verse they say, "have revived" = ἀνεθάλετε (better and more faithful was the A. V., "have caused to flourish again"); and in the 11th and 12th verses they put "have learned" alike for ἔμαθον and for μεμύημαι. Cf. John xvii.

19. "Every need of yours" for "all your need" = πᾶσαν χρείαν ὑμῶν. Articular nicety?

COLOSSIANS.

I.

5. "In the heavens" for "in heaven" = ἐν τοῖς οὐρανοῖς. But see Matt. v. 12, 45, and the Lord's Prayer.

6. "For you" = ὑπέρ,—not "in your behalf." We make this and the like notes, because the Revisers so often and needlessly substitute "in behalf of" for the simple "for" of the A. V., as a translation of ὑπέρ.

12. "Made" for "hath made;" also "delivered" and "translated;" but followed by "we have."

16, 20. "The heavens," "the earth," for "heaven," "earth." Cf. the Lord's Prayer, Mark ii. 10, etc., etc. "Things visible and things invisible" = τὰ ὁρατὰ καὶ τὰ ἀόρατα: but what of the article? Cf. the faithful correction at iii. 2,—"the things that are" for "things."
22. "Hath reconciled,"—an aorist.
26. "Hath been manifested,"—an aorist.
27. "Was pleased to" for "would" = ἠθέλησεν = "willed to," "it was God's will to."
29. "Which worketh" = τὴν ἐνεργουμένην, without any marginal alternate.

II.

1. "Would have you know" for "would that ye knew;" but see Luke xix. 14; 1 Tim. ii. 4.
3. "In whom are all . . . hidden" for "in whom are hid all . . ." The A. V. is better English, if the R. V. is better Greek. Which do we want? The sense remains the same.
4. "That no one" for "lest any man;" how faithful! but see 1 Tim. iii. 7; Rev. xvi. 15, etc.
5. "In the flesh" = τῇ σαρκί (as to the flesh).
7. "Builded" for "built,"—excruciating faithfulness! And yet "our Father which," and "we be." "Your faith" for "the faith" = τῇ πίστει. (?)
8. "His philosophy" = τῆς φιλοσοφίας. (?)
11. "Were circumcised" for "are (have been) circumcised" = περιετμήθητε. (?)
12. "Were raised" for "are risen." Cf. Matt. xxviii. 6, etc. "Raised" for "hath raised (Christ)" is right, for this is historical.
13. "Did quicken" for "hath he quickened." (?)
14. "Nailing" = προσηλώσας: but above they have translated aorist participles in connection with preterite verbs,—"having been buried," for "buried," "having blotted" for "blotting;" and below they say,—"having put off," and then "triumphing over."
18. "By a voluntary humility" for "in," etc. = θέλων ἐν ταπεινοφροσύνῃ.

20. "Died" for "be dead,"—the aorist. (?)

23. "But are not of any value against the indulgence of the flesh;"—a very doubtful rendering of a very difficult passage, and "indulgence" (= $πλησμονήν$) is without article in the Greek;—"not in any honour or reverence,—to an indulgence of the flesh;" *i.e.*, "not in any reverence towards God,—rather and really to a greater indulgence of the flesh." For construction see 2 Tim. ii. 14.

III.

1. "Were raised" for "be risen" (so [3] "died" for "are dead"); "is seated" for "sitteth" = $ἐστιν$ . . . $καθήμενος$:—say "is sitting," if we *must* make a change.
2. "The things that are" for "things" (bis) = $τά$. But cf. i. 20.
5. "The which" for "which" = $ἥτις$: also 1 Tim. i. 4. But cf. ii. 23, etc.
7. "In the which" (so A. V.) = $ἐν οἷς$: also at verse 15.
10. "Is being renewed" = $ἀνακαινούμενον$. (?) Cf. Luke xxii. 19, 20, etc., etc.
18. "Is fitting" = $ἀνῆκεν$.
22. "That not" for "lest;" but see again 1 Tim. iii. 7 and Rev. xvi. 15, etc.

IV.

8. "Have sent,"—an aorist.
11. "Workers unto the kingdom of God" = $εἰς$: not "in furtherance of." Cf. Phil. i. 4, 5.
12, 13. "For you" = $ὑπὲρ ὑμῶν$, not "in your behalf."
15. "The church that" for "the church which" (is in their house);—amazing faithfulness! Cf. 1 Cor. ii. 12, "the Spirit which"; iii. 10, "the grace which"; iv. 6, "the things which"; etc., etc. And see 2 Cor. i. 4, note.
16. "Hath been read" for "is read" = $ἀναγνωσθῇ$: but see "it is written."
17. "Hast received,"—an aorist.

I. THESSALONIANS.

I.

5. "How that" for "for" = ὅτι. (?) *Marg.* "Fulness" (for "assurance") = πληροφορία: but see new reading at Col. iv. 12, πεπληροφορημένοι, rendered, without marginal alternate, "fully assured," instead of the "complete" of the A. V. "Showed ourselves" for "were" = ἐγενήθημεν.
9. "A living and true God" for "the," etc. Cf. 1 Tim. iv. 10; Heb. xii. 22; Rev. vii. 2.

II.

1. "Hath been found' for "was" = γέγονεν. But see Gal. iii. 17, and see here the development' in subsequent preterites.
2. "Waxed bold" for "were bold" = ἐπαρρησιασάμεθα. But see Acts xiii. 46, corrected just contrariwise.
5. "Were found using" for "used" = ἐγενήθημεν.
13. "We also" for "also we" (thank God).
14. "Which are in Judea in Christ Jesus" for "which in Judea are in Christ Jesus"—oh, faithfulness!
15. The antecedent of "who" is doubtful; in consistency they should have said, "for the Jews both killed," etc. Cf. Phil. iv. 3, where their change is not needed.
18. "Once and again" = ἅπαξ καὶ δίς,—"once and twice;" but see "two witnesses or three."

III.

5. "Sent that I might know" for "sent to know" = εἰς τὸ γνῶναι.
11. "May our God direct." The added "may" is not needed; see the Lord's Prayer, and the next verse (12), where (with the A. V.) they say "and the Lord make," without any "may."

IV.

1, 3, 4. The needless omission of *would* and *should* makes the sense less clear.

9. "That one write unto you" for "that I," etc. But see their translation at James i. 27, etc. The A. V. could not use this "one" in 1611.

14. "That are fallen asleep" = τοὺς κοιμηθέντας,—not "that slept." So for the saints in general; but "Jesus died" (ἀπέθανε) is right, for this is historical. Cf. 2 Cor. v. 14, etc.

V.

1. "Concerning the times" for "of;"—faithfulness!

6. *Quære*—whether "the others" would not be better than "the rest," which they use here and elsewhere.

13. "Exceeding highly" for "very highly" = ὑπὲρ ἐκπερισσοῦ. A very exceeding superfluity of faithfulness.

15. "Unto any one evil for evil" for "evil for evil unto any man"! And the A. V. is in the Greek order.

16. "Rejoice alway" for "rejoice evermore." Cf. Phil. iv. 4, and its *marg.* "Farewell."

II. THESSALONIANS.

I.

9. "Who" = οἵτινες. Why not say "for they"? Cf. Phil. iv. 3. There is more danger of misunderstanding here than there.

10. "To be marvelled at" for "to be admired" = θαυμασθῆναι. "Admired" is according to the later usage of the Greek; and is it not better here?

11. "Desire (or *marg.* 'good pleasure') of goodness." Whose desire? Whose goodness?

II.

1. "Concerning" for "by" = ὑπέρ. Would not "upon," or "by reason of," or "in view of" be better?

2. "To the end that" for "that" = εἰς τό, etc. Is not this illogical? It answers to *why* and not to *what*; and it would remain to know what he beseeches of them after all. "Is now present" for "is at hand" = ἐνέστηκεν,—"is imminent." Has this word lately lost this meaning?

7. "There is one that restraineth now" = ὁ κατέχων ἄρτι. Why not say "he that restraineth (or 'the restrainer') restraineth now"? Cf. ὁ σπείρων, "the sower."

10. "Are perishing" for "perish." (?)

13. "For that" for "because" = ὅτι. Is the sense any clearer? Is the English any better?

15. "So then" for "therefore" = ἄρα οὖν. The same questions may be asked again.

16. "Loved" and "gave" for "hath," etc. (?)

III.

1. "Brethren, pray" = προσεύχεσθε, ἀδελφοί. Why did they not follow the Greek order, and say "pray brethren"? Cf. Gal. iv. 12; vi. 18; Matt. xxvi. 22, 25.

2. "All have not faith"=οὐ πάντες, not πάντες οὐ. Why not follow both the Greek and good logic—and good English too—and say " not all men have (the) faith"? Cf. Heb. ii. 5 and 1 Cor. vi. 12.

I. TIMOTHY.

I.

2. "My true child in faith" = γνησίῳ τέκνῳ ἐν πίστει = "a true child in the faith;"— cf. 1 Thess. i. 9. There is neither "my" nor "the" with "child," and the Revisers are themselves accustomed to insert the article after ἐν.

3. "Exhorted" for "besought" Why? See Phil. iv. 2. (note). "Charge" = παραγγέλλω. This rendering is here retained; but "command" is put for "charge" at v. 7, and is retained at iv. 11; also at 2 Thess. iii. 4, 6, 10, 12; Luke viii. 29; ix. 21; Acts xvii. 30; Mark viii. 6;—while "charge" is put for "command" at Matt. x. 5; Mark vi. 8; Acts i. 4; iv. 18; v. 28, 40; x. 42; xv. 5; xvi. 18; xxiii.

30; 1 Cor. vii. 10; 1 Thess. iv. 11; 1 Tim. i. 5; and is retained at Luke viii. 56; v. 14; Acts xvi. 23; xxiii. 22; 1 Tim. vi. 13, 17. This is one of the words which seems to have been a special exercise to the Revisers' faithfulness; but the ground of their distinctions it is hard to divine. Cf. *e.g.* Mark vi. 8 with viii. 6; or 1 Cor. vii. 10 with 2 Thess. iii. 4, 6, 10, 12 and 1 Tim. iv. 11; v. 7.

4. "The which" for "which" = $αἵτινες$,—also Col. iii.
5. But see $οἵτινες$, 2 Thess. i. 9; Heb. xiii. 7, etc., where they say simply "who" or "which."
5. "Charge" for "commandment" = $παραγγελίας$. (?)
7. "Though they understand" for "understanding." The A. V. is literally correct. Cf. Heb. vi. 6, "if they shall fall away" changed to "and then fell away," to render an aorist participle.
9. "As knowing this" for "knowing this = $εἰδὼς$ $τοῦτο$. The "as" is not even *italicized*. "Law" for "the law," but what is the difference? Both must here mean *law* in general.
10. "Doctrine," *marg.* "teaching," = $διδασκαλία$. But see iv. 6—with no *marg.* reading. It is extremely difficult for the uninitiated to apprehend the nice distinctions of such faithfulness.
17. "Incorruptible" for "immortal" = $ἀφθάρτῳ$,—of God?
18. "By them" = $ἐν αὐταῖς$.
19. "Made" for "have made." (?)

II.

2. "Tranquil and quiet" for "quiet and peaceable," (?) or, say, "peaceful"?
4. "Willeth that" for "will have to;" but see 1 Cor. x. 1 and Col. ii. 1; corrected contrariwise.

III.

2. "Without reproach" for "blameless" = $ἀνεπίληπτον$ = blameless, or unblamable, or irreproachable, *i.e.* (that ought) not to be attacked or blamed. Cf. verse 10 and iv.

4; and see, by analogy, Col. i. 22 and 1 Thess. iii. 13. "The husband of one wife,"—no article; cf. verse 12.

3. "No brawler" for "not given to wine" = πάροινον. Marg. of A. V.,—"*i.e.*, not ready to quarrel and offer wrong as one in wine." The Revisers leave the *wine* out entirely.

7. Lest" = ἵνα μή,—not "that not," and so at Rev. xvi. 15. But cf. Col. iii. 22; ii. 4; Phil. ii. 27; Heb. iv. 11, etc., etc. See note John xii. 35.

12. "Husbands of one wife" for "the husbands," etc. But cf. verse 2. Whether the subject be "deacons" or "the deacons" can make no difference in the predicate.

15. "The church," "the pillar,"—no article in Greek.

IV.

2. "Through" = ἐν. Here their whole construction is doubtful; cf. verses 2 and 3.

10. "The living God" = ἐπὶ Θεῷ ζῶντι.

13. "To reading," etc.—articles omitted thrice; cf. "the weeping and gnashing." "Teaching" for "doctrine" = διδασκαλία. Do they eschew *doctrine* altogether?

V.

7. "Without reproach," again, for "blameless." See iii. 2 (note).

9. "*Having been;*" why italicized? It is the translation of γεγονυῖα, if that is translated at all.

11. "They desire to marry" for "they will marry" = γαμεῖν θέλουσιν. ("They choose to marry" or "are bent upon marrying.")

VI.

1. "The doctrine" for "his doctrine." (?)

2. "Partake of the benefit" = ἀντιλαμβανόμενοι. Better "reap the benefit," *i.e.* the *masters* do?

9. "Desire to be rich" for "will be rich;"—*i.e.* will to be, or aim or seek to be,—lay their plans and make their efforts to be;—it is more than an idle "desire." There is no ambiguity in the A. V. according to the laws of good English. The "they that" is here indefinite, like "whoever."

10. "A root" for "the root,"—predicate; but the Revisers familiarly render anarthrous predicates with the English article. See above iii. 2, 15; iv. 10; and John ix. 5, etc., etc. "A root of all evils" or "of all the evils" (πάντων τῶν κακῶν, which they render "all kinds of evil," forgetting their faithfulness with "all the nations") either is nonsense or is subject to much the same difficulty in its strictly universal application which was supposed to be involved in "the root of all evil." Instead of being the universal cause, it simply becomes a universal *con-cause*. But the definite article in English is not absolutely exclusive, and the apostle's words are not to be interpreted with mathematical rigor. The A. V. has given the natural English expression for the apostle's meaning: "The love of money is the root of all evil,"—an expression whose rhetorical character and simple sense are perfectly clear to every common-sense reader.

14. "Without reproach," again, for "unrebukable." See iii. 2.

17. "Have their hope set" = ἠλπικέναι. But this is not the English perfect; that would be, "have set their hope." Did they mean to throw a little dust in our eyes?

21. "Have erred,"—an aorist.

II. TIMOTHY.

I.

1. "The promise of the life which" for "the promise of life which" = ἐπαγγελίαν ζωῆς τῆς: they do not say "of life, even *the life* which." But cf. Gal. ii. 20.

3. "My" for "*my;*" neither pronoun nor article in the Greek. "Supplications" for "prayers" = δεήσεσι :—consequential.

5. "Having been reminded" for "when I call to remembrance" = ὑπόμνησιν λαβών = "while I call (or having called) to remembrance." "In thee also" for "that in thee also," ὅτι not being rendered *oratione rectâ*.

6. "For the which cause" for "wherefore" = δι' ἣν αἰτίαν. Wherefore, with "the which" and all? At Eph.

v. 31, "for this cause" stands for ἀντὶ τούτου. At Tit. i. 13, "for which cause" = δι' ἣν αἰτίαν.

8. "Suffer hardship with the gospel" for "be partaker of the afflictions of the Gospel ;"—is it not rather "be partaker (with me) of afflictions for the Gospel"?—the "with" is not with *the gospel* but with *me ;* see ii. 3.

10. "Hath been manifested" for "is made manifest" = φανερωθεῖσαν. But cf. 2 Cor. v. 11, where "we are made manifest" renders the perfect of the same verb.

12. "Yet'' for "nevertheless'' = ἀλλά,—this is not ill,— if some change *must* be made. But it is strange they should have forgotten their favorite "howbeit;" which they are accustomed to substitute for "but" in rendering ἀλλά, as at John v. 34 ; viii. 26 ; xix. 34 ; Acts v. 13 ; 1 Cor. x. 5 ; xiv. 19 ; Phil. iii. 7 ; 1 Tim. i. 13.

II.

6. "The first'' for "first" = πρῶτον.

9. "Malefactor" for "evil-doer" = κακοῦργος. Consequential ; but is it necessary ? Is it any improvement ?

10. Cf. "the salvation which" with Gal. ii. 20.

11. "Faithful is the saying" for "it is a faithful saying ;" and so, often ; but what's the faithful difference ? "Died" for " be dead;" but note the connection following.

17. "Gangrene" for "canker." So, the margin of the A. V.; but *quære?*

18. "Men who" for "who" = οἵτινες. But see 2 Thess. i. 9 ; Eph. iv. 19 ; also Rom. iv. 18; not to say Matt. vii. 15. "Have erred" = ἠστόχησαν.

19. "Howbeit" for "nevertheless" = μέντοι. This is also the favorite translation for πλήν, ἀλλά, μὲν οὖν, etc., etc.

24. "The Lord's servant" for "the servant of the Lord." If they proposed to make any difference, they should have said "a servant of the Lord." See Matt. x. 24, and cf. Matt. xvii. 22 ; xxv. 31 ; James i. 20; Acts vii. 35; Rev. viii. 4.

26. Read—"They having been taken captive by the

devil, may recover themselves out of his snare unto the will of God"? Cf. Tit. iii. 4; and Matt. xxvi. 24.

III.

10. "Thou didst follow" for "hast fully known." The Greek text is changed for the tense; but see the context for the sense.

12. "Would" for "will" = οἱ θέλοντες. But cf. Matt. xxiii. 4—"they will not move them," and Acts xxv. 9— "wilt thou go up?"

16. " Every scripture inspired of God is also profitable," etc. = πᾶσα γραφὴ θεόπνευστος καὶ ὠφέλιμος, κ.τ.λ. The marginal reading, which is substantially the same as that of the A. V., is by all means to be preferred: for (1) the natural use of the καί, in its ordinary sense, is, to connect θεόπνευστος and ὠφέλιμος, and thus they of course fall into the predicate;—and, in any event, the "is," which remains to be inserted somewhere, may quite as properly be inserted before the "inspired" as after it. (2) Even if the "inspired of God" is put before the "is," it must still have a predicative and not an attributive character,—not "every God-inspired scripture" (that would be πᾶσα θεόπνευστος γραφή), nor "every scripture *which is* inspired of God" (that would require ἡ θεόπνευστος), but "every scripture being inspired of God" (as it is); cf. Heb. v. 1, "Every high priest being taken from among men" (as he is),—not "which is taken," etc.; so also Heb. iv. 2, "because they were not united,"—not "them which were not united." And thus the sense (though not clearly expressed in the Revisers' text) will remain substantially the same after all their unnatural change of construction.

It is noticeable that they render καὶ ὠφέλιμος "also profitable" and not "profitable also." But see their painstaking corrections in the construction of "also," *e.g.* at 1 Thess. ii. 13, "we also" for "also we" = καὶ ἡμεῖς.—cf. Heb. iv. 12, 13, where they do not say: "The word of God living is also active," and "all things naked are also laid open." Why then adopt this strange construction just here?

IV.

6. "Am already being offered" = $ἤδη\ σπένδομαι$. Is this better English than to say "I am now offered"?—if indeed the A. V. need be changed at all. "Is come" for "is at hand" = $ἐφέστηκε$. (?)

10. Preterites for perfects ; but with Crescens and Titus are not perfects much more naturally to be understood ?

TITUS.
I.

1-4. The rendering of articles here is worthy of examination. Why is it "the truth which," and then "eternal life, which," and then "the message which," and then "my true son," and then "a common faith"? "When" for "after that" = $ὅτε$: cf. 1 Cor. xiii. 11.

6. "That believe" for "faithful" = $πιστά$. (?)

7. "God's steward" for "the steward of God." But what is the difference? Is this rendering given in such cases because the Greek is without the article? But if the A. V. expressed the exact sense, did faithfulness require a change of the form?

8. "A lover of good." Good what? They might have said "of that which is good" (or " of good things") or "of good men;" but must it not be one or the other?

11. "Men who" for "who" = $οἵτινες$. See 2 Tim. ii. 18 (note).

13. "For which cause" for "wherefore" = $δι'\ ἥν\ αἰτίαν$. At 2 Tim. i. 6, they say "for the which cause" for the same Greek. What becomes then of their boasted and painstaking uniformity of rendering, as with "straightway," for example? And wherefore make any change either there or here, the sense remaining the same?

15. "Are defiled" = $μεμίανται$ (perfect).

II.

3. "Enslaved" = $δεδουλωμένας$ = "having been enslaved." Cf. Matt. v. 10.

5. "To be ... being in subjection to" for "to be ... obedient to"= ὑποτασσομένας. (?) And so at verse 9.
7. "Ensample" for "pattern" = τύπον. (?)
11. "Hath appeared"—an aorist.

III.

3. "Aforetime" for "sometimes" = ποτέ = once.
5. "Done" = τῶν = "which were."
6. "Poured out upon" for "shed on" = ἐξέχεεν. But see Acts ii. 17, 18 and 33, etc., where the Revisers insist upon "poured forth," and (17, 18) correct the "poured out" of the A. V.
9. "Strifes" for "contentions" = ἔρεις. But at 1 Cor. i. 11, they have left "contentions;" is the sense different there for the case-increment? "Fightings" for "strivings" (about the law) = μάχας νομικάς (legal battles).
15. "In faith" for "in the faith" = ἐν πίστει. (?)

PHILEMON.

8. "Have all boldness" for "might be much bold" = πολλὴν παρρησίαν ἔχων. (?)
12. "Have sent back"—an aorist.
13. "In thy behalf" for "instead of thee" = ὑπέρ. Suppose we give the simple and true rendering, "for," and then let common-sense decide which is the right meaning in this connection?
19. "Write" for "have written"—an aorist. "That I say not" for "albeit I say not" = ἵνα μὴ λέγω = "not to say" (see 2 Cor. xii. 7; Phil. ii. 30; 2 Thess. iii. 9, etc.), and proceed with "that" instead of "how that" = ὅτι.
21. "Beyond" for "more than" = ὑπέρ: but at verse 16, "more than" for "above," with the same case and ὑπέρ.

HEBREWS.

I.

1. The many and divers changes in this verse are well enough in themselves; but are they necessary? For the

translation of the aorist participle, cf. 1 Cor. viii. 5; John iv. 39 and v. 44, note.

2. "In *his* son," *marg.* "a son." What occasion for this marginal reading? After ἐν the Revisers are accustomed freely to insert the article; it is, or may be, therefore, "the son" or "his son."

3. "Effulgence" for "brightness." (?) "Substance" for "person." (?) "Sins" = τῶν ἁμαρτιῶν: but does not this mean "our sins," even without the ἡμῶν? Think of "the weeping and gnashing"; and cf. "its sanctuary" at ix. 1, "their deliverance" at xi. 35, and "their faith" at xi. 40.

7. "Who maketh his angels winds" = πνεύματα. This might be well enough in itself, but is it quite consistent? At verse 13, of the angels they say: "Are they not all ministering spirits"—not "winds" = πνεύματα. As to the suggestion that "winds" and "flame of fire" are here for the Hebrew accusative of material, that is not likely—(1) from the nature of the case, which is not one of moulding or fashioning; (2) from the fact that the Psalmist had just said, "who maketh the clouds his chariot," in a different order; and (3) from the fact that the Septuagint, in almost all cases, translate the Hebrew accusative of material with ἐκ. And that "angels" and "ministers" must be accusative subjects and not predicates appears from this, that it is, with ministers, "a flame of fire" or "a flaming fire," and not "flames of fire"; it could not be said, "he maketh a flame of fire his ministers."

14. "To do service" for "to minister" = εἰς διακονίαν. This is generally rendered by the Revisers "ministry;" see 2 Tim. iv. 11, "for ministering" = εἰς διακονίαν. They should rather have changed the rendering of λειτουργικά—(if they *must* change something): say, *e.g.*, "Spirits that do service, sent forth to minister," etc.?

II.

1. "Things that were heard"—(not "have been") = τοῖς ἀκουσθεῖσι. Cf. Rom. vi. 7.

2. "Proved" for "was" = ἐγένετο. (?)

5. "Not unto angels did he" for "unto the angels hath he not." Why not, then, following the Greek, say, at 2 Thess. iii. 2, "Not all men have faith"? That would have been logically correct; while here the order makes no difference in the logic or in the sense. As for the article and the tense—*quære?*

9. "Behold" for "see"= βλέπομεν: but they render this verb by "see," ten to one.

16. "For verily not of angels doth he take hold, but he taketh hold of the seed of Abraham." After all, this must refer to the *Incarnation*; otherwise, why say "seed of Abraham," and not "seed of Adam," or "mankind"? If *aiding* or *helping* is what is meant by ἐπιλαμβάνεται, surely the *help*, the *benefits of the salvation* are for all men, and not for the "seed of Abraham" only; see verse 9. He taketh hold of the seed of Abraham—he taketh to himself the seed of Abraham—the seed of David—that he might *help*, might save, mankind. For ἐπιλαμβάνομαι, cf. Matt. xiv. 31; Luke ix. 47; xxiii. 26; Acts xvi. 19; xvii. 19; xviii. 17; xxi. 30, 33; and particularly, 1 Tim. vi. 12, 19;—to lay hold on, to take to one's self, to take as one's own.

III.

5. "Afterward to be spoken" for "to be spoken after;" but see iv. 8, "have spoken afterward" is put for "afterward have spoken." What is the key? Why either change? Why both? Under such criticism the A. V. is in hard case.

IV.

1. "Let us fear therefore" for "let us therefore fear." How consistent! Cf. Acts xxv. 17; 2 Cor. v. 20, etc. etc.

3. "Have believed" = πιστεύσαντες: "that" = τήν: cf. verse 11, "that" = ἐκείνην τήν, and verse 4, "the" for "this."

6. "That some should enter thereinto" = τινὰς εἰσελθεῖν εἰς αὐτήν,—not, "that some enter." "Failed to enter in" for "entered not in"= οὐκ εἰσῆλθον. Which is the true

rendering? The most faithful translation need not be clearer than the original.

    10. "Is entered," "hath rested"—aorists.

    11. "That no man fall" for "lest any man fall." The difference? But see John v. 14; xii. 40; 1 Tim. iii. 7; Matt. xvii. 27; xxvi. 5; Rev. xvi. 15, etc.

    12. "Active" for "powerful" = $\dot{\varepsilon}\nu\varepsilon\rho\gamma\acute{\eta}s$. (?) "The dividing" = $\mu\varepsilon\rho\iota\sigma\mu o\tilde{v}$,—no article.

    13. "Before the" for "unto the" = $\tau o\tilde{\iota}s$.

    15. "But one" for "but;"—no "one" in text.

V.

    5. "This day" for "to-day" = $\sigma\acute{\eta}\mu\varepsilon\rho o\nu$, and so at Acts xiii. 33; but see iv. 7, 8, and Luke xxiii. 43.

    6. "For ever" = $\varepsilon\iota s\ \tau\grave{o}\nu\ \alpha\iota\tilde{\omega}\nu\alpha$:—*no marg.*

    7. "For his godly fear" = $\dot{\alpha}\pi\grave{o}\ \tau\tilde{\eta}s\ \varepsilon\dot{v}\lambda\alpha\beta\varepsilon\acute{\iota}\alpha s$: A. V. *marg.*, "For his piety." But *quaere?*

    12. "For" = $\varkappa\alpha\grave{\iota}\ \gamma\acute{\alpha}\rho$: but at iv. 2, "for indeed" for "for"=the same Greek.

    14. "But solid food is for full grown men" = $\tau\varepsilon\lambda\varepsilon\acute{\iota}\omega\nu\ \delta\acute{\varepsilon}\ \dot{\varepsilon}\sigma\tau\iota\nu\ \dot{\eta}\ \sigma\tau\varepsilon\rho\varepsilon\grave{\alpha}\ \tau\rho o\varphi\acute{\eta}$ = "but for full grown men is the solid food." Where was their faithfulness to Greek order and emphasis and article? "The weeping and gnashing."

VI.

    1. "Wherefore" for "therefore" = $\delta\iota\acute{o}$. But is this better English at the beginning of a paragraph?—"for which" instead of "for this"? And see 2 Cor. iv. 13. "Let us cease to speak of the first principles of Christ" for "leaving the principles of the doctrine of Christ" = $\dot{\alpha}\varphi\acute{\varepsilon}\nu\tau\varepsilon s\ \tau\grave{o}\nu\ \tau\tilde{\eta}s\ \dot{\alpha}\rho\chi\tilde{\eta}s\ \tau o\tilde{v}\ X\rho\iota\sigma\tau o\tilde{v}\ \lambda\acute{o}\gamma o\nu$. The A. V. has the advantage of the literal participial construction, and there is no more in the Greek about "speak" than about "doctrine." After all, have they made the sense any clearer?

    4-6. Are the changes here necessary? Are they authorized? It is not likely that actual historical cases are here described; and the Revisers have no more right to insert "then" before the *falling away* than the A. V. had to insert "if,"—and cf. their own construction at vii. 5 and 1 Cor. viii. 10; xi. 29. The present tenses in verse 6 indicate that probably the preceding aorists are conceived of as perfects. And immediately after, at verse 7, they render ἡ πιοῦσα "that hath drunk,"—not "that drank." (!)

10. "Not unrighteous to forget;" cf. Acts xv. 10. "Showed" and "ministered" for "have," etc.; followed by the present "still do,"—was there an *interval*?

11. "May show" for "do show,"—infinitive with accusative. Better, simply "show."

12. "Imitators" for "followers." So, constantly; but which is the more current English?

13. "Since" for "because" = ἐπεί. Consequential.

15. "And thus" for "and so" = καὶ οὕτω. How faithful! "Having" for "after he had," and what of it?

16. "And in every dispute of theirs, the oath is final for confirmation," for "and an oath for confirmation *is* to them an end of all strife" = Gr., "And of all controversy to them the oath is an end for confirmation." The A. V. is quite as near the Greek as is the Revision.

18. "Lay hold of" for "lay hold upon." (?)

19. "Which we have as . . . a *hope* both sure," etc., for "which *hope* we have as . . . both sure," etc. Is the revised sense quite certain?

VII.

6. "That hath" for "that had" = τὸν ἔχοντα, governed by a verb in the perfect. It means simply "the possessor," and so, here, "that had," if we would have natural English. Cf. xiii. 7; Rev. iv. 9, 10 and v. 1; also xi. 28.

7. "Dispute" for "contradiction" = ἀντιλογία.

11. "Now if" for "if therefore" = εἰ μὲν οὖν. So also at viii. 4. "Arise" for "rise" = ἀνίστασθαι. "Be reckoned" for "be called" = λέγεσθαι, cf. ix. 2.

16. Note: "Indissoluble (ἀκαταλύτου) life" is proved by "priest forever" (εἰς τὸν αἰῶνα); therefore the last phrase means "everlastingly," "without end."

18. "There is a disannulling" (so also A. V.)—not "is

made" = γίνεται. " Of a foregoing" for "of the," etc. ;—
but a *definite* commandment is intended.

20. "The taking of an oath" for "an oath" = ὁρκωμο-
σίας :—no article; and the very same word is immediately
rendered "oath" simply, as in the A. V., and as also at
verse 28.

21, 23. "Have been made" = εἰσὶν γεγονότες = " have
become," or "are (priests) having become (such)." 22.
" Hath become" for " was made" = γέγονεν. Cf. xi. 28 ;
Gal. iii. 17; 2 Cor. ii. 13; John vi. 25, etc.

25. "Draw near unto God" for "come to God" =
προσερχομένους τῷ Θεῷ : see note at x. 1 ; and cf. xi.
6, etc.

26. "Made = γενόμενος,—not " become."
27. "Like" for "as" = ὥσπερ.
28. "Perfected" for "consecrated." (?) So the A. V. in
margin.

VIII.

5. "Who," not "the which" = οἵτινες : " is warned when
he is about to" = κεχρημάτισται μέλλων = "has been
warned when about to."

IX.

1. "Now even" for "then verily . . . also" = μὲν οὖν
καί. It is nothing strange that the first covenant, because it
was first, should have ordinances of divine service ; and so
the "even" would seem out of place. Note the revised rendering of τό τε ἅγιον κοσμικόν :—"its sanctuary, *a sanctuary* of this world" for "a worldly sanctuary." What a
contortion in order to avoid putting "a" for τό,—and yet
putting it after all !

2. "The Holy place" = ἅγια : no "the," no "place,"—
literally, " is called (not "is reckoned") holy." And so
below " Holy of holies," no "the."

4. "Having" for "which had." (?)

11. "Having come" for "being come" = παραγενόμε-
νος. How could this be required by faithfulness ? "Being
come " may be archaic, but is it unintelligible ? The Revi-

sers retain and multiply archaisms ("howbeit," etc.). They even retain the *be* for *have* in unnumbered cases as the auxiliary of *come, go,* etc.; and so, if that is unintelligible they are unfaithful, and if it is intelligible they are inconsistent (" straightway," etc.).

15. "A death" for " death." *His* death is evidently implied in the connection. Cf. verse 1.

16. "The death," subject of φέρεσθαι,—no article. And "death," not "a death," at verse 17. Διαθήκη is translated "covenant" from viii. 6, to this verse; and here, where evidently the same thing is meant, it is translated "testament;" and, again, thenceforward it is rendered "covenant." In the A. V. it is "testament" from verse 15 through the chapter.

17. "Where there hath been death," (*marg.* "over the dead,") for "after men are dead"= ἐπὶ νεκροῖς. Certainly the word is "dead" and not "death."

X.

1. "Them that draw nigh" for "the comers thereunto" = τοὺς προσερχομένους. The Revisers have rendered this verb, with the A. V., 68 times by "come," "come to," "come unto," and at Matt. xxvii. 58; Luke xxiii. 52; Acts ix. 1; xxii. 26, by "went to." They agree with the A. V. in the Gospels throughout, except at Luke vii. 14, where they say "came nigh." They agree with the A. V. in rendering it "draw near" at Acts vii. 31; Heb. x. 22; "go near" at Acts viii. 29; and "consent" at 1 Tim. vi. 3. They put "draw near" for "come to" at Heb. iv. 16 and vii. 25, and here at x. 1, they say "draw nigh" (for a little variety?—see "straightway"). At Heb. xi. 6, where they (with the A. V.) translate it by "come," it is *coming to God;* and so, at xii. 18, 22, "coming to a mount," "to Mount Zion;" and at 1 Pet. ii. 4, "coming to the Lord."

8, 11. "The which" for "which" = αἵτινες. Cf. viii. 5; xiii. 7; 2 Thess. i. 9.

10. "Which" for "the which" = ᾧ. Oh! how faithful!

11. "Day by day" for "daily." (?)

13. "Footstool of his feet"—once more.

16. "*Then saith he*" is an entirely unnecessary insertion. We need only put the semicolon after "make with them;" and a comma after "saith the Lord," and the whole becomes consecutive and clear. See the punctuation of the A. V. in the original prophecy at Jeremiah xxxi. 33.

19. "Holy place" for "Holiest" = τῶν ἁγίων. Also ix. 8. (?).

20. If "way" is repeated, the last ought to be in *italics*. Note their servile construction. Cf. 2 Pet. iii. 1.

23. "That it waver not" for "without wavering" = ἀκλινῆ. Is all that verbal construction in an adjective?

25. Day "drawing nigh" for "approaching" = ἐγγίζουσαν. Required by faithfulness!

28. "A man that hath set at naught" for "he that despised" = ἀθετήσας τις. This is a remarkable case, where the Revisers put a perfect for the preterite of the A. V. in rendering an aorist. And it is further remarkable that just here they are wrong, and the A. V. is probably right; that is to say, the tense should be either preterite or pluperfect,—in no event perfect;—"one (or he) that set (or had set) at nought," or "treated (or had treated) with contempt, . . . died without mercy," etc.

29. "Judged" for "thought" worthy = ἀξιωθήσεται. (?)

30. "Said" for "hath said," aorist. (?)

32. "After ye were enlightened" for "after ye were illuminated" = φωτισθέντες. Here they retain "after," but cf. verses 12 and 36, etc.

37. "He that cometh shall come" for "he that shall come will come" = ὁ ἐρχόμενος ἥξει. Cf. Luke. xviii. 30, "He that is to come."

38. The text in the first clause is changed, by adding μοῦ after δίκαιος, (righteous one). The "and" which begins the second clause does not belong to the quotation, not being in the prophet; see Septuagint; and cf. Luke iv. 11, and above at i. 10, "and, Thou Lord."—The same mode of printing should have been adopted here. The "and" connects two separate quotations; and it is remarkable that, in the prophet, that which is here the second comes first; so that the "he" (or the subject of "shrink back") cannot there

refer to "the righteous one," who is not mentioned till afterward. The Revisers have treated the passage as a citation,—and rightly ; for, if the apostle had constructed his sentence without reference to the prophet, he would naturally have connected the two clauses with δέ and not with καί,—with "but" (as the A. V.) and not with "and." As to the insertion of "any man" by the A. V., see John viii. 44 marg. ; 2 Cor. viii. 12 and 1 Pet. iv. 16, etc.

XI.

1. The margin or the A. V. is to be preferred for ὑπόστασις, "substance;" the text or A. V. for ἔλεγχος, "evidence" or "proving."

5. "Translated" for "had translated," after διότι: but cf. Phil. ii. 26 and 1 Thess. ii. 8.

6. "Is a rewarder,"—not "becomes" = γίνεται.

9. "Became a sojourner . . . in a land not his own" for "sojourned . . . in a strange country" = παρῴκησεν εἰς γῆν . . . ἀλλοτρίαν. But see their own translation at Acts vii. 6, "that his seed should sojourn in a strange land" = ὅτι ἔσται τὸ σπέρμα αὐτοῦ πάροικον ἐν γῇ ἀλλοτρίᾳ. Above they put "became a sojourner" for one aorist verb, παρῴκησεν = "sojourned," and in Acts they put "sojourn" alone for ἔσται πάροικον, which might fairly be rendered "should be (or become) sojourners," — plural, for they immediately say "them" for "seed." And as to their *strange* rendering of ἀλλοτρίαν here, cf. also Matt. xvii. 25 and John x. 5 ("strangers") ; Luke xvi. 12 ; Rom. xiv. 4 ; xv. 20 ; 2 Cor. x. 15, 16 ; 1 Tim. v. 22, ("another's," "another man's," "other men's") ; and verse 34 ("aliens").

11. "Even Sarah herself" for "also Sarah herself." (Cf. "also" for "even," verse 12.) Who should have received the power rather than Sarah herself ? Say rather "by faith, also, Sarah herself (= πίστει καὶ αὐτὴ Σάρρα) received power to conceive seed, even when she was past age" (καὶ παρὰ καιρὸν ἡλικίας). This "even" (καί) they omit entirely. Extraordinary faithfulness! The logic of the case must prevail over the order of the first καί.

12. "Wherefore" for "therefore" = $\delta\iota\acute{o}$: see vi. 1 and cf. 2 Cor. iv. 13. "Also ... of one" for "even of one," cf. verse 11. Literally, "wherefore even of one sprang there —and him already dead (as it were)—so many," etc. Their "also" is, by their own apparent rule, connected solely with "wherefore," implying an added "wherefore," or an added inference, and implying moreover, according to their apparent Greek rule, that the $\varkappa\alpha\acute{\iota}$ stood before the $\delta\iota\acute{o}$.

16. "Hath prepared"—an aorist.

17. In the text, a perfect is designedly and deliberately rendered in the preterite,—see margin;—"offered up" = $\pi\rho o\sigma\varepsilon\nu\acute{\eta}\nu o\chi\varepsilon\nu$: and then an imperfect is carefully rendered "was offering up." Literally, "and his only begotten was he offering up who had (gladly) received the promises, to whom it was (or had been) said," etc. And thus their crabbed and intercalated construction might be quite avoided. They say "that had received" = $\acute{o}\ \acute{\alpha}\nu\alpha\delta\varepsilon\xi\acute{\alpha}\mu\varepsilon$-$\nu o\varsigma$, not, "that received"; but cf. Matt. xxv. 18, 20, 22. For $\pi\rho\grave{o}\varsigma\ \ddot{o}\nu$ the A. V. "of whom" (or "in reference to whom") is better. Their margin, which is the same as the A. V., would require the "he" of their text to be changed to "him" before the "of" of their margin.

19. The A. V. is better, with "him" inserted. What immediately follows implies it. "Parable" here is not English.

21. "When he was a dying" retained = $\acute{\alpha}\pi o\vartheta\nu\acute{\eta}\sigma\varkappa\omega\nu$.

22. "When his end was nigh" = $\tau\varepsilon\lambda\varepsilon\upsilon\tau\tilde{\omega}\nu$.

28. "Kept" = $\pi\varepsilon\pi o\acute{\iota}\eta\varkappa\varepsilon$,— perfect. "That not" for "lest." Wanton faithfulness. Cf. John xii. 40; 1 Tim. iii. 7; Rev. xvi. 15; Matt. xvii. 27; xxvi. 5, etc. "The destroyer of" for "he that destroyed" = $\acute{o}\ \acute{o}\lambda o\theta\rho\varepsilon\acute{\upsilon}\omega\nu$. Cf. xiii. 7; Rev. iv. 9, 10.

30. "After they had been compassed about" for "after they were," etc. = $\varkappa\upsilon\varkappa\lambda\omega\theta\acute{\varepsilon}\nu\tau\alpha$ = "having been compassed about," cf. next verse.

32. What shall I more say? = $\tau\acute{\iota}\ \acute{\varepsilon}\tau\iota\ \lambda\acute{\varepsilon}\gamma\omega$; retained. "If I tell" = $\delta\iota\eta\gamma o\acute{\upsilon}\mu\varepsilon\nu o\nu$: see vi. 6.

35. "Their deliverance;" *marg.* "Gr. the redemption." Say " the *proffered* deliverance,"—if we *must* have " the."

40. "Through their faith" for "through faith" = διὰ τῆς πίστεως. But ἡ πίστις they freely render simply "faith," see James ii. 17, 22; Rom. iii. 25, 30, 31; Gal. iii. 23, etc.

XII.

4, 5. "Have resisted" = ἀντικατέστητε: "have forgotten" = ἐκλέλησθε,—aorist and perfect co-ordinated. See also Acts xxv. 10; Phil. iii. 12; iv. 11; Mark v. 19, etc. Cf. John xvii.

9. "Had" for "have had" = εἴχομεν,—"used to have." "Have had" is as good an expression for it as we can command in English.

11. "Peaceable fruit . . . *even the fruit* of righteousness" for "the peaceable fruit of righteousness." Another wrestling with the article. See also ix. 1; xiii. 20, and Gal. ii. 16, 20. Cf. 2 Tim. iii. 15, *ad fin.*

13. "That not" for "lest" = ἵνα μή. But cf. John xii. 40; 1 Tim. iii. 7; Rev. xvi. 15; Matt. xvii. 27; xxvi. 5, etc.

17. "Desired" for "would have" = θέλων,—"sought to." (?) It is remarkable that in Spanish they use *querer* (from the Latin quaerere), for the French *vouloir*, the German *wollen*, the Latin *volo*, and the Greek θέλω. All these correspond more nearly to our *will* than to our *wish* or *desire*.

22, 23. From the Revisers' suggestion of "a Son of God" at Matt. xxv. 54, and from the rendering "*the* Son of God" at John x. 36; "sons of God" at Rom. viii. 14; "children of God" at John i. 12 and John iii. 3; "sons of thunder," Mark iii. 17; "son of exhortation," Acts iv. 36; "an unknown God," Acts xvii. 23; "a root of all kinds of evil," 1 Tim. vi. 10, etc., etc.,—it would have seemed only consistent if, in this passage, they had translated: "But ye are come to a mount Zion, and unto a city of a living God, a heavenly Jerusalem, and to innumerable hosts of angels, to a general assembly and church of men firstborn enrolled in heaven, and to God a judge of all, and to spirits of just men made perfect, and to Jesus a mediator of a new covenant, and to a blood of sprinkling," etc. At all events, if it is to be, as they translate, "innumerable hosts of angels," then it should also be "a general assembly and church of men firstborn enrolled in heaven" (—not "who are"); and if it is to be "of a new covenant," then it should also be "of a living God." Moreover, "who are enrolled" and "made perfect" they put for perfect participles in the Greek,—not "who have been" and "having been;" but cf. Matt. v. 10, etc.

28. "Offer service well-pleasing" for "serve acceptably" = λατρεύωμεν εὐαρέστως. Cf. Rom. xii. 1, 2—"acceptable;" also Matt. iv. 10; Luke i. 74; iv. 8; Acts vii. 7; xxvi. 7; xxvii. 23, etc.—"serve."

XIII.

1. "Love of the brethren" for "brotherly love" = φιλαδελφία. (?)

7. "Them that had the rule over you, which spake" for "them which have the rule over you, who have spoken"= τῶν ἡγουμένων ὑμῶν, οἵτινες ἐλάλησαν. The present participle they here render as a past, and οἵτινες by "which" and not "the which;"—the change of "who" to "which" seems to have contented them. The ἡγουμένων might be rendered "rulers," without regard to time (see vii. 6); but ἐλάλησαν should rather be rendered, with A. V., as a perfect. The "rulers" spoken of were probably still living and in office; see verse 17. The verb μνημονεύω means simply "think of," "bear in mind."

15. "Then" for "therefore." (?) "A sacrifice" for "the sacrifice," and then "the fruit,"—why? No article in Greek, but see xii. 22, 23.

18. "Desiring" for "willing" = "seeking." (?)

20, 21. "The great shepherd . . . *even* our Lord Jesus" for "our Lord Jesus, that great shepherd." What need of Grecizing? Is the sense affected? "The" for "that" is well enough, though trifling; cf. iv. 3; James ii. 14, etc., etc.

JAMES.

I.

9. "In his high estate" for "in that he is exalted" = ἐν τῷ ὕψει αὐτοῦ, and then "in that he is made low" = ἐν τῇ ταπεινώσει αὐτοῦ. Cf. Luke i. 48, where they render this very ταπείνωσις "low estate." "Straightway"!

11. "Ariseth," "withereth," "falleth," "perisheth," are all for Greek aorists.

12. "Promised" for "hath promised,"—aorist. (?)

15. "Then the lust, when it" for "then when lust . . . it." (?) "The lust," "the sin," for "lust," "sin,"—article generic;—"mint, anise, cummin."

17. "'Boon" for "gift." There is no need of using *two* English words, unless we have fit words to use. The two Greek words are of the same etymology. "Shadow that is cast by turning" for "shadow of turning" = τροπῆς ἀποσκίασμα. How does turning cast a shadow? The A. V. is literal and correct. If we *must* have it explained in the translation, we might say, "shadow whose direction is changed by turning," or, better, "shadow that turneth;" cf. verse 25, "a hearer that forgetteth = ἀκροατὴς ἐπιλησμονῆς.

18. "Of his own will" = βουληθείς,—notice "will," not *wish* or *desire*.

20. "The wrath," "the righteousness,"—no article in the Greek. Why did they not say, "man's wrath worketh not God's righteousness"? Cf. 2 Tim. ii. 24, "the Lord's servant" faithfully substituted for "the servant of the Lord,"—thus making believe to get rid of the article. (?)

25. "The perfect law, the *law* of liberty" for "the perfect law of liberty" = νόμον τὸν τῆς ἐλευθερίας. And why not "a perfect law, the *law*," etc.? Cf. Gal. ii. 20; Heb. ix. 1; xii. 11; 1 Pet. i. 19.—"Being" = γενόμενος,—not "becoming;" "that forgetteth" for "forgetful,"—who is "forgetful" but he "that forgetteth"? = τῆς ἐπιλησμονῆς: "that worketh" for "of the work," = (ποιητής)

ἔργου = "a doer of work," or "the doer of the work." cf. verse 20, etc.

27. "Himself" = one's self. Cf. 1 Thess. iv. 9.

II.

1. "Hold" for "have" = ἔχετε. Cf. Mark xi. 22; Matt. xvii. 20; xxi. 21, etc.,—"have faith."

4. "Are ye not divided . . . and become,"—aorists rendered as presents or perfects. "With" for "of;"—"of" is exact but ambiguous; = κριταὶ διαλογισμῶν πονηρῶν = "judges who are led by, or who think, evil thoughts." For the construction, cf. i. 25.

5. "Did . . . choose" for "hath chosen;" "promised" for "hath promised,"—aorists. (?)

6. "Have dishonored" for "have despised" = ἠτιμάσατε :—aorist; but is not "dishonored" rather too strong—too *positive*—here? Cf. "disbelief."

8. "Howbeit if" for "if" = εἰ μέντοι. The pet "howbeit" again! It seems to stand ready for any Greek particle somewhat obscure or idiomatic. Why not say here, "if now," or "if then," or rather, "if indeed"? See the following εἰ δέ in the apodosis.

12. "Men that are to be judged by a law of liberty" for "they that shall be judged by the law of liberty." What is the advantage of "men that are to be" over "they that shall be"? And as to "a law" for "the law," cf. i. 20; Heb. ix. 15; xii. 5, 22, 23, etc.

13. "Hath shewed"—an aorist.

14. "That faith" for "faith" = ἡ πίστις: but cf. verse 17.

18. "In itself" for "being alone" = καθ' ἑαυτήν. Say "by itself;" the A. V. is not far wrong.

21. "In that" for "when" (he offered) = ἀνενέγκας,— "having offered;" so verse 25.

22. "By works" = ἐκ τῶν ἔργων: "faith" = ἡ πίστις How happened they to forget the articles? Surely it is: "by the works was the faith made perfect," *i.e.*, "by his works was his faith," etc.

III.

1. "Be not" = μὴ γίνεσθε—not "become." "Heavier judgement" for "the greater condemnation." Does not μεῖζον itself show that κρῖμα really means condemnation? With "judgement" they are compelled to assume a change in its proper meaning.

2. "The whole body also" = καὶ ὅλον τὸ σῶμα. Why didn't they say: "even the whole body"? See Luke vii. 49.

6. "The world of iniquity among our members is the tongue" = ὁ κόσμος τῆς ἀδικίας ἡ γλῶσσα καθίσταται ἐν τοῖς μέλεσιν ἡμῶν = "the world of iniquity doth the tongue make itself among our members." They render τὸ ὅλον and ὅλον τό alike, "the whole." See verses 2 and 3, cf. Matt. xxii. 37; Luke x. 27.

10. "Cometh forth" for "proceedeth" = ἐξέρχεται. But the Revisers very often render this verb by "go" instead of "come" forth; in St. Matthew, for example, the instances are two to one. See Matt. ix. 26, 31, 32, etc.

14. "Faction" (in your heart), for "strife" = ἐριθείαν. Faction in the heart?

15. (*A wisdom* that) "cometh down" for "descendeth" = ἐστὶ κατερχομένη. Why not "is coming down" or "descending"? or "is one that cometh down or descendeth." Cf. Col. iii. 10; Matt. xix. 22, also Heb. i. 1, etc.

IV.

4. "Maketh himself" for "is" = καθίσταται. But see iii. 6. Consequential?—"straightway"!

V.

1. "Ye rich" for "ye rich men" = οἱ πλούσιοι. But presumably they were men; and if so the A. V. is the better English. They might have said "ye who are rich," very literally, and idiomatically also.

4. "Who mowed," "reaped" for "have," etc., equivalent to "the mowers," "the reapers of." But, if put in the

verbal form, the more natural English in the connection is in the perfect;—observe " which is (not, which was) kept back."

5, 6. "Have lived," "have taken," "have nourished," "have condemned," "have killed,"—all aorists. So, at verse 11, "have heard," "have seen."

7. "The early and latter rain,"—no article in the Greek.

10. Inversion of order, after the Greek, but not necessary to faithfulness; for the sense is the same, only the A. V. follows the English idiom for emphasis. Cf. 2 Pet. iii. 1.

12. "The heaven," "the earth," for "heaven," "earth." (?) Cf. Matt. xxiv. 35.

16. Having said "the supplication," where there is no article with a nominative case, they might have rendered ἐνεργουμένη, "effectual" or "being effectual" (A. V.) instead of "in its working." ("A righteous man's prayer works with mighty effect.")

I. PETER.

I.

1, 2. There is no Greek article in these verses, but the Revisers have inserted "the" six times. "Elect" they have separated from its connection with "according to," following the Greek construction; but is there any doubt of the sense? Here they seem to have felt the duty of being no clearer than the original.

5. "A salvation" for "salvation"? See verse 9, where they say "the salvation," though there is no more article there than here. There, however, "salvation" is with a genitive; but cf. Luke xix. 9; 1 Thess. v. 9; Heb. i. 14; ii. 3; vi. 9, etc., etc.; where they familiarly use "salvation" in an absolute way;—and it is here, at most, only a question of punctuation.

6. "Have been put to grief" for "are in heaviness" = λυπηθέντες,—literally "were grieved,"—aorist.

7. "Proof" for "trial" = δοκίμιον = "proving"? "Though it is proved" for "though it be;"—the proving is not affirmed, but the Revision makes it seem so.

12. "Have been announced" for "are reported" = ἀνηγγέλη: two forms of the perfect, alike for an aorist.

19. Here is another of the characteristic elaborate inversions to conform to the order of the Greek words. "With precious blood . . . *even the blood* of Christ" for "with the precious blood of Christ." But is it really greater faithfulness to the original, to say "precious blood, *even the blood*," than to say "the precious blood"? If "even the blood" may be implied, cannot "the" be implied, and that too when followed by a genitive? But oh, the modern mysteries of the Greek article! Even if the order of the Greek must be followed, we should still have,—"By the precious blood, as of a lamb without blemish and without spot, of Christ," *i.e.* (re-arranging) exactly as the A.V. stands.

20. Here a Greek perfect and an aorist are co-ordinated, and both rendered in the preterite.

23. "Having been begotten" for "being born;"—but see "it is written."

24. "Withereth," "falleth,"—aorists.

II.

2. "Spiritual" for "of the word" = λογικόν. Marg. "reasonable." So, most of the former translations. The A. V. follows the Geneva version. It is remarkable that for the same word at Rom. xii. 1, the Revisers put "reasonable" in the text and "spiritual" in the margin.

7. "Was made" for "is made" (or "has been made") = ἐγενήθη. (?)

9. "For *God's* own possession" for "peculiar;"—but *his own* is the peculiar meaning of peculiar," from *peculium*.

10. "Which had not obtained mercy, but now have obtained mercy" = οἱ οὐκ ἠλεημένοι, νῦν δὲ ἐλεηθέντες. Note the tenses, and compare i. 20.

11. "Which" = αἵτινες,—not "the which," nor "for they," cf. Heb. x. 8, 11.

12. "Seemly" for "honest." Is this *seemly*? Why not say "honorable" or "becoming?"

15. "By" for "with." But *with* or *in* is certainly more

consonant to the participial construction than "by;" "with well doing" = ἀγαθοποιοῦντας.

19. "Acceptable" for "thankworthy," marg. "Gr. grace;" say rather "Gr. thanks."

24. "Having died unto sins" for "being dead to sins" = ἀπογενόμενοι?—two forms of the perfect, but the former having a preterite meaning.

25. "Ye were going astray like sheep" for "ye were as sheep going astray." Gr. "as sheep ye were going astray." "Are now returned" = ἐπεστράφητε νῦν.

III.

4. "A meek," etc. = τοῦ πραέος, etc. How happened their faithfulness not to say, "the meek and quiet spirit?" Cf. "The sower," etc.; see v. 11, and "the weeping and gnashing," etc. They insert "*apparel*" for "ornament;" but the gender and number in the original require the latter.

6. "Ye now are" for "ye are = ἐγενήθητε. Aorist and no νῦν: cf. ii. 7, where "was made" for "is made."

12. "Upon" for "against." The rendering of ἐπί should of course be changed according to its connection. Does "upon" give the sense here in English?

14. "But and if," again; here for ἀλλ' εἰ καί. See 1 Cor. vii. 11 and 2 Cor. iv. 3.

20. "Wherein" = εἰς ἥν. Marg. to be preferred, *i.e.* "entering into which."

21. "Interrogation" = ἐπερώτημα. Marg. better, *i.e.* "the appeal of a good conscience to God." (Note, if it was the *ark* that saved the others, *i.e.* brought them safely through the water, how should it be "after a true likeness" that the *water* should now save us? It would seem that it must be, not the water that saves, but baptism in its concrete spiritual sense, as an act of faith and of a good conscience.)

IV.

1. "Suffered" = παθόντος, by the preterite when spoken of Christ; "hath suffered" = παθών, by the perfect, of the

Christian. What becomes then of the faithfulness of persistently rendering ἀπέθανε, "died," when speaking of the Christian as well as of Christ?

3. "And to have walked" for "when we walked" = πεπορευμένους = "having walked" or "while we have walked." Cf. the change made in verse 8, in just the contrary sense.

5. "Who;" but is not this ambiguous? Why did they not render, "and they" or "but they" or "for they," as they do sometimes elsewhere?

6. "Even to the dead" for "also to them that are dead" = καὶ νεκροῖς: i.e. "to them also that are (now) dead;" say, then, "to the dead also."

10. "Hath received" = an aorist. "A gift" for "the gift" =χάρισμα. (?) Cf. v. 1.

11. "Any man" = τις,—not "any one." "As it were oracles of God" for "as the oracles of God" = ὡς λόγια Θεοῦ. Cf. v. 1, and ῥῆμα Θεοῦ at Heb. vi. 5 and xi. 3, and see John vi. 68; James v. 16, etc. See also "the manifold grace of God," just before, without Greek article; and why should ὡς be rendered "as" immediately before and after, but "as it were" here?

V.

1. "The elders,"—no article; in the direct accusative. Cf. Eph. iii. 15.

2. "Of constraint" for "by constraint" = ἀναγκαστῶς. Wherefore the change? Did they suppose that "by constraint" might be understood for "by constraining"? So may "of constraint" be understood for "of constraining" if one *will*. But the next words forbid any such interpretation.

4. "Shall receive" = κομιεῖσθε,—not, "receive again." But see Matt. xxv. 27; Eph. vi. 8; Col. iii. 25; Heb. xi. 19; where they put "receive back" or "again," for "receive;" while at i. 9; 2 Cor. v. 10; Heb. x. 36; xi. 39, they render as here, simply "receive."

5. "To serve one another" = ἀλλήλοις, "for" or "towards one another." They use no italics here.

9. Marg. "Gr. being accomplished" = ἐπιτελεῖσθαι = "to be accomplished." Do they mean that it is, "to be being accomplished"?

12. "Have written" = ἔγραψα.

II. PETER.

I.

1, 3. "That have obtained" = τοῖς λαχοῦσι (aorist), and then (3) "that called" for "that hath called" = τοῦ καλέσαντος. "Virtue" = ἀρετῆς :—being referred to God, it had better be "excellency," as at 1 Pet. ii. 9.

7. "In love of the brethren supply love" for "to brotherly kindness add charity." If "love" is to be substituted for "charity" = ἀγάπη, "brotherly kindness" is surely better than "love of the brethren," not only for sound's sake, but because the Greek word (φιλία) for the love that is "kindness" is different from that (ἀγάπη) for the "love" that is "charity." The simple reader might, from the Revision, suppose them to be the same; and then be puzzled to know how, "in love of the brethren," "love" was to be "supplied." And, in general, this "supplying in" may be very good Greek, but after all "adding to" expresses the same sense in better English.

12. "Are established" = ἐστηριγμένους,—not "have been established."

14. "Signified" for "hath showed" = ἐδήλωσε. But there is nothing expressed about the mode of showing,—no sign or token referred to. Cf. Rev. i. 1.

18. "We ourselves" for "we" = ἡμεῖς: but cf. Tit. iii. 3, where they correct just contrariwise.

II.

12. "Creatures without reason, born mere animals" for "natural brute beasts, made," etc. There is nothing in the text of "creatures," and "mere animals" is put for "natural beasts" (ζῶα φυσικά). Does the slight change of order in the new text necessitate all this change, and is it an improvement? If ζῶα is to be rendered "living creatures,"

it does not follow that we can drop the "living" and retain the "creatures." "Living" is the essence of the original word, and "creatures" no more belongs to it, and has no more right to represent it, than would "things" or "objects," after having been inserted with "living."

15. "Went astray, having followed" for "have gone astray, following." (Aorists.) But did they "follow" before "forsaking the right way," and before they "went astray"? And why did the Revisers not say "a right way" as well as "a root of evil"? They have no article in their text, and it is a direct accusative, without a genitive.

16. "A dumb ass spake with man's voice and stayed" for "the dumb ass speaking with man's voice forbad" = ὑποζύγιον ἄφωνον, ἐν ἀνθρώπου φωνῇ φθεγξάμενον, ἐκώλυσε. For the article, compare "the dog" and "the sow," at verse 22; and for the construction of the participle, as well as for the article, compare "forsaking the right way" at verse 15.

17. "Hath been reserved" for "is reserved;" but see "it is written;" and see next below.

19. "Is overcome," "is brought,"—perfects.

20, 21. "After they have escaped,"—aorist participle. "After knowing" for "after they have known,"—also an aorist participle.

22. Why not translate *faithfully*, and say: "a dog when he turned upon his own vomit again, and a sow when she washed herself to wallowing in mire"?

III.

1. "This is now, beloved, the second epistle that I write unto you; and in both of them," etc., for "This second epistle, beloved, I now write unto you, in both which," etc. The A. V. is here an exact literal translation of the Greek, unless the position of the "now" should be called in question; and is it not intelligible, if the R. V. is? What then of "faithfulness"? In the original, "epistle" is in the accusative case after "write," and there is neither "is" nor "that;" and the whole phrase of the R. V., "and in both of them," is, in the Greek, simply ἐν αἷς, as in A. V., "in

both which." It may be said the literal translation is harsh and the R. V. is smoother; but this the Revisers can scarcely urge without abundant self-contradiction. Cf. Mark v. 15; Acts xxvi. 24; Rom. i. 3, 4; viii. 28, 38, 39; Gal. ii. 9; Eph. v. 12, 20; Heb. x. 20; Ja. v. 10, etc.

2. "Should" for "may." Why?

3. "That in the last days mockers shall come" for "that there shall come in the last days scoffers" = ὅτι ἐλεύσονται ἐπ' ἐσχάτων τῶν ἡμερῶν ἐμπαῖκται. The A. V. follows the exact order and sense of the original. The "with mockery" of the new reading could be added perfectly well after "scoffers" or "mockers." Do the Revisers pretend to set English euphony against the order and form of the Greek text?

5. "That there were heavens from of old, and an earth compacted out of water and amidst water, by the word of God; by which means," etc. Transposing the phrase "by the word of God," a very literal translation of the Greek would stand thus: "That, by the word of God, heaven was from of old, and earth of water and in water consisting; by means of which," etc. One would understand from the Revision—and perhaps it was intended to be so understood—that the "compacting" (συνεστῶσα = "consisting"), and not "heaven and earth," was "by the word of God;" and "by which means" (δι' ὧν) might in English be also referred to "the word of God," instead of the conditions of the earth as related to water.

9. "Not wishing" for "not willing" = μὴ βουλόμενος.(?) Cf. 3 John 13. "Not designing," or "not intending," or "not being pleased." "Wishing" seems too idle a thing to predicate of God.

14. "In his sight" for "of him," = αὐτῷ.

16. "All his epistles" = πάσαις ἐπιστολαῖς. Cf. Rev. iii. 2. "Ignorant" for "unlearned" = ἀμαθεῖς. "Ignorant" is elsewhere always a translation from ἀγνοέω.

17. "Lest" = ἵνα μή. See Heb. xii. 13, note.

I. JOHN.

I.

1. "Beheld" for "have looked upon" (cf. John iv. 35). It is not likely that the apostle means to make a distinction between the time of the " seeing" and of the "beholding," although he says ἑωράκαμεν and ἐθεασάμεθα:—both forms being so used in Greek as to be properly expressed by our perfect, while our preterite and perfect are not thus interchangeable. For some of the cases in which the Revisers have rendered the Greek aorist and perfect co-ordinated as perfects, cf. Acts xxv. 10, 11; xxi. 21–24; John xiii. 14, 15; Matt. xxvi. 12, 13 (an aorist as a preterite and then a perfect); Phil. iii. 12; iv. 11, 12; Rev. xviii. 2, 3; and especially Acts xxii. 15. The repetition of "that which" is unnecessary and not literal. " What" might have been literal, and, so, repeated.

2. " The life, the eternal *life*" for "that eternal life" = τὴν ζωὴν τὴν αἰώνιον. But see the "daily bread" of the Lord's Prayer, etc. As for the construction and the emphatic "that" of the A. V., cf. Eph. i. 13, 19; James ii. 14, etc.

II.

5. "Hath been perfected" for "is perfected" = τετελείωται. Cf. τετέλεσται, John xix. 30, and see below, iv. 12, 17, and v. 1; where we have τετελειωμένη ἐστίν rendered "is perfected," and this very τετελείωται rendered "is made perfect," and γεγέννηται rendered "is begotten."

7. "No new commandment write I" for "I write no new commandment." But cf. 2. Thess. iii. 2, where the order of the Greek is (what there, too, logic requires) "not all have faith." Here one order is as logical and as intelligible as the other, with precisely the same sense. If *emphasis* is appealed to, it will apply in Thess. as well as here.

8. "Write I" for "I write." Oh, exquisite faithfulness!

11. "Hath blinded,"—an aorist.

13, 14. "Have written" (tris)—an aorist.
15. "Any man" = τις,—not their usual "any one."
18. "Heard" for "have heard." (?)
19. The marg., "That not all are of us," is singularly ἄτοπον, as being contrary to the order of the Greek and inconsistent with the manifest sense and logic of the passage. Cf. 2 Thess. iii. 2, also 1 Cor. vi. 12.
24. "Heard from the beginning" for "have heard," etc.
26. "Have I written,"—an aorist. "Would lead astray" for "seduce" = πλανώντων. There is nothing for "would;"—faithfulness.
27. "Received," "taught," for "have," etc. (?)
28. "At his coming" = ἐν τῇ παρουσίᾳ. Cf. Phil. ii. 10, ἐν τῷ ὀνόματι Ἰησοῦ.

III.

1. "For this cause" for "therefore" = διὰ τοῦτο, and then "because" (euphony?). They themselves render διὰ τοῦτο by "therefore" at iv. 5; Matt. vi. 25; xii. 27; xiii. 13, 52; xiv. 2; xviii. 23; xxi. 43; xxiv. 44; Mark vi. 14; xi. 24; Luke xi. 19, 49; xii. 22; xiv. 20; John ix. 23; xiii. 11; xv. 19; xvi. 15; xix. 11; Acts ii. 26; 2 Cor. iv. 1; vii. 13; 2 Tim. ii. 10; Philemon 15; Heb. i. 9; ii. 1; Rev. vii. 15; xii. 12; xviii. 8; and at John x. 17, where it is followed by "because," just as it is here. They have put "for this cause" instead of "therefore" at Mark xii. 24; John i. 31; v. 16, 18; vi. 65; vii. 22; viii. 47; xii. 39; Rom. iv. 16; 2 Cor. xiii. 10; 1 Thess. iii. 7, and here. Under these circumstances of course Greek scholarship can decide nothing. Let every intelligent reader, noting the context in each case, say whether it was not possible to avoid making these changes consistently with faithfulness. To my own apprehension they are not even improvements in any sense or degree; but, in the case before us, for example, the change seems to me decidedly and entirely for the worse. At all events, think of "straightway," and remember that διὰ ταύτην αἰτίαν is the proper Greek for "for this cause;" see Acts xxviii. 20, etc.

3. "Every one" for "every man." Cf. ii. 15.

4. "Every one that" for "whosoever" = πᾶς ὁ. This is a frequent correction of the faithfulness of the Revisers. But see the 6th, 9th, 10th, and 15th verses of this very chapter, where we have "whosoever" for πᾶς ὁ five times over.

8. "To this end" for "for this purpose" = εἰς τοῦτο. To what purpose the change?

9. "Is begotten" (bis) for the perfect. Cf. ii. 5.

16. "Hereby know we love,"—τὴν ἀγάπην = "his love"? "He" immediately follows without antecedent. But cf. Rom. v. 9, "The wrath *of God*" = τῆς ὀργῆς.

17. "Beholdeth" is dragged in again for θεωρῇ: but with it they have "shutteth up" for κλείσῃ. How happened they to overlook that this last is an aorist and requires "shall shut up"?

24. "Gave" for "hath given." (?)

IV.

6. "Who for "that;" why? "Heareth us not" for "heareth not us;" why? Faithfulness! In "heareth us," here, the "us" is not enclitic, but has an accent or emphasis; and therefore in the contrasted phrase "heareth not us," propriety of utterance requires "us" to come last.

V.

4. "That hath overcome" for "that overcometh" = ἡ νικήσασα, literally, "that overcame." See verse 6, "that came" = ὁ ἐλθών: and verse 18, ὁ γεννηθείς = "that was begotten;" and this last is expressly contradistinguished from a perfect participle, ὁ γεγεννημένος, which is rendered "is begotten." Why not then, here, say, "that overcometh," if it is once assumed that ἡ νικήσασα may be rendered as if it were a perfect or present? And see Matt. iii. 17, "in whom I am well pleased."

9. "For the witness of God is this, that he hath borne witness," etc., for "For this is the witness of God, which

he hath testified," etc. Their Greek will permit the rendering, " For this is the witness of God (for he hath borne witness," etc.) See verse 11 for the *content* of the testimony ; and see 2 John 6 for the construction of " this."

16. " Not concerning this do I say that he should make request" for " I do not say that he should pray for it" = οὐ περὶ ἐκείνης λέγω ἵνα ἐρωτήσῃ. Cf. 2 Thess. iii. 2, etc.

19. " Lieth in the evil one" for " lieth in wickedness" = ἐν τῷ πονηρῷ. (? ?) Grant the sense ; is this English ?

II. JOHN.

4. " I rejoice" for " I rejoiced" = ἐχάρην : with " have found" for " found," perfect. Cf. 3 John 3. " Commandment" for " a commandment" = ἐντολήν. But what's the difference ? And if there is any, how did the Greek determine for them which to prefer ? As for the rendering of the perfect by "found" in the A. V., cf. Gal. iii. 17 ; Heb. xi. 17, 28 ; 2 Cor. ii. 13 ; John vi. 25 ; Matt. xiii. 46 ; 1 Pet. i. 20 ; Mark xv. 47 (plup. ?).

7. " Are gone forth"—an aorist. " *Even* they that confess not" for " who confess not" = οἱ μὴ ὁμολογοῦντες. Cf. Rom. ix. 5 ; John xix. 39, etc., etc.

III. JOHN.

5. " A faithful work in" for " faithfully" = πιστόν. There is no word for " work." " Doest" = ποιεῖς and ἐργάσῃ alike. Render, "thou doest faithfully whatever thou workest" ?

7. " The name" for " his name" = τοῦ ὀνόματος. (?) " His name" in St. John's language means Christ's name, and that is what is meant here.

13. " Am unwilling" for " will not" = οὐ θέλω. Cf. 2 Peter iii. 9, where they say of *the Lord* " not wishing."

JUDE.

1. They say "Jude" in the title and then "Judas" in the text. Is the epistle ascribed to the wrong person? "For Jesus Christ" for "in Jesus Christ." The ἐν naturally and probably goes over from ἐν Θεῷ πατρί: or else "Jesus Christ" may be in the instrumental dative. How happened they thus to transpose "called" from its proper position in the text?

3. "I was constrained" for "it was needful for me" = ἀνάγκην ἔσχον. The "diligence" is consistent with "need," but is it with "constraint"?

4. "*Even* they who" for "who" = οἱ. But cf. verse 6, John xix. 39; Rom. ix. 5, etc. "Were set forth" for "were ordained" = οἱ προγεγραμμένοι. Where does "set forth" come from? And why did they not say "have been set forth"? This is a perfect participle, and belongs to the subject of another (English) perfect,—not a preterite. Cf. Rev. v. 12.

5. "A people" for "the people" = λαόν, *i.e.* λαὸν Ἰσραήλ. The Israelites are plainly referred to; and "the people" is the more natural English.

10. "Whatsoever things" for "those things which" = ὅσα—"as many things as." Immediately after, they (with the A. V.) render ὅσα by "what." If "whatsoever" differs from "what" or "those which," one or the other of their renderings is wrong, and their change from the A. V. is without reason, or worse. "Creatures without reason" for "brute beasts" = ἄλογα ζῶα. But ζῶα does not mean mere "creatures," but "animals" or "beasts," or, at most, "living creatures;" and the "living" is essential.

11. "Woe unto them;"—better, "alas for them." "Went" for "have gone," and so on; but these aorists are required, by their relation to presents, to be rendered as perfects.

13. "Hath been reserved" for "is reserved;" but see "it is written."

15. "Have wrought," "have spoken,"—aorists.

24. "To set without blemish" for "to present faultless"

= στῆσαι ἀμώμους. (?) "Without stumbling" for "from falling" = ἀπταίστους. See also "stumble," James iii. 2; but compare σκανδαλίζω and "straightway."

REVELATION.

I.

1. "Signified" = ἐσήμαινεν: right, but cf. 2 Peter i. 14.
4. "Which is to come" = ὁ ἐρχόμενος: right, but cf. Matt. xi. 3; Heb. x. 37, etc.
5, 6. "Loosed" and "made" for "hath," etc. (?)
9, 10. "I was" = ἐγενόμην.
13. "A son of man" for "the Son of man" = υἱῷ ἀνθρώπου. But see "the voice of many waters" at verse 15; and see ii. 18:—He was "the Son of God."
15. "As if it had been refined" for "as if they burned" = πεπυρωμένης for πεπυρωμένοι. What is the syntax of this reading? What is the "it" which "had been refined"? "Brass"? But χαλκολιβάνῳ is of the neuter gender. The Vatican MS. and Tischendorf (3d) read as A. V. "As the voice of many waters" = ὡς φωνή, etc. Why not "a voice"? Cf. verse 13, and vi. 1.

II.

2–9. Here are six aorists co-ordinated with two perfects, all of which should be rendered as perfects. Cf. Acts xxi. 21–24; Phil. iii. 12; iv. 11, 12; John xiii. 14, 15; Matt. xxvi. 12, 13; Rev. xxviii. 2, 3; Acts xxv. 10, 11; Mark v. 19; Heb. xii. 45.

9. "A synagogue" for "the synagogue,"—predicate.
12. "The sharp two-edged sword" for "the sharp sword with two edges" = τὴν ῥομφαίαν τὴν δίστομον τὴν ὀξεῖαν. How important the difference! How impossible consistently with faithfulness to avoid the change! And how could they consistently with faithfulness fail to say: "the sharp, the two-edged sword," or rather, "the sword, *even* the two-edged, the sharp one"? Let us, by all means, have the full force of the Greek; did they not see all those

articles? Surely they are not so repeated for nothing; and cf. the next verse.

13. "My witness, my faithful one" for "my faithful martyr" = ὁ μάρτυς μου ὁ πιστός μου. Cf. the "daily bread" of the Lord's Prayer. And as for the term "martyr," this was plainly a "martyr" in the full modern sense, *i.e.*, one who died in attestation of the truth.

23. "Each one of you" for "every one of you." The Revisers often render ἕκαστος by "every," and if it may be so rendered anywhere, why not here?

III.

2. "Be thou watchful" for "be watchful" = γίνου γρηγορῶν. "Works of thine" for "thy works" = σου ἔργα. Very nice; but cf. 2 Cor. vi. 16; Eph. ii. 10; Rom. ix. 7; 2 Pet. iii. 16.

3. A co-ordinated perfect and aorist here distinguished. See ii. 2–9, note.

4. "Did not defile" for "have not defiled." (?)

5. "In no wise" for "not" = οὐ μή. But at verse 3 they had just rendered these particles by the simple "not."

8. "A door opened" for "an open door" = θύραν ἀνεῳγμένην. How necessary to faithfulness! "That" for "for" = ὅτι. This may be well here; cf. verses 2 and 4. Here are two aorists, and another at verse 10, which should have been rendered perfects instead of preterites, as appears from their connection and co-ordination with verbs in the present as well as in the perfect tense.

12. "*I will write upon him*" is omitted; but is the sense expressed clearly? Is the omission *necessary* to "faithfulness"?

17. "Have gotten riches" for "am increased in goods" = πεπλούτηκα. (?)

19. The emphatic ἐγώ is not so rendered; cf. 2 Pet. i. 18.

IV.

2. "There was a throne set" for "a throne was set" = θρόνος ἔκειτο. Say: "a throne was set, and there was one

sitting upon the throne." "There was" does not belong where they have put it. It implies κείμενος (for ἔκειτο), like the following καθήμενος. Cf. Matt. ii. 18.

3. "To look upon" for "in sight" = ὁράσει. Faithful?

4. "Thrones" for "seats;" literal consequential faithfulness. But is it not rather "seats" always, if we *must* always have one word? We have two English words for the one Greek word; but, while every "throne" in English is a "seat," not every "seat" is a "throne."

7. "Creature" = ζῶον : again, without "living." How is the English reader to know that these "creatures" in the 7th verse are living, as well as those in the 6th and the 8th? And see "straightway;" also Acts xxvi. 24, 25; 1 Cor. xv. 27, 28.

V.

3. "In the heaven" for "in heaven" = ἐν τῷ οὐρανῷ : but cf. iv. 1, where they say "in heaven" for the same ἐν τῷ οὐρανῷ.

6. "As though it had been slain" for "as it had been slain." But cf. viii. 8; Acts vi. 15; ix. 18; and x. 11, where they introduce no "though."

7. "Came and taketh" for "came and took,"—marg. "hath taken" = ἦλθε καὶ εἴληφε. What contortions! Manifestly these two tenses are here co-ordinated, and are both to be rendered as perfect, or both as preterite.

11. "Ten thousand times ten thousand" is equal only to μυριάς μυριάδων. Μυριάδες μυριάδων should be rendered "ten thousands of ten thousands." "Ten thousand times ten thousand" is just 100,000,000; but μυριάδες μυριάδων is several times 100,000,000; and is, I believe, the largest expression of number found in the Bible. The "two myriads of myriads" of ix. 16 is the *least* number included under this *plural*.

12. "Great voice" for "loud voice" = φωνὴ μεγάλη. It is curious that the Revisers make everybody in the book of the Revelation, whether man or angel, cry with a "great" voice. They have changed "loud" to "great" twelve times; but in one instance, at xix. 17,—by way of being "straightway" consistent—they let the angel cry with a "loud" voice.

In the other books of the New Testament, they always let people cry with a "loud" voice,—an expression which, in those books, occurs some twenty times. The original word is the same throughout. One is tempted to inquire what there was special in the air of the Apocalypse which hindered a "great" voice from being "loud"?

13. "The blessing, the honour," etc., for "blessing, honour," etc.; and so at iv. 11; v. 13, etc. But cf. vii. 10, 12 and xix. 1, where they omit the articles; and so make the current, as well as the good old, English. But see "the weeping and gnashing" at Matt. viii. 12, etc.

VI.

1. "As with a voice of thunder" for "as it were the noise of thunder" = ὡς φωνὴ (not φωνῆς) βροντῆς = "as it were the voice of thunder." For "as it were" see viii. 8, and for "the voice" (not "a voice") see i. 15.

2. "Came forth" for "went forth" = ἐξῆλθε. "There was given" for "was given." (?)—As to *came* or *went*, the question is whether the movement is to be conceived as *towards* the speaker, or as *across* his vision,—or, perhaps, *away from him;* and whether from an objective or subjective point of view.

3. "Opened" for "had opened." But either may be used; and so the A. V. used both. As to the Revision, cf. v. 8 and x. 10, for examples of the pluperfect rendering.

4. "And another horse came forth, a red horse" for "and there went out another horse, *that was* red" = ἐξῆλθεν ἄλλος ἵππος πυρρός. For the order, cf. the next clause and verse 2. Is "a horse, a red horse" better than "a horse, *that was* red"? And if the A. V may be interpreted as meaning "another red horse," so may the R. V., after all.

8. "With" = ἐν (tris).

9. "Had been slain" for "were slain" = ἐσφαγμένων. But these are merely two forms in English for the same tense. The A. V. is the simpler and more natural. Cf. xx. 12, "out of the things which were written" = ἐκ τῶν γεγραμμένων. And compare vii. 5–8, where ἐσφραγισμένοι

is rendered "were sealed" twelve times, though "were sealed," there, can scarcely be understood as pluperfect.

12. "There was" = ἐγένετο,—not "came" or "followed," cf. viii. 1, etc.

VII.

1. "That no wind should" for "that the wind should not" = ἵνα μὴ πνέῃ ἄνεμος = "that wind should not blow." Cf. 1 Cor. ii. 9 and Luke xxii. 34. An articular throe.

2. "Great" for "loud" (voice), again. See v. 12, note.

3. "Till we shall have sealed" for "till we have sealed." But one is only the shortened, and the ordinary and easy, form for the other. Cf. their own translation at John viii. 28; Rom. xi. 25; Gal. iv. 19 ("be" for "shall be"); 1 Cor. xi. 26, "come" for "shall come;" etc., etc,

12. "Blessing and glory and wisdom," etc. Here they at length omit the articles with which they encumber the sense elsewhere. Cf. iv. 11; v. 13, etc.; also Matt. viii. 12, etc., "the weeping."

14. "I say" for "I said" = εἴρηκα, followed immediately by the co-ordinated εἶπε = "he said." (?)

15. "Spread his tabernacle" for "dwell." Cf. xxi. 3, and John i. 14.

VIII.

1. "There followed a silence" for "there was silence" = ἐγένετο σιγή. But see verse 7 and vi. 12 and xvi. 18. And what would be the Greek for "silence," which should be neither "the silence" nor "a silence"? "In heaven" = ἐν τῷ οὐρανῷ.

2. "There were given unto them" for "to them were given" = ἐδόθησαν αὐτοῖς. Cf. Matt. x. 32, 33, and Mark iii. 17, "them he surnamed" for "he surnamed them" = ἐπέθηκεν αὐτοῖς ὀνόματα.

3. "Add it unto the prayers" for "offer [give] it with the prayers." So the margin of A. V. But cf. the next verse, where they say "with the prayers" for the very same construction, *i.e.* the simple dative with a verb of action.

5. "Taketh" for "took" = εἴληφεν, "and filled" = ἐγέμισεν. Here again we have a perfect coördinated with

an aorist, where both should be translated either in the perfect or in the preterite (see note, ii. 2–9). "Followed" for "were" = ἐγένοντο: but cf. xvi. 18, etc. It is true that, in verse 7, the A. V. put "followed" for ἐγένετο: but they professedly study variety; and why should the Revisers change in *some* places, while yet they retain the *variety?* Remember "straightway."

9. "Even they that had" for "that had" = τὰ ἔχοντα. This follows the change of case; but does it give the real sense? Is it meant that *all* that had life died? or only a third part of them?

10. "From heaven a great star,"—ἐκ τοῦ οὐρανοῦ. See also ix. 1. Not "out of heaven," nor "out of the heaven."

IX.

1. "Heaven" and "the earth;"—both with articles in the Greek. Cf. vi. 13, and Acts iv. 24.

6. "Men shall seek" for [then] "shall men seek" = ζητήσουσιν οἱ ἄνθρωποι. "In no wise" for "not" = οὐ μή. But cf. iii. 3, etc.

7. "Men's faces" for "the faces of men" = πρόσωπα ἀνθρώπων,—as though, in English, the one did not imply the article which the other expresses. Is not the change simply *puerile?* And why did not the learned Revisers say "women's hair" for "the hair of women" = τρίχας γυναικῶν, immediately afterwards? According to their apparent principles of translation one would have a right to infer that there was an article with "the hair" and none with "faces." Yet they are inconsistent even with their apparent principle; for, at x. 10, they render ἐκ τῆς χειρὸς τοῦ ἀγγέλου "out of the angel's hand;" while at Matt. xii. 40, they change "the whale's belly" into "the belly of the whale." And then, too, what becomes of the articular precision of "the Lord's servant" at 2 Tim. ii. 24?

9. "War" for "battle" = πόλεμον. But the context requires "battle." See note, 1 Cor. xiv. 8.

14. "At the great river Euphrates" = τῷ ποταμῷ τῷ μεγάλῳ Εὐφράτῃ. Why did they not say: "the river, *even* the great," etc.? Cf. xiv. 19, etc.

17. "Breastplates *as* of fire" for "breastplates of fire." The A. V. is faithful. "As heads of lions" follows in the Greek with ώς: there is therefore a difference in the two cases. "Like brimstone" they might have said, for the Greek has θειώδεις.

19, 20. "With" = ἐν (bis).

20. "Devils and the idols" = τὰ δαιμονια καὶ τὰ εἴδωλα—alike with the article in the Greek.

X.

1. "Arrayed" for "clothed" = περιβεβλημένον. Why didn't they say, "enveloped in," and have done with it? The A. V., indeed, uses "arrayed" elsewhere; but why should faithfulness require a change here? What is the difference? See note, at viii. 5, upon ἐγένετο.

4. "A voice from heaven" = φωνὴν ἐκ τοῦ οὐρανοῦ: and so at xiv. 13 and xviii. 4. But cf. Matt. iii. 17; Mark i. 11, "a voice out of the heavens" = φωνὴ ἐκ τῶν οὐρανῶν: and Luke iii. 22; John xii. 28; Acts xi. 9, etc., "out of heaven" = ἐκ τοῦ οὐρανοῦ.

7. "Is finished,"—an aorist.

9. "Saying unto him that he should give me" = λέγων αὐτῷ δοῦναί μοι (a new text) = "telling (or asking) him to give me." And see "to" for "unto" at ii. 1, 8, 12, 18; iii. 1, 7, 14, etc., etc. Yet here, in an original translation of theirs, and having no A. V. to correct, they say "unto"! What irresistible constraint of faithfulness! See Acts xxi. 21, note.

10. "When I had eaten" = ὅτε ἔφαγον: but cf. "opened" for "had opened" (with the 2d and the 7th seals).

XI.

2. "Nations" for "Gentiles;" but cf. Luke xxi. 24; Rom. ix. 24, etc. The "nations" are here contradistinguished from the Jews.

3. "Give" for "give *power*." But what, then, *do* they give?

5. "Desireth to" for "will" = θέλει: and so again in this, and in the 6th verse. But is it the mere *desire* that is

meant, without the executive purpose or volition? There is no ambiguity in the A. V. from the use of *will*, for it cannot properly stand in these connections as the auxiliary to form the future tense;—that would be *shall*.

10. "Dwell" for "dwelt." But see "tormented." The tense of the participle in the translation follows that of the governing verb. See xiv. 18. "He called to him that had the sharp sickle," where "him that had" is for a present participle.

17. "Hast taken and didst reign;"—another instance of εἴληφας coördinated with an aorist. Cf. viii. 5; v. 7, there rendered by a present.

18. "The small and the great" for "small and great;" but cf. "heaven and earth," Luke xxi. 33, etc.

19 and 15. "Followed" for "were" = ἐγένοντο. So the A. V. at viii. 7; but see vi. 12; Matt. viii. 26, etc.; and note at viii. 5.

XII.

5. "Was delivered of" for "brought forth" = ἔτεκεν: consequential; — but see verse 13, where they render "brought forth" for this identical case, word, and tense.

15. "River," "stream" = ποταμόν, ποταμοφόρητον— for "flood" in both cases (fluvius). Cf. "straightway," and Acts xxvi. 24; 1 Cor. xv. 27, 28.

17. "Waxed wroth" for "was wroth" = ὠργίσθη. Cf. Matt. xviii. 34; xxii. 7; Luke xiv. 21; xv. 28; and above at xi. 18, where they translate by "being wroth" or "angry;"—consequential? "Straightway." "Hold" for "have" = ἐχόντων :—consequential again?

XIII.

6. "*Even* them that dwell in the heaven." Here heaven seems to be the abode of the blessed, and not the visible sky; and yet they give it the article in English.

8. "Hath been written" for "is [are] written" = γέγραπται! "That hath been slain" for "slain" = τοῦ ἐσφαγμένου. (?)

10. "With" = ἐν (bis).

12. "Death stroke" for "deadly wound" = πληγὴ τοῦ

θανάτου. *Death stroke* is often used in English for no "wound" (πληγή) at all.

13. "That he should make" for "so that he maketh" = ἵνα ποιῇ. (?) Cf. verse 15.

15. "That the image should," etc. (ἵνα). Here "that" = "so that." Cf. 13, and the relation in the two cases.

16. "The small and the great, and the rich and the poor, and the free and the bond" for "both small and great, rich and poor," etc. What is the difference in the sense? And see "heaven and earth," etc., etc. "That there be given them" for "to receive" = ἵνα δῶσιν αὐτοῖς = "that they should give them." So, after all, the Revisers are not *literal*, if that is what is meant by *faithful ;* and meantime the A. V. gives the simple resultant sense.

17. "He that hath" for "he that had" = ὁ ἔχων :—then they should have omitted their "should" just before, as in verse 16.

XIV.

2. "As the voice" (bis) ; no article in the Greek.

3. "Out of the earth" for "from the earth" = ἀπὸ τῆς γῆς.

6. "An eternal Gospel" for "the everlasting Gospel." No article in the Greek; but *quære?* and cf. "the heavenly Jerusalem." "To proclaim" for "to preach" = εὐαγγελίσαι. But cf. Matt. xi. 5; Luke iii. 18; iv. 18, 43; xvi. 16; 1 Cor. i. 17; Gal. i. 8; Eph. ii. 17.

11. "They that worship." There is no ground in the Greek for this repeated "they." Cf. John ii. 9, where they do not say "the servants, they which." "Whoso" = εἴ τις = "if any one." Cf. xx. 15, where they substitute "if any" for "whosoever." Cf. also verse 9.

12. "They that" for "here *are* they that." The insertion is grammatically necessary, although the "here" is not repeated in the new text.

14. "A son of man" for "the Son of man." Wherefore, then, "son" at all? Why "a son of man" rather than simply "a man," if that is all that is meant? Christians had, from prophecy, from Jewish tradition, and from the teaching of our Lord, a vivid idea of the glory of "the Son

of man." See Stephen's dying vision. Even if it was "a son of man" to the prophet Daniel, it was nevertheless "the Son of man" to those who applied the prophecy. The angel, in verse 15, may utter a prayer or request rather than a command.

16. "Cast his sickle upon the earth" for "thrust in his sickle," etc., = ἔβαλεν τὸ δρέπανον αὐτοῦ ἐπὶ τὴν γῆν. What does this mean? faithfulness to the Greek βάλλω? But compare verse 15; and see Matt. x. 34, where they say "to send peace on the earth" for βαλεῖν εἰρήνην ἐπὶ τὴν γῆν.

18. "He that hath" for "that had" = ὁ ἔχων. (?) The "he" is unnecessary. Cf. Rom. ix. 5; and "had" is required in connection with the preterite verb. Cf. the following words, "him that had the sharp sickle."

19. "Cast his sickle," again, for "thrust," etc. "The wine-press, the great *wine-press* of the wrath of God" for "the great wine-press of the wrath of God" = τὴν ληνὸν τοῦ θυμοῦ τοῦ Θεοῦ τὴν μεγάλην = "the wine-press of the wrath of God, the great (one)." So, after all, they have not retained the order of the Greek; and why have they any more right to put in "wine-press" twice in English for once in Greek, than to make the order of the words in English different from that in the Greek—the sense remaining the same? Cf. ix. 14 (xvi. 12); Mark i. 26; and the "daily bread" of the Lord's Prayer.

20. "The bridles of the horses" for "the horse bridles." "As far as" for "by the space of" = ἀπό. What is the difference of sense?

XV.

1. "Is finished,"—an aorist.
2. "Come victorious" for "had gotten the victory" = νικῶντας. After "I saw," the participle should be rendered by a preterite verb;—"came" for "come," or still better "were victorious," or "had gotten the victory;"—there is no "come" in the text.
3. "O Lord God the Almighty" for "O Lord God Almighty;" and so, often, in this book. It is true, the Greek has the article; but is not English usage settled to have

"Almighty" in such connections without the article? And why does faithfulness to the original require its insertion with "Almighty" any more than with "God"? The Greek is ὁ Θεός as well as ὁ παντοκράτωρ. English usage settles one case, and why not the other? By way of showing their diligent consistency, however, the Revisers, at xix. 15, have put "Almighty God" for τοῦ Θεοῦ τοῦ παντοκράτορος,—not "the Almighty God," nor "God the Almighty."

6. "And there came out from the temple the seven angels that had" for "and the seven angels came out of the temple having." This important change is made because their text has οἱ before ἔχοντες. "Arrayed with *precious* stone pure *and* bright" for "clothed (ἐνδεδυμένοι) in pure and (the old text has καί) white linen." If we *must* have "stone" (not "stones") for "linen," why insert "precious" out of the whole cloth, and "and" too, which is especially thrown out of their text? Why not boldly say, "clothed in pure, bright stone," and be faithful to the original? "Arrayed," in the Revision, elsewhere = περιβεβλημένος.

XVI.

1. "Go ye" for "go your ways" = ὑπάγετε: but cf. Matt. xxvii. 65; Luke x. 3 and xix. 30. In the last passage they *substitute* "go your way" for "go ye" = ὑπάγετε!

3. "Even the things that were" = τά = "whatever *was*" (or *were*). (?)

5. "Didst thus judge" for "hast judged thus." (?) This aorist is coördinated with a perfect "hast given;" and, in the connection, the simple English naturally is a perfect. See note, ii. 2-9.

7, 14. "God the Almighty" for "God Almighty." Cf. xix. 15.

9. "The God which" for "God which." Why did they not say just above, "O Lord, the God, the Almighty"? Is the author a polytheist?

12. "The great river, the *river* Euphrates." "*River*" is utterly unnecessary, if not the "the" also. But let us be thankful that their faithfulness did not lead them to say

"the river, the great *river*, the *river* Euphrates," exactly after the Greek order. "The kings that *come* from the sunrising" for "... of the East"= τῶν ἀπὸ ἀνατολῶν ἡλίου. There is no need of the "*come ;*" and, if they could not say "East" for "sunrising," why did they not render "from the risings of the sun"? Is not ἀνατολῶν plural?

15. "Lest" = ἵνα μή. But cf. Col. ii. 4; iii. 22; Phil. ii. 27; Heb. iv. 11, etc., etc., where they change to "that not." But in several other places, as at 1 Tim. iii. 7, they render "lest."

18. "Were" and "was" = ἐγένετο. This they have many times changed to "followed"—see viii. 1, 5, etc., etc. —consequential—"straightway."

21. "Hail cometh down out of heaven" = ἐκ τοῦ οὐρανοῦ,—not "the heaven." And cf. viii. 10, "from heaven." Did it then come from the abode of the blessed? Cf. Acts xi. 9, etc. ;—"a voice out of heaven." But perhaps, after all, they have no rule, but insert or omit the article with "heaven" *ad lib.*—provided only they may diverge from the A. V. But see x. 8; xi. 12; xiv. 2, 13; xviii. 4, where they render "a voice from heaven," not "out of heaven."

XVII.

8. "They" is needless.
10. "Are fallen,"—an aorist.
12. "Have received,"—an aorist.
14. "*Also shall overcome*" for "*are.*" (?)
17. "Did put" for "hath put" = ἔδωκεν. (?) "To come to one mind" for "to agree" = ποιῆσαι μίαν γνώμην. (?)
17. "Should be accomplished" for "shall be fulfilled" = τελεσθήσονται. This change of tense follows from "did put," above; but the future here tends to show that it should have been "hath put," as in the A. V.

XVIII.

2. "Fallen is,"—the aorist. "Is become,"—the aorist.
3. "Are fallen,"—the perfect. Thus they rightly render an aorist and a perfect alike in coördinated phrases; and see note, ii. 2–9. But again, "committed" for "have com-

mitted,"—an aorist. "Waxed rich" for "are waxen rich," —an aorist; and then, verse 5, "have reached" = ἐκολλή-θησαν, and "hath remembered" = ἐμνημόνευσεν.

10. If, instead of putting "woe" for "alas" in this and several other instances, they had put "alas" for "woe" in many cases where the A. V. has the latter, as in the Gospels, they would have secured the true sense and prevented mistakes. Here the sense may be the same with either word, for it is plain a malediction is not intended, even if "woe" is used. Say "woe" for the noun and "alas" for the interjection?

14. "Are gone," "are perished," for aorists.

17, 19. "Is made desolate," for the aorist.

21. "A strong angel" for "a mighty angel" = ἰσχυρός. But cf. xix. 18, where ἰσχυρῶν are "mighty men." Consequential, "straightway."

21. "A mighty fall" for "violence" = ὁρμήματι = "with a sudden ruin"?

23. "The princes" for "the great men" = μεγιστᾶνες. Etymology favors the A. V.

24. "That have been slain" for "that were slain" = τῶν ἐσφαγμένων = "that had been slain," in connection with a preterite verb as here; and "were slain" comes nearer this than "have been slain" does. Indeed, the Revisers often use it as a form of the pluperfect. Cf. xx. 4; Matt. xxii. 3, etc.

XIX.

1. "Salvation and glory," etc. Here again, as at vii. 12, they omit the articles which they have so often inserted in similar ascriptions; but they insert "belong" as though it were certainly in the text;—*quære?*

2. "Hath judged,"—aorist; "hath avenged,"—aorist.

4. "That sitteth" for "that sat." Do they forget that it is told as a vision? Cf. verses 19 and 21.

5. "Give praise to" for "praise" = αἰνεῖτε. (?)

6. "Reigneth,"—aorist.

7. "Is come," "hath made,"—aorists.

8. "Was given,"—aorist.

9. "These are true words of God" for "these are the

true sayings of God" = Οὗτοι οἱ λόγοι ἀληθινοὶ τοῦ Θεοῦ εἰσι. But what has become of the article, and that after "these"? (Cf. Mark xii. 31.) " Bidden" for "called" = κεκλημένοι. It was not possible to refrain from this important emendation consistently with faithfulness?

11. "Saw the heaven [for 'heaven'] opened" = τὸν οὐρανόν. See Acts x. 11, note.

12, 13. "*Are*" for "*were.*" (?) The latter is probably preferable—not certain. Some of the verbs describing this vision are in the present and some in the past; but the visions are generally described in the past.

14. Here they say, "the armies which are [for 'were'] in heaven followed him." This is certainly harsh, but is printed as if "are" were in the *text*, which it is not.

15. "Wrath of Almighty God" = τῆς ὀργῆς τοῦ Θεοῦ τοῦ παντοκράτορος. They forget their article with Almighty. Cf. xvi. 7, 14, where they have "God the Almighty," for the very same Greek.

17. "A loud voice" = φωνῇ μεγάλῃ. They forget their apocalyptic "great voice."

18. "Mighty men" = ἰσχυρῶν. They forget their "strong angel" at xviii. 21.

20. "Them that had received" = τοὺς λαβόντας: "them that worshipped" = τοὺς προσκυνοῦντας—with a preterite verb—right; aorist participle as a pluperfect, and present participle as a preterite,—and so the A. V. Cf. Matt. xxv. 16, 17, 18. "They twain" for "these both" = οἱ δύο. How important! And, after all, it is not "they twain" but simply "the twain" or "the two" or (*tous les deux*) "both." At Matt. xix. 5, the Revisers *substitute* "the twain" for "they twain" as the rendering for οἱ δύο!

21. "The sword of him that sat (τοῦ καθημένου) *even the sword* which came forth" for "which *sword* proceeded," (τῇ ἐξελθούσῃ:)—one participle is present and the other aorist, and they are rendered alike in the preterite.

XX.

4. "Such as" for "which" = οἵτινες = "who" or "those who." "Had been" for "were"; but either makes a plu-

perfect passive. "Worshipped" and "received" for "had," etc.; but this would imply the *imperfect*, here.

12. "And I saw the dead, the great and the small";—articular faithfulness; Greek for English idiom, see "heaven and earth." "Out of the things which were written" = ἐκ τῶν γεγραμμένων,—not "have been" nor "had been." Cf. verse 4 and vi. 9; v. 12, etc.

XXI.

1. "Are passed away" for "were passed away" = an aorist!
2. "Made ready" for "prepared" = ἡτοιμασμένην. See note, Matt. iii. 3.
9. "The wife of the lamb" for "the lamb's wife." Faithfulness! And cf. x. 10, "the angel's hand."
17. "*According* to the measure of a man" = μέτρον ἀνθρώπου. No article with μέτρον. Why did not they compromise upon "a man's measure"? "Of an angel" for "of the angel." (?)

XXII.

17. "He that heareth let him say" for "let him that heareth say" = ὁ ἀκούων εἰπάτω: and similarly twice more, "he that is athirst," "he that will" . . . "let him." And so also, both the Revisers and the A. V. in the Epistles to the Churches at ii. 7, 11, 17, etc. But at Mark iv. 9, the Revisers put "who . . . let him" for "he that . . . let him"; while at Matt. xiii. 9, 43 they put "he that . . . let him" for "who . . . let him"; at Matt. xxiii. 20, 21, they put "he that" for "whosoever." The A. V. uses different renderings, and so do the Revisers. In correcting the A.V. here, they have preferred the more cumbrous and ungrammatical English to the simpler and more grammatical. And it may be observed that the reason why the A. V. translated as it did in the Gospels and in the Epistles to the Churches, is that the law of euphony required it. The *ear* would have been offended with "let him that hath an ear, hear"; or, still worse, "let him that hath an ear to hear, hear." But that the Revisers *need* not have made their correction in this

place, is evident from their own rendering at Rom. xiv. 3, where, with the A. V., they translate this same construction of the Greek "let not him that eateth set at naught him that eateth not; and let not him that eateth not judge him that eateth'"= ὁ ἐσθίων τὸν μὴ ἐσθίοντα μὴ ἐξουθενείτω, ὁ δὲ μὴ ἐσθίων τὸν ἐσθίοντα μὴ κρινέτω. See also 1 Cor. x. 12, "Let him that thinketh he standeth take heed lest he fall." They do not say "he that eateth let him not," etc.; wherefore, then, did faithfulness compel them to amend the A. V. here, and say "he that heareth let him say come," etc., instead of the simple, dear, old, familiar words, "let him that heareth say, Come; and let him that is athirst come; and whosoever will, let him take the water of life freely"?

www.ingramcontent.com/pod-product-compliance
Lightning Source LLC
Chambersburg PA
CBHW050148170426
43197CB00011B/2007